Persia Blues

Persia Blues

volume 1
Leaving Home

Dara Naraghi
Brent Bowman

ComicsLit

ISBN 978-1-56163-706-5
© 2013 Dara Naraghi and Brent Bowman
www.nbmpub.com
Library of Congress Control Number
2013938100
1st printing May 2013

Comicslit is an imprint
and trademark of

NANTIER • BEALL • MINOUSTCHINE
Publishing inc.
new york

To Wendy and Hanna, for brightening and completing my life.
To mom and dad, for all your love and support.
To Bahman, for being a good sport about your
unfortunate demise on page 5.
--Dara

To Holly, Nevan and Nayson for their love and support.
To my parents for always telling me to follow my dreams.
To all of my friends and family for the encouragement,
especially my colleagues in the PANEL Collective for
the great feedback and critiques.
--Brent

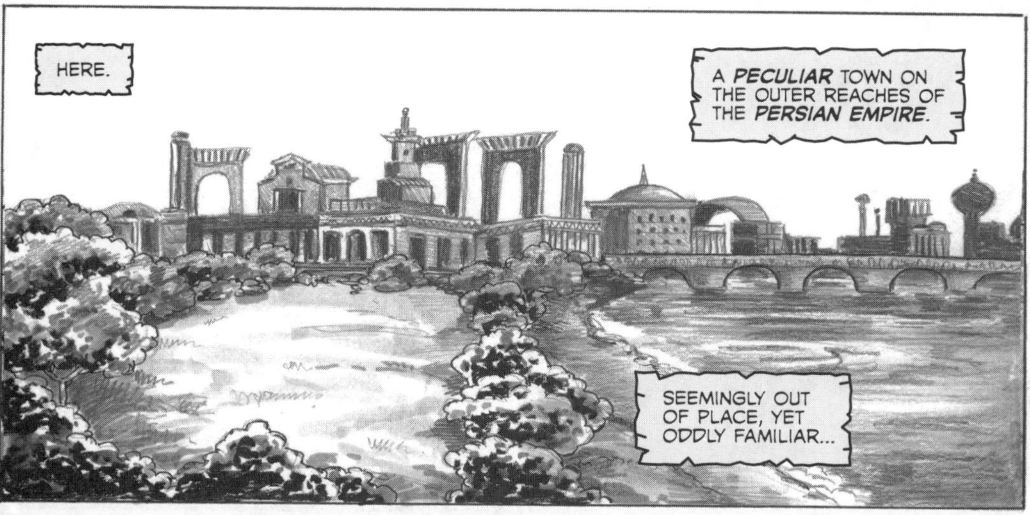
HERE.
A PECULIAR TOWN ON THE OUTER REACHES OF THE PERSIAN EMPIRE.
SEEMINGLY OUT OF PLACE, YET ODDLY FAMILIAR...

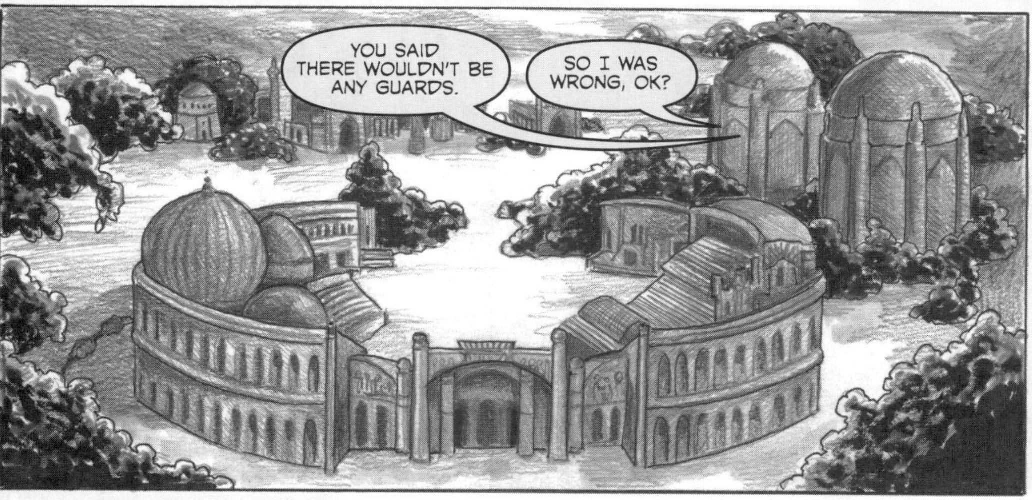
YOU SAID THERE WOULDN'T BE ANY GUARDS.
SO I WAS WRONG, OK?

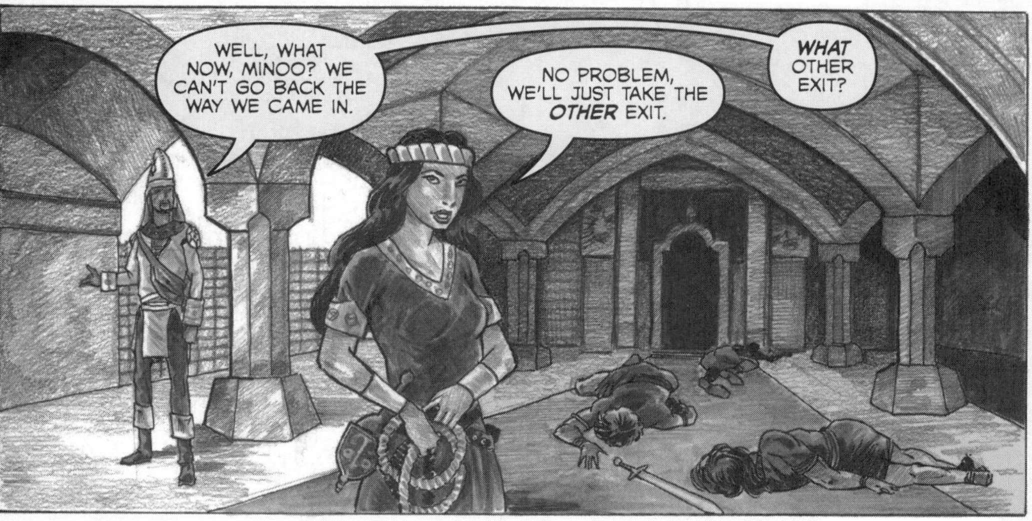
WELL, WHAT NOW, MINOO? WE CAN'T GO BACK THE WAY WE CAME IN.
NO PROBLEM, WE'LL JUST TAKE THE OTHER EXIT.
WHAT OTHER EXIT?

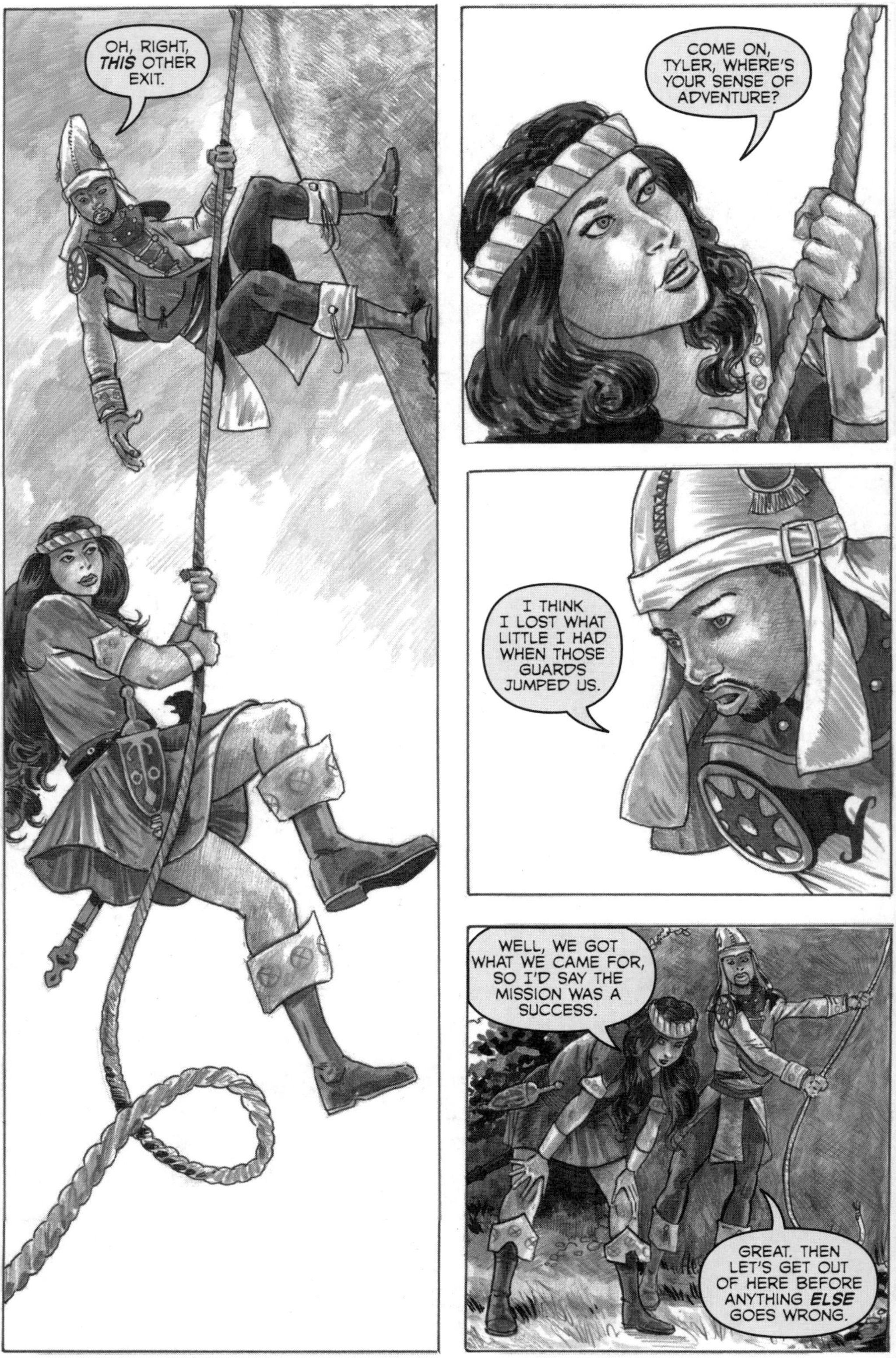

OH, RIGHT, *THIS* OTHER EXIT.
COME ON, TYLER, WHERE'S YOUR SENSE OF ADVENTURE?
I THINK I LOST WHAT LITTLE I HAD WHEN THOSE GUARDS JUMPED US.
WELL, WE GOT WHAT WE CAME FOR, SO I'D SAY THE MISSION WAS A SUCCESS.
GREAT. THEN LET'S GET OUT OF HERE BEFORE ANYTHING *ELSE* GOES WRONG.

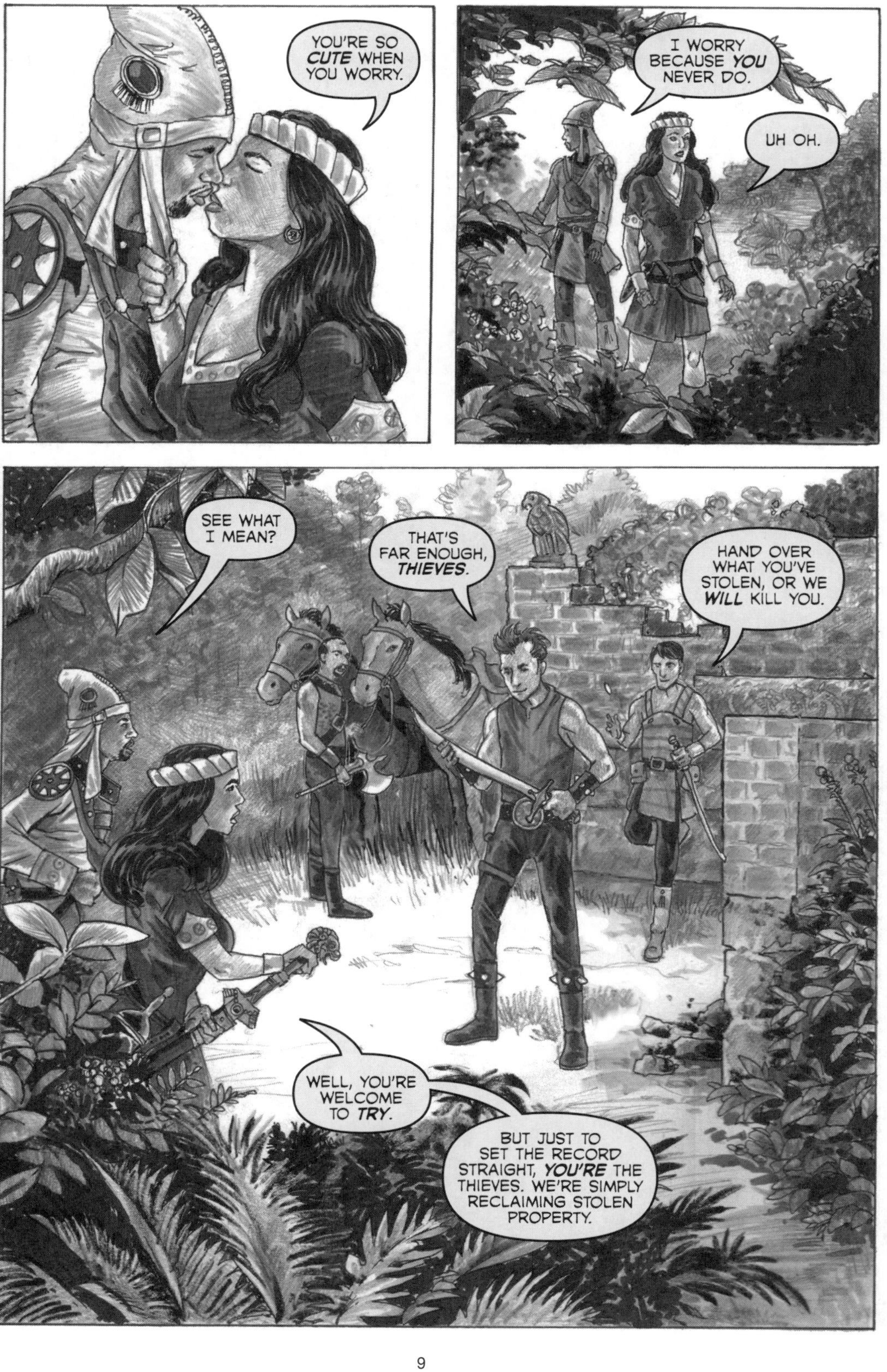
YOU'RE SO *CUTE* WHEN YOU WORRY.
I WORRY BECAUSE *YOU* NEVER DO.
UH OH.
SEE WHAT I MEAN?
THAT'S FAR ENOUGH, *THIEVES*.
HAND OVER WHAT YOU'VE STOLEN, OR WE *WILL* KILL YOU.
WELL, YOU'RE WELCOME TO *TRY*.
BUT JUST TO SET THE RECORD STRAIGHT, *YOU'RE* THE THIEVES. WE'RE SIMPLY RECLAIMING STOLEN PROPERTY.

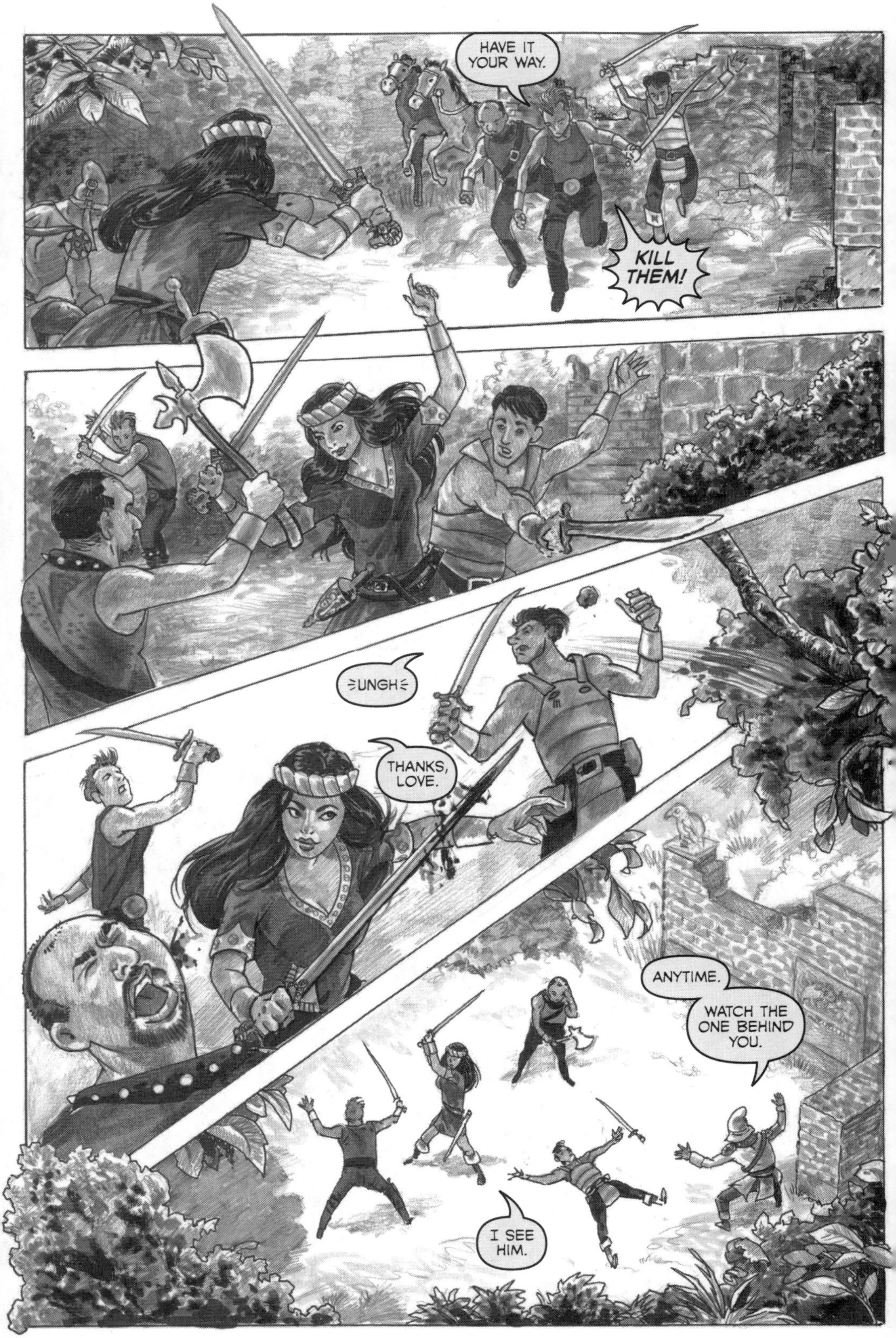
HAVE IT YOUR WAY.
KILL THEM!
UNGH
THANKS, LOVE.
ANYTIME.
WATCH THE ONE BEHIND YOU.
I SEE HIM.

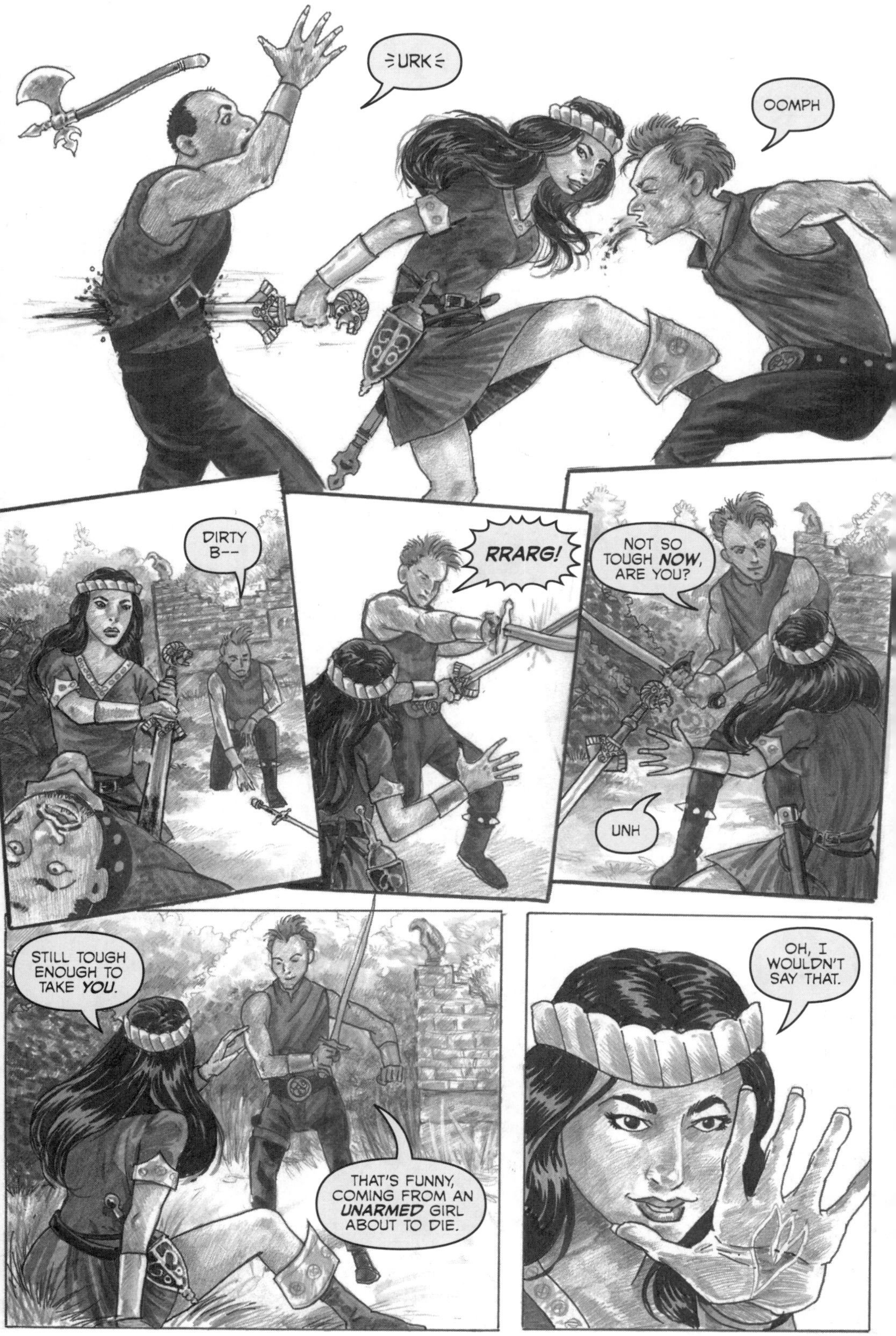
URK
OOMPH
DIRTY B--
RRARG!
NOT SO TOUGH NOW, ARE YOU?
UNH
STILL TOUGH ENOUGH TO TAKE YOU.
THAT'S FUNNY, COMING FROM AN UNARMED GIRL ABOUT TO DIE.
OH, I WOULDN'T SAY THAT.

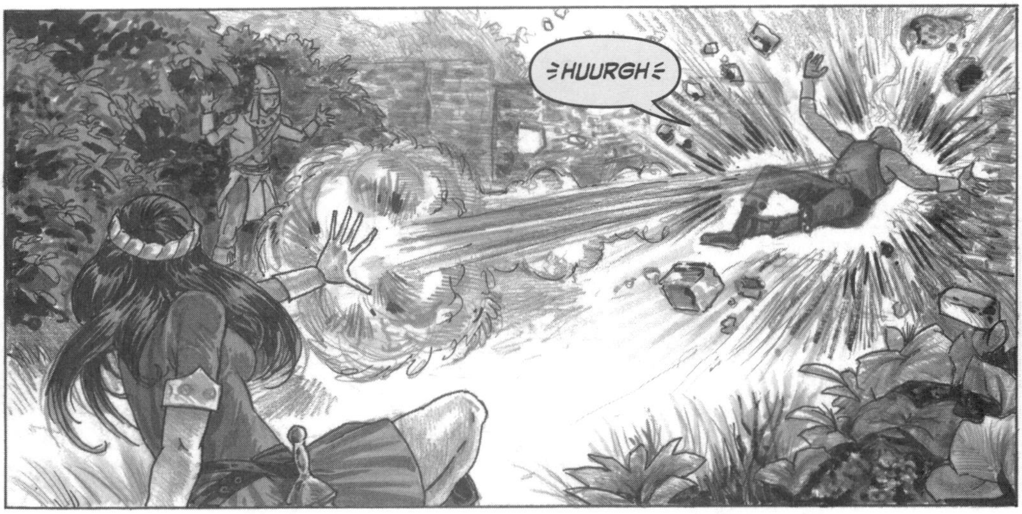
HUURGH

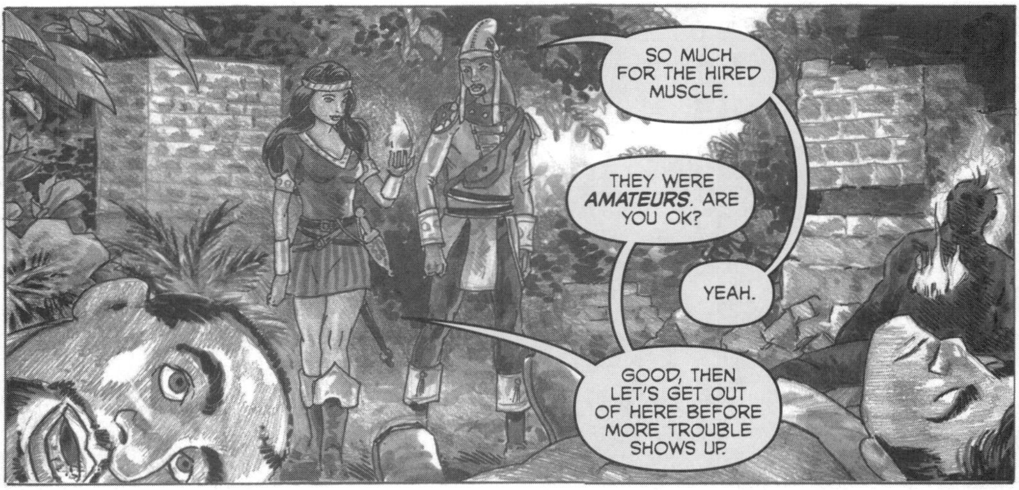
SO MUCH FOR THE HIRED MUSCLE.
THEY WERE **AMATEURS**. ARE YOU OK?
YEAH.
GOOD, THEN LET'S GET OUT OF HERE BEFORE MORE TROUBLE SHOWS UP.

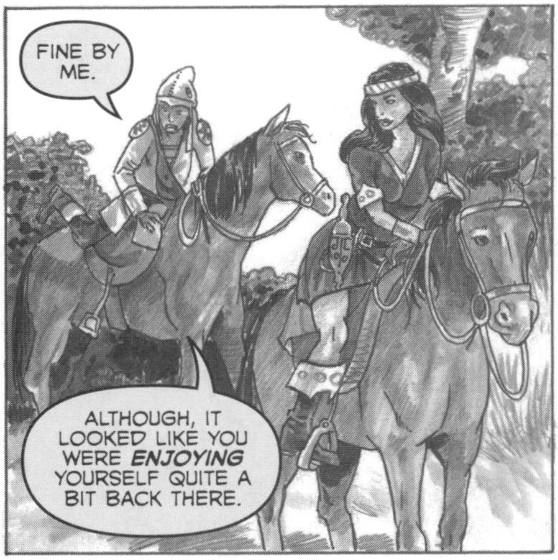
FINE BY ME.
ALTHOUGH, IT LOOKED LIKE YOU WERE **ENJOYING** YOURSELF QUITE A BIT BACK THERE.

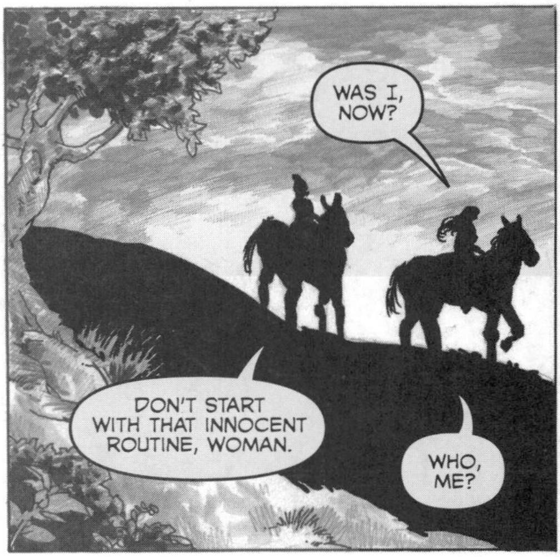
WAS I, NOW?
DON'T START WITH THAT INNOCENT ROUTINE, WOMAN.
WHO, ME?

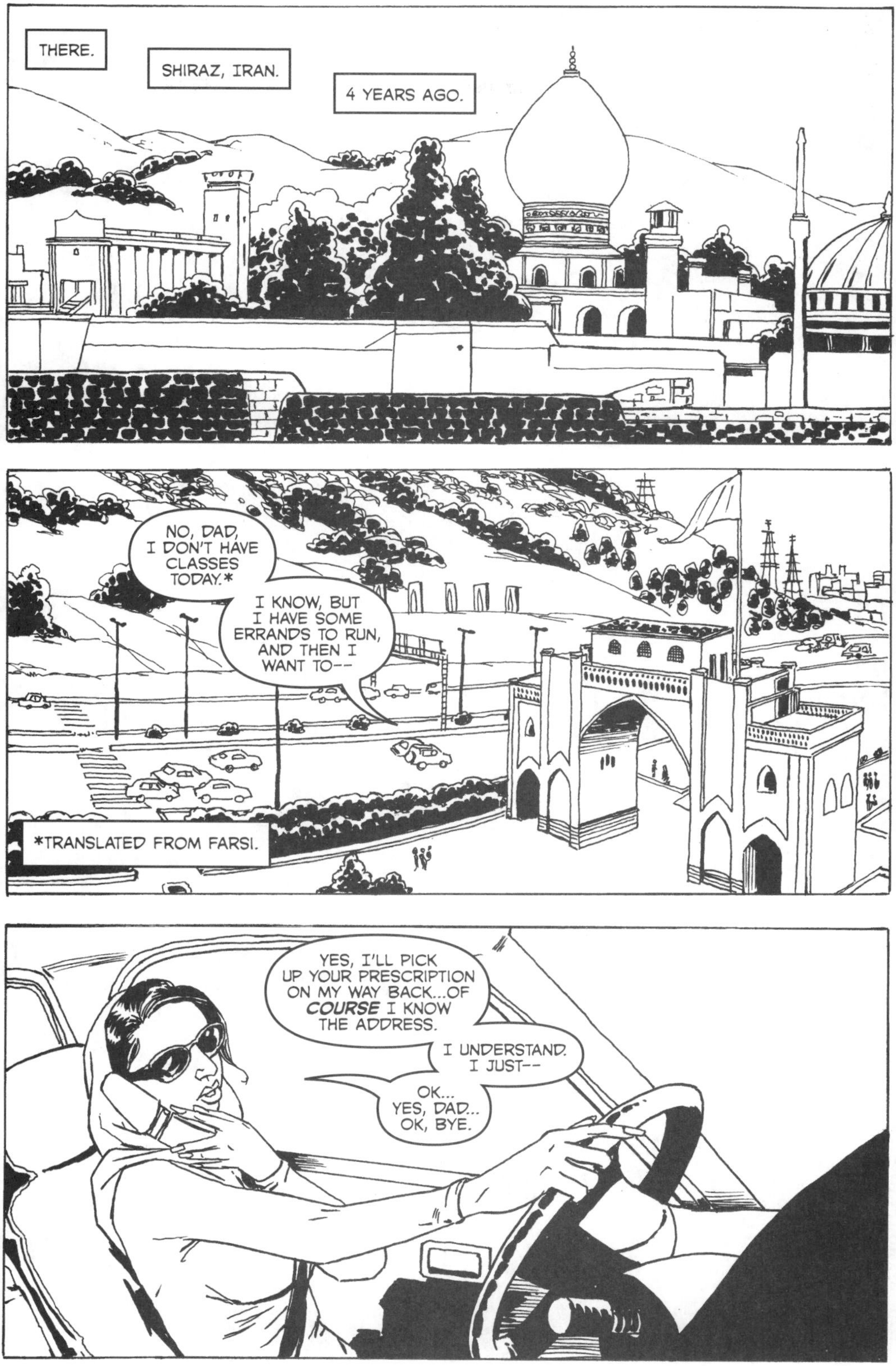
THERE.
SHIRAZ, IRAN.
4 YEARS AGO.
NO, DAD, I DON'T HAVE CLASSES TODAY.*
I KNOW, BUT I HAVE SOME ERRANDS TO RUN, AND THEN I WANT TO--
*TRANSLATED FROM FARSI.
YES, I'LL PICK UP YOUR PRESCRIPTION ON MY WAY BACK...OF *COURSE* I KNOW THE ADDRESS.
I UNDERSTAND. I JUST--
OK... YES, DAD... OK, BYE.

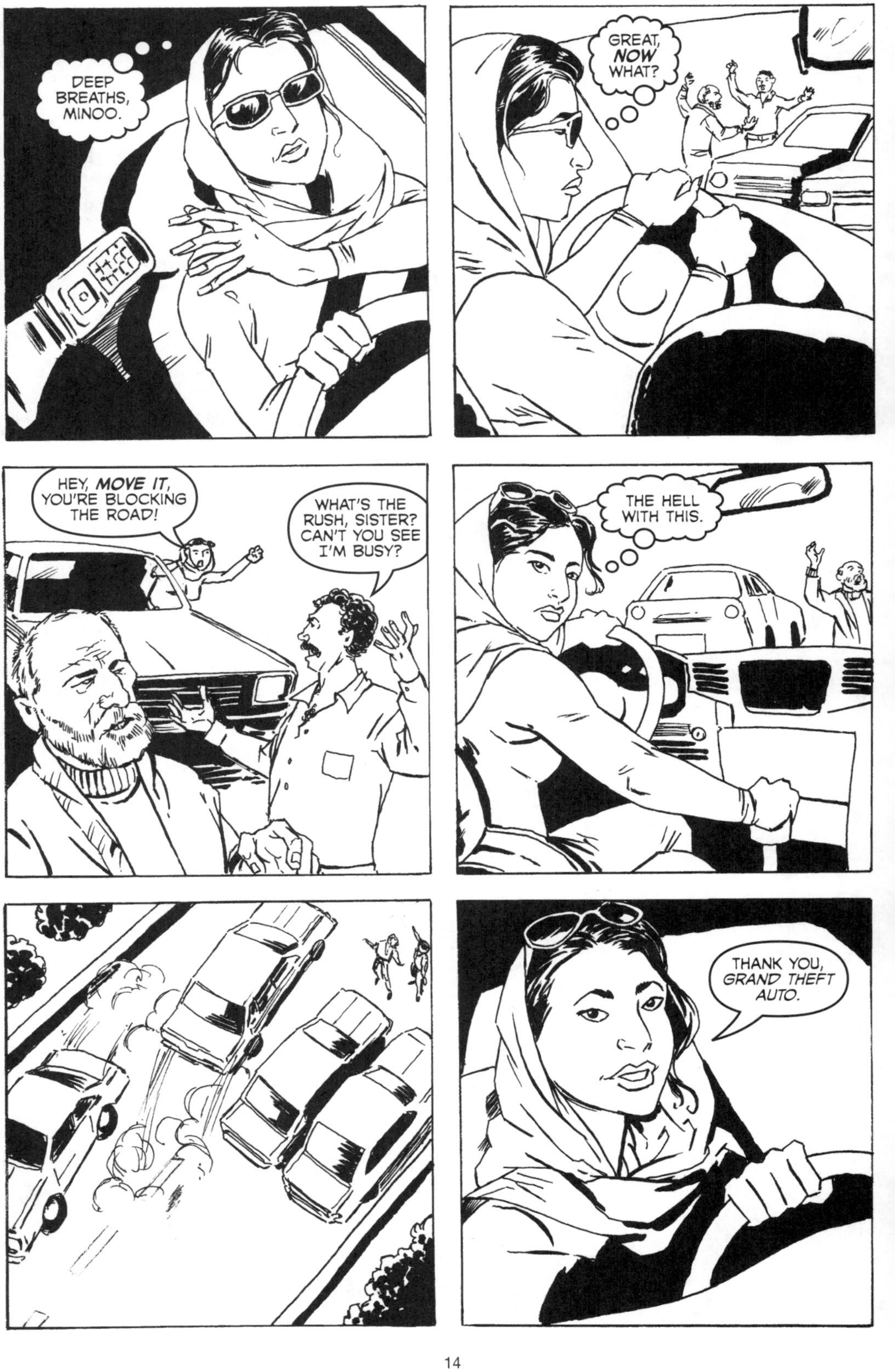
DEEP BREATHS, MINOO.
GREAT, NOW WHAT?
HEY, MOVE IT, YOU'RE BLOCKING THE ROAD!
WHAT'S THE RUSH, SISTER? CAN'T YOU SEE I'M BUSY?
THE HELL WITH THIS.
THANK YOU, GRAND THEFT AUTO.

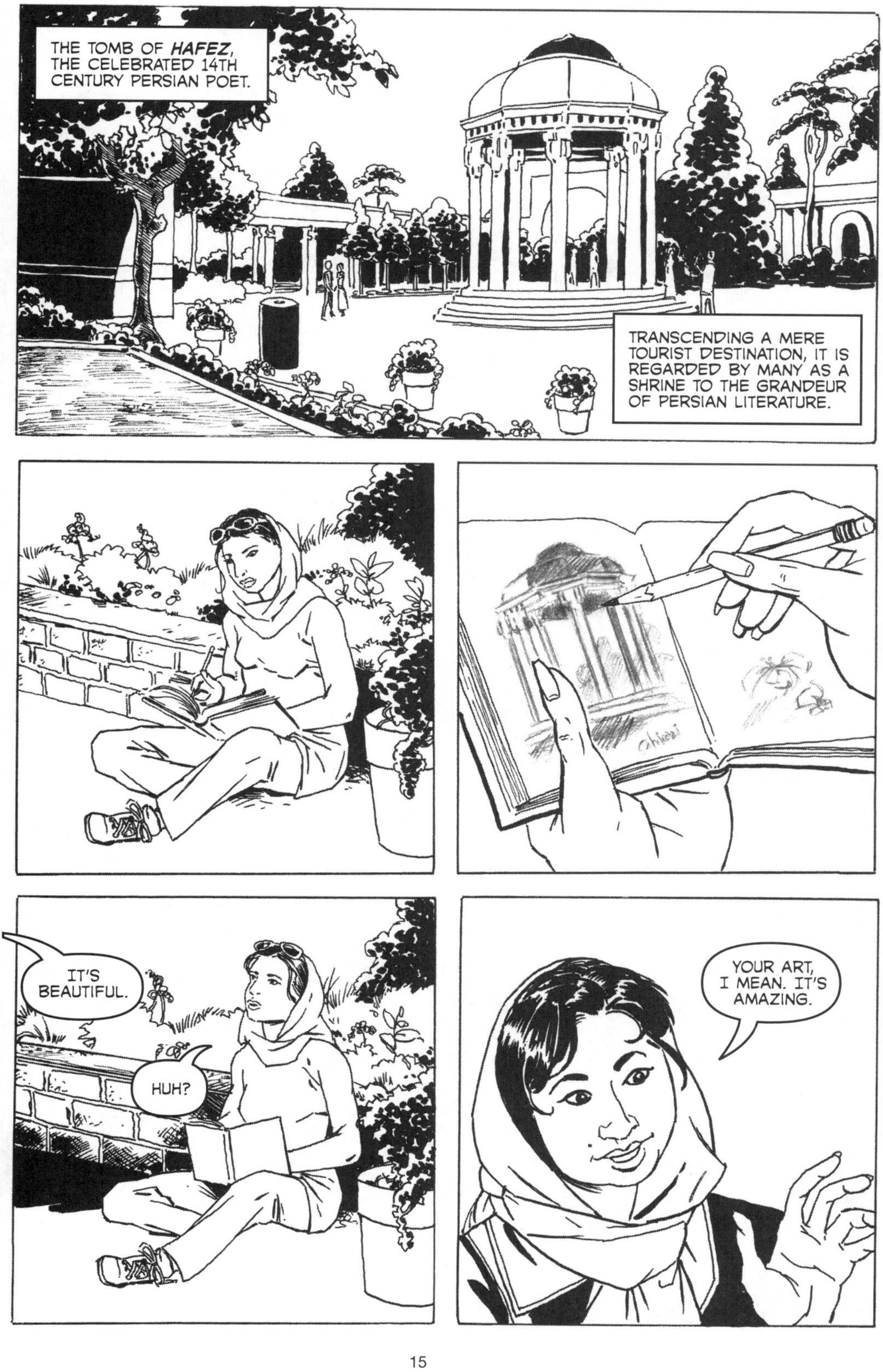
THE TOMB OF *HAFEZ*, THE CELEBRATED 14TH CENTURY PERSIAN POET.
TRANSCENDING A MERE TOURIST DESTINATION, IT IS REGARDED BY MANY AS A SHRINE TO THE GRANDEUR OF PERSIAN LITERATURE.
IT'S BEAUTIFUL.
HUH?
YOUR ART, I MEAN. IT'S AMAZING.

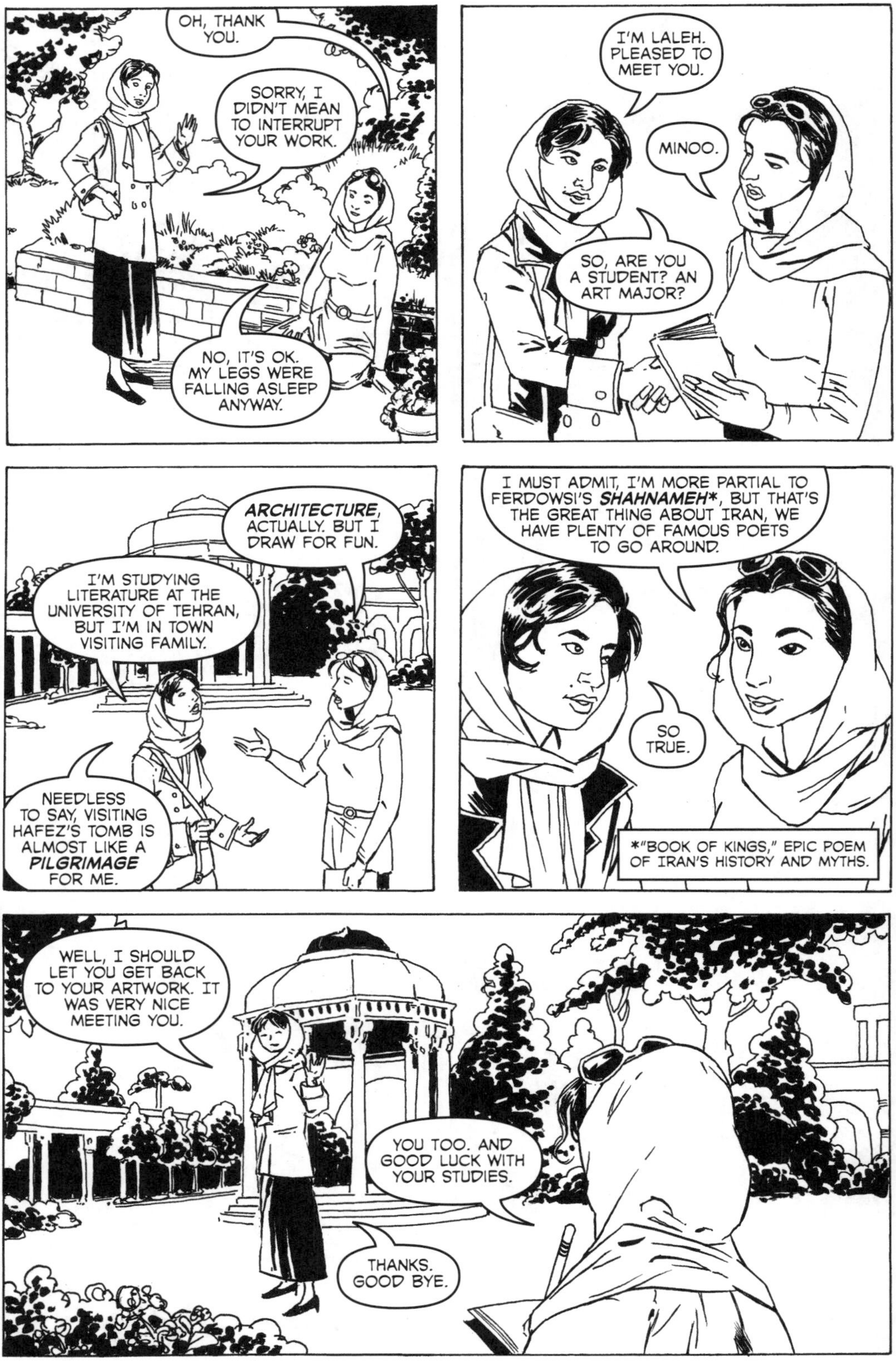
OH, THANK YOU.
SORRY, I DIDN'T MEAN TO INTERRUPT YOUR WORK.
NO, IT'S OK. MY LEGS WERE FALLING ASLEEP ANYWAY.
I'M LALEH. PLEASED TO MEET YOU.
MINOO.
SO, ARE YOU A STUDENT? AN ART MAJOR?
ARCHITECTURE, ACTUALLY. BUT I DRAW FOR FUN.
I'M STUDYING LITERATURE AT THE UNIVERSITY OF TEHRAN, BUT I'M IN TOWN VISITING FAMILY.
NEEDLESS TO SAY, VISITING HAFEZ'S TOMB IS ALMOST LIKE A PILGRIMAGE FOR ME.
I MUST ADMIT, I'M MORE PARTIAL TO FERDOWSI'S SHAHNAMEH*, BUT THAT'S THE GREAT THING ABOUT IRAN, WE HAVE PLENTY OF FAMOUS POETS TO GO AROUND.
SO TRUE.
*"BOOK OF KINGS," EPIC POEM OF IRAN'S HISTORY AND MYTHS.
WELL, I SHOULD LET YOU GET BACK TO YOUR ARTWORK. IT WAS VERY NICE MEETING YOU.
YOU TOO. AND GOOD LUCK WITH YOUR STUDIES.
THANKS. GOOD BYE.

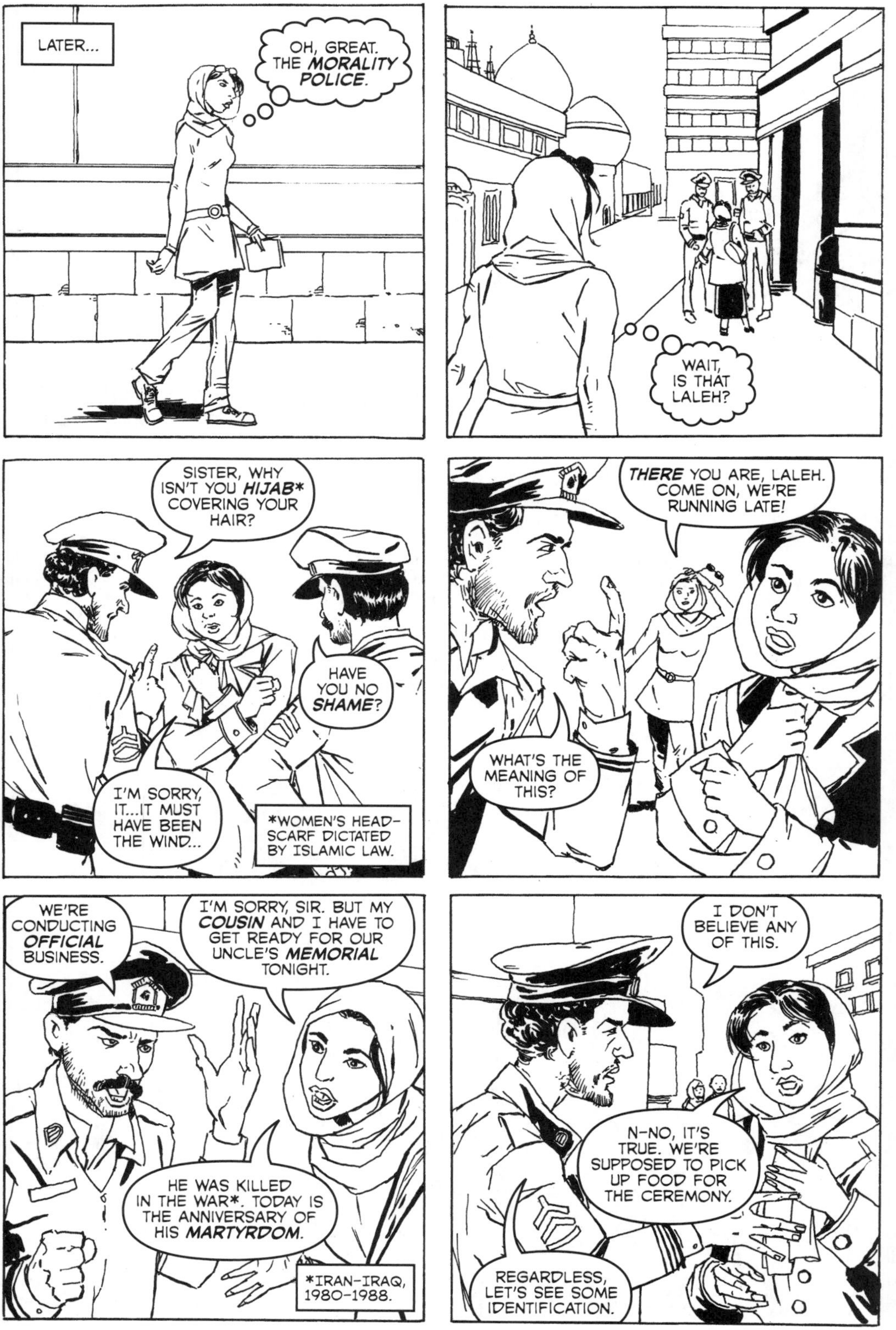
LATER...
OH, GREAT. THE MORALITY POLICE.
WAIT, IS THAT LALEH?
SISTER, WHY ISN'T YOU HIJAB* COVERING YOUR HAIR?
HAVE YOU NO SHAME?
I'M SORRY, IT...IT MUST HAVE BEEN THE WIND...
*WOMEN'S HEAD-SCARF DICTATED BY ISLAMIC LAW.
THERE YOU ARE, LALEH. COME ON, WE'RE RUNNING LATE!
WHAT'S THE MEANING OF THIS?
WE'RE CONDUCTING OFFICIAL BUSINESS.
I'M SORRY, SIR. BUT MY COUSIN AND I HAVE TO GET READY FOR OUR UNCLE'S MEMORIAL TONIGHT.
HE WAS KILLED IN THE WAR*. TODAY IS THE ANNIVERSARY OF HIS MARTYRDOM.
*IRAN-IRAQ, 1980-1988.
I DON'T BELIEVE ANY OF THIS.
N-NO, IT'S TRUE. WE'RE SUPPOSED TO PICK UP FOOD FOR THE CEREMONY.
REGARDLESS, LET'S SEE SOME IDENTIFICATION.

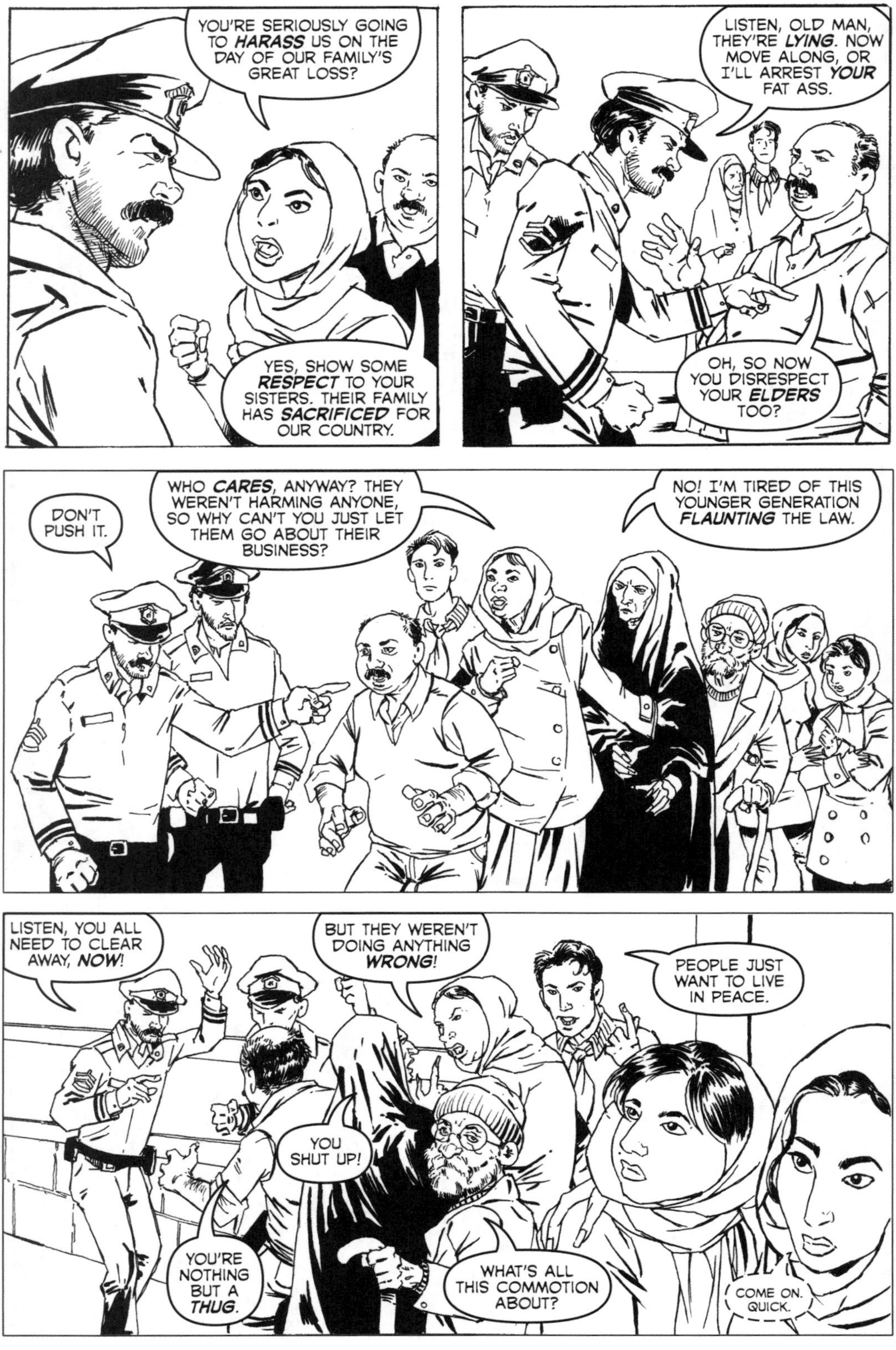
YOU'RE SERIOUSLY GOING TO HARASS US ON THE DAY OF OUR FAMILY'S GREAT LOSS?
YES, SHOW SOME RESPECT TO YOUR SISTERS. THEIR FAMILY HAS SACRIFICED FOR OUR COUNTRY.
LISTEN, OLD MAN, THEY'RE LYING. NOW MOVE ALONG, OR I'LL ARREST YOUR FAT ASS.
OH, SO NOW YOU DISRESPECT YOUR ELDERS TOO?
DON'T PUSH IT.
WHO CARES, ANYWAY? THEY WEREN'T HARMING ANYONE, SO WHY CAN'T YOU JUST LET THEM GO ABOUT THEIR BUSINESS?
NO! I'M TIRED OF THIS YOUNGER GENERATION FLAUNTING THE LAW.
LISTEN, YOU ALL NEED TO CLEAR AWAY, NOW!
BUT THEY WEREN'T DOING ANYTHING WRONG!
PEOPLE JUST WANT TO LIVE IN PEACE.
YOU SHUT UP!
YOU'RE NOTHING BUT A THUG.
WHAT'S ALL THIS COMMOTION ABOUT?
COME ON. QUICK.

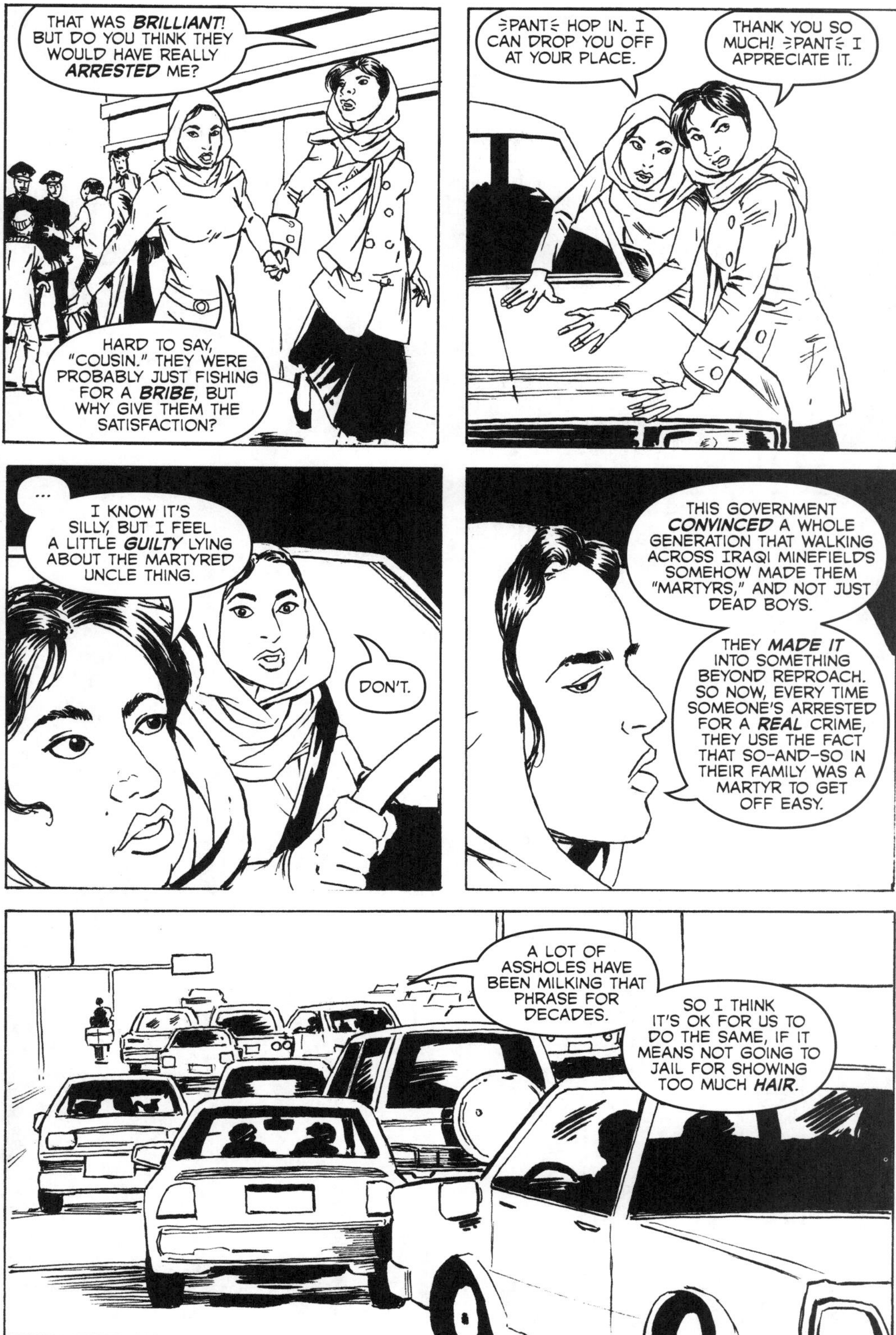
THAT WAS BRILLIANT! BUT DO YOU THINK THEY WOULD HAVE REALLY ARRESTED ME?
HARD TO SAY, "COUSIN." THEY WERE PROBABLY JUST FISHING FOR A BRIBE, BUT WHY GIVE THEM THE SATISFACTION?
⋛PANT⋚ HOP IN. I CAN DROP YOU OFF AT YOUR PLACE.
THANK YOU SO MUCH! ⋛PANT⋚ I APPRECIATE IT.
...
I KNOW IT'S SILLY, BUT I FEEL A LITTLE GUILTY LYING ABOUT THE MARTYRED UNCLE THING.
DON'T.
THIS GOVERNMENT CONVINCED A WHOLE GENERATION THAT WALKING ACROSS IRAQI MINEFIELDS SOMEHOW MADE THEM "MARTYRS," AND NOT JUST DEAD BOYS.
THEY MADE IT INTO SOMETHING BEYOND REPROACH. SO NOW, EVERY TIME SOMEONE'S ARRESTED FOR A REAL CRIME, THEY USE THE FACT THAT SO-AND-SO IN THEIR FAMILY WAS A MARTYR TO GET OFF EASY.
A LOT OF ASSHOLES HAVE BEEN MILKING THAT PHRASE FOR DECADES.
SO I THINK IT'S OK FOR US TO DO THE SAME, IF IT MEANS NOT GOING TO JAIL FOR SHOWING TOO MUCH HAIR.

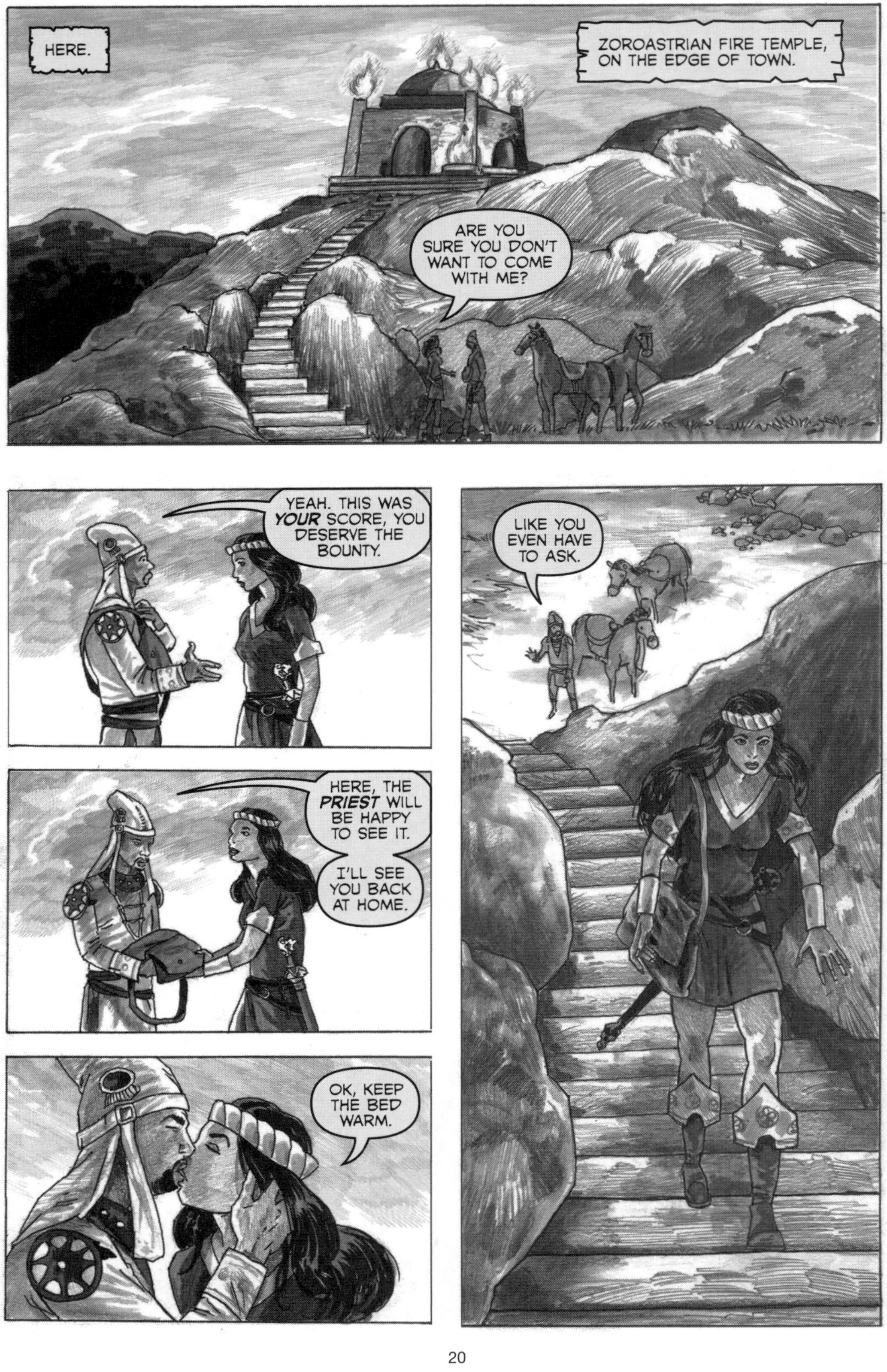

HERE.
ZOROASTRIAN FIRE TEMPLE, ON THE EDGE OF TOWN.
ARE YOU SURE YOU DON'T WANT TO COME WITH ME?
YEAH. THIS WAS ***YOUR*** SCORE, YOU DESERVE THE BOUNTY.
HERE, THE ***PRIEST*** WILL BE HAPPY TO SEE IT.
I'LL SEE YOU BACK AT HOME.
OK, KEEP THE BED WARM.
LIKE YOU EVEN HAVE TO ASK.

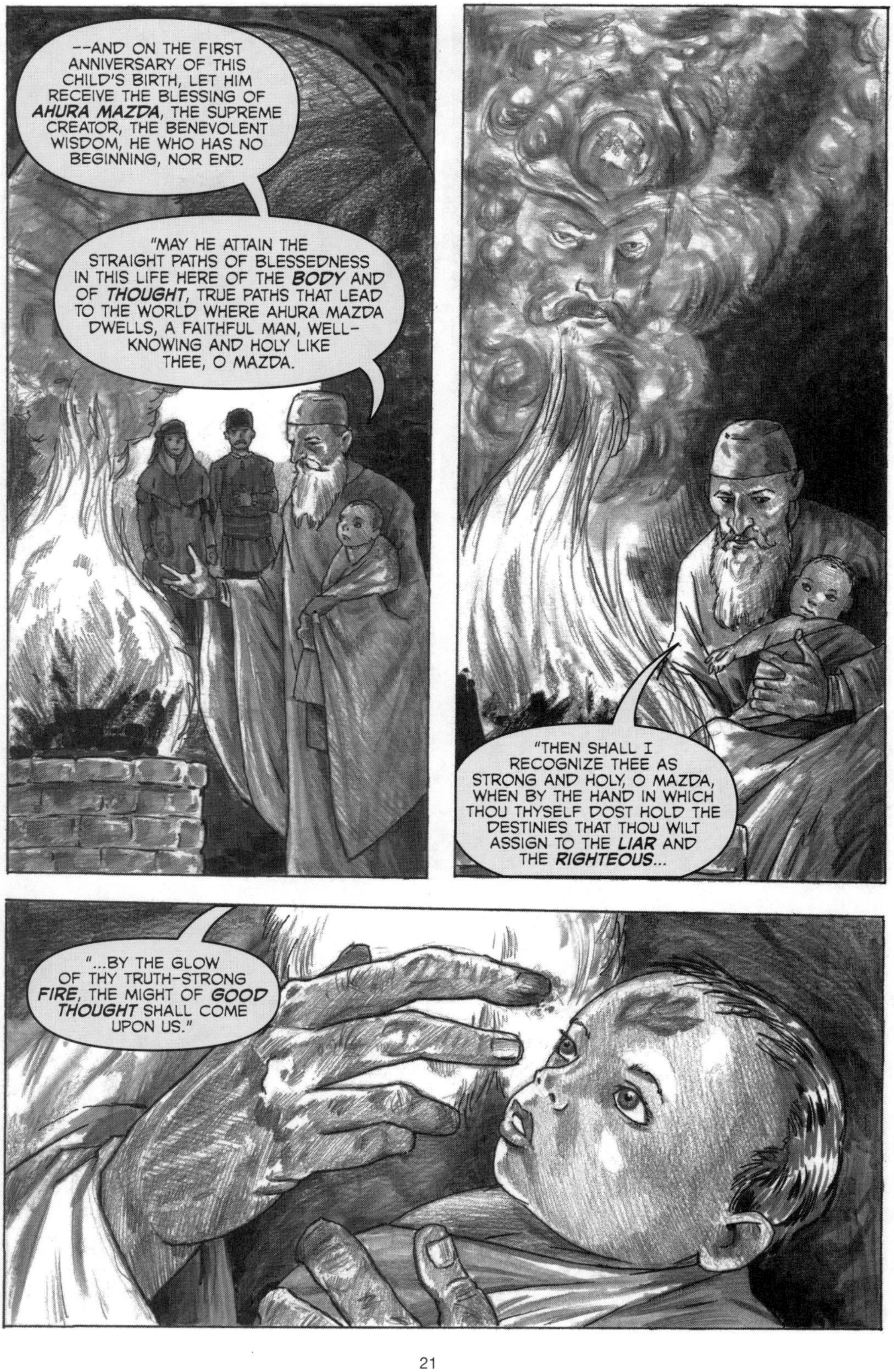
--AND ON THE FIRST ANNIVERSARY OF THIS CHILD'S BIRTH, LET HIM RECEIVE THE BLESSING OF AHURA MAZDA, THE SUPREME CREATOR, THE BENEVOLENT WISDOM, HE WHO HAS NO BEGINNING, NOR END.
"MAY HE ATTAIN THE STRAIGHT PATHS OF BLESSEDNESS IN THIS LIFE HERE OF THE BODY AND OF THOUGHT, TRUE PATHS THAT LEAD TO THE WORLD WHERE AHURA MAZDA DWELLS, A FAITHFUL MAN, WELL-KNOWING AND HOLY LIKE THEE, O MAZDA.
"THEN SHALL I RECOGNIZE THEE AS STRONG AND HOLY, O MAZDA, WHEN BY THE HAND IN WHICH THOU THYSELF DOST HOLD THE DESTINIES THAT THOU WILT ASSIGN TO THE LIAR AND THE RIGHTEOUS...
"...BY THE GLOW OF THY TRUTH-STRONG FIRE, THE MIGHT OF GOOD THOUGHT SHALL COME UPON US."

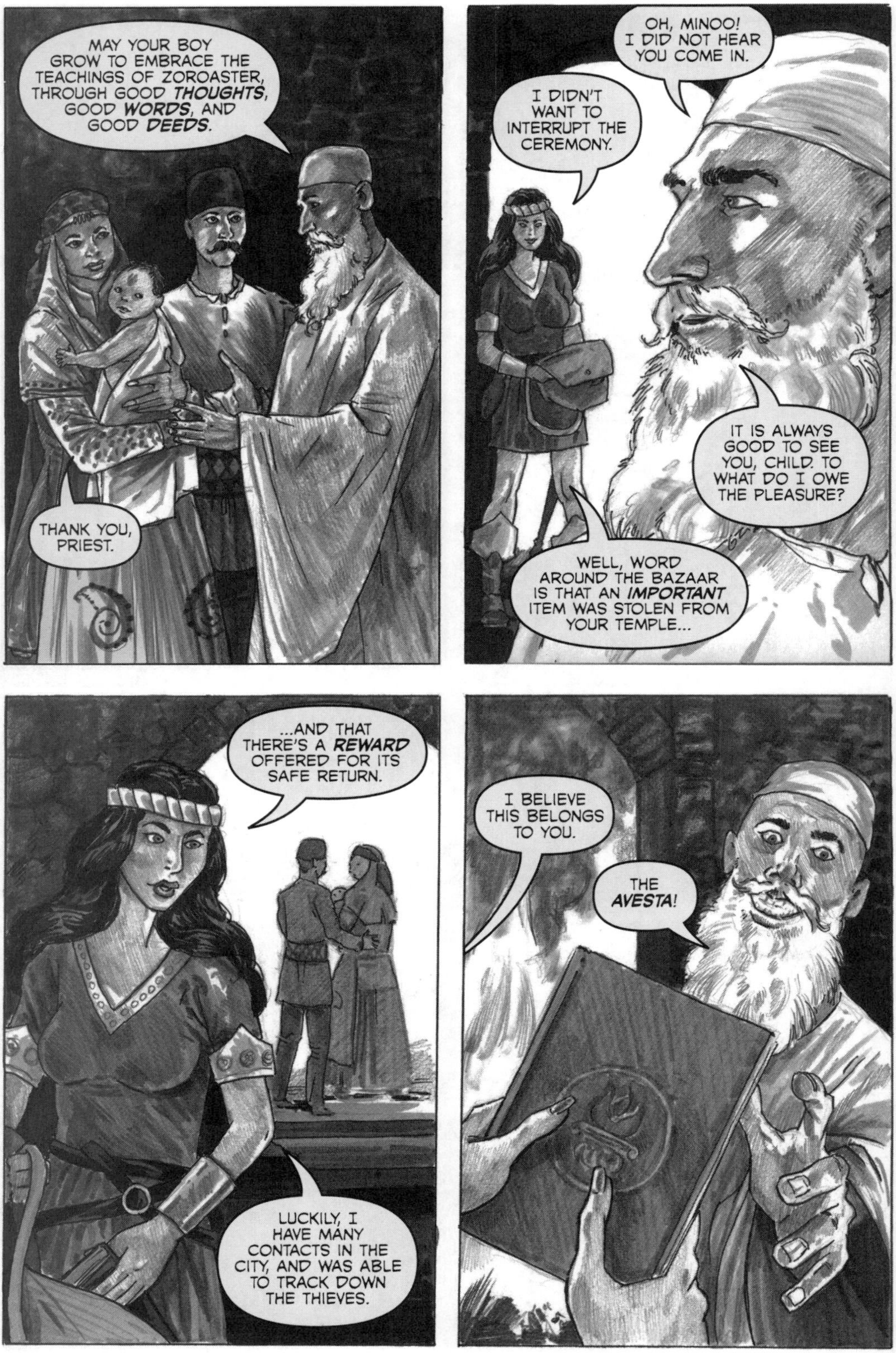
MAY YOUR BOY GROW TO EMBRACE THE TEACHINGS OF ZOROASTER, THROUGH GOOD *THOUGHTS*, GOOD *WORDS*, AND GOOD *DEEDS*.
THANK YOU, PRIEST.
OH, MINOO! I DID NOT HEAR YOU COME IN.
I DIDN'T WANT TO INTERRUPT THE CEREMONY.
IT IS ALWAYS GOOD TO SEE YOU, CHILD. TO WHAT DO I OWE THE PLEASURE?
WELL, WORD AROUND THE BAZAAR IS THAT AN *IMPORTANT* ITEM WAS STOLEN FROM YOUR TEMPLE...
...AND THAT THERE'S A *REWARD* OFFERED FOR ITS SAFE RETURN.
LUCKILY, I HAVE MANY CONTACTS IN THE CITY, AND WAS ABLE TO TRACK DOWN THE THIEVES.
I BELIEVE THIS BELONGS TO YOU.
THE *AVESTA*!

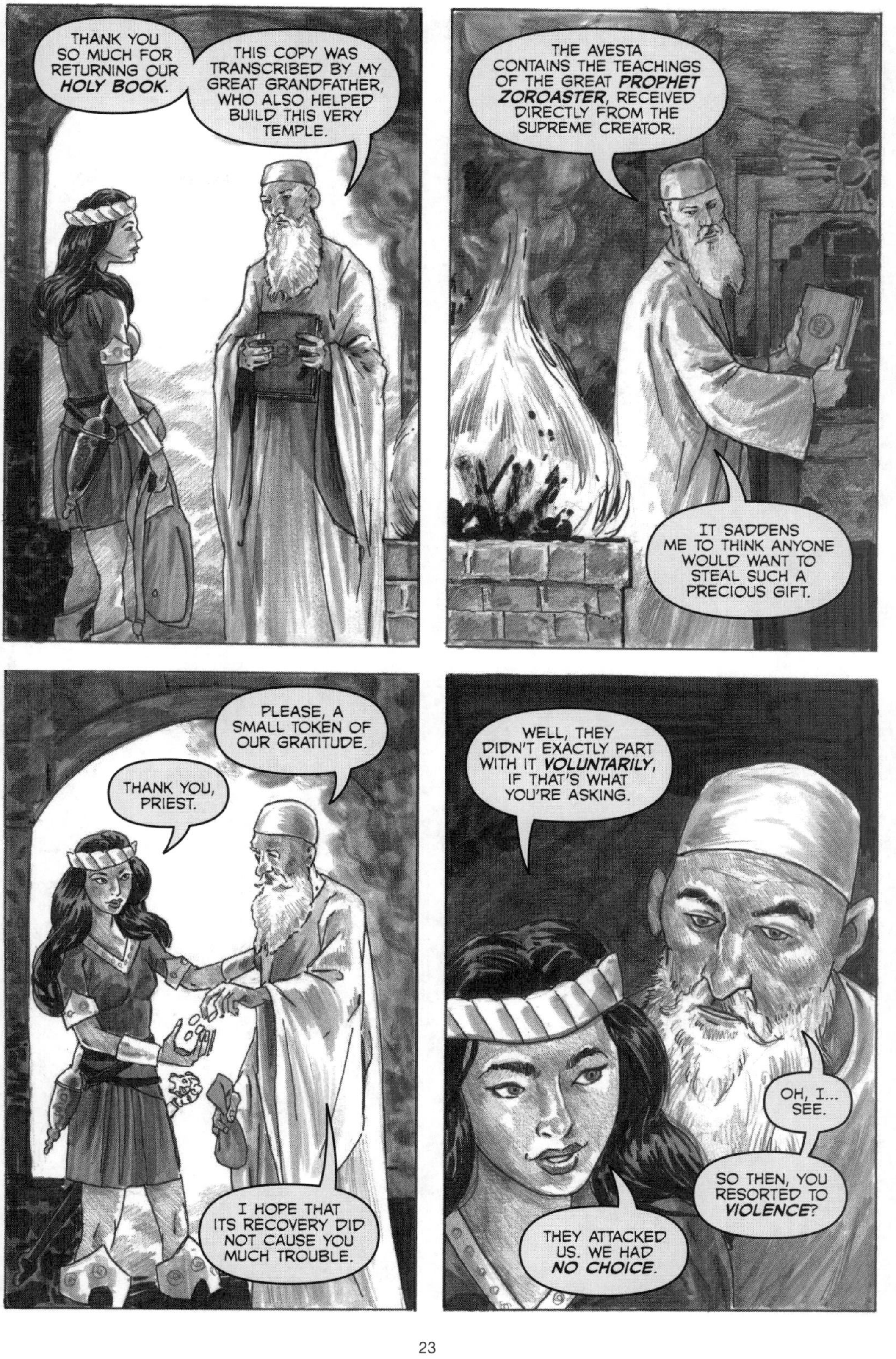

THANK YOU SO MUCH FOR RETURNING OUR HOLY BOOK.
THIS COPY WAS TRANSCRIBED BY MY GREAT GRANDFATHER, WHO ALSO HELPED BUILD THIS VERY TEMPLE.
THE AVESTA CONTAINS THE TEACHINGS OF THE GREAT PROPHET ZOROASTER, RECEIVED DIRECTLY FROM THE SUPREME CREATOR.
IT SADDENS ME TO THINK ANYONE WOULD WANT TO STEAL SUCH A PRECIOUS GIFT.
PLEASE, A SMALL TOKEN OF OUR GRATITUDE.
THANK YOU, PRIEST.
I HOPE THAT ITS RECOVERY DID NOT CAUSE YOU MUCH TROUBLE.
WELL, THEY DIDN'T EXACTLY PART WITH IT VOLUNTARILY, IF THAT'S WHAT YOU'RE ASKING.
OH, I... SEE.
SO THEN, YOU RESORTED TO VIOLENCE?
THEY ATTACKED US. WE HAD NO CHOICE.

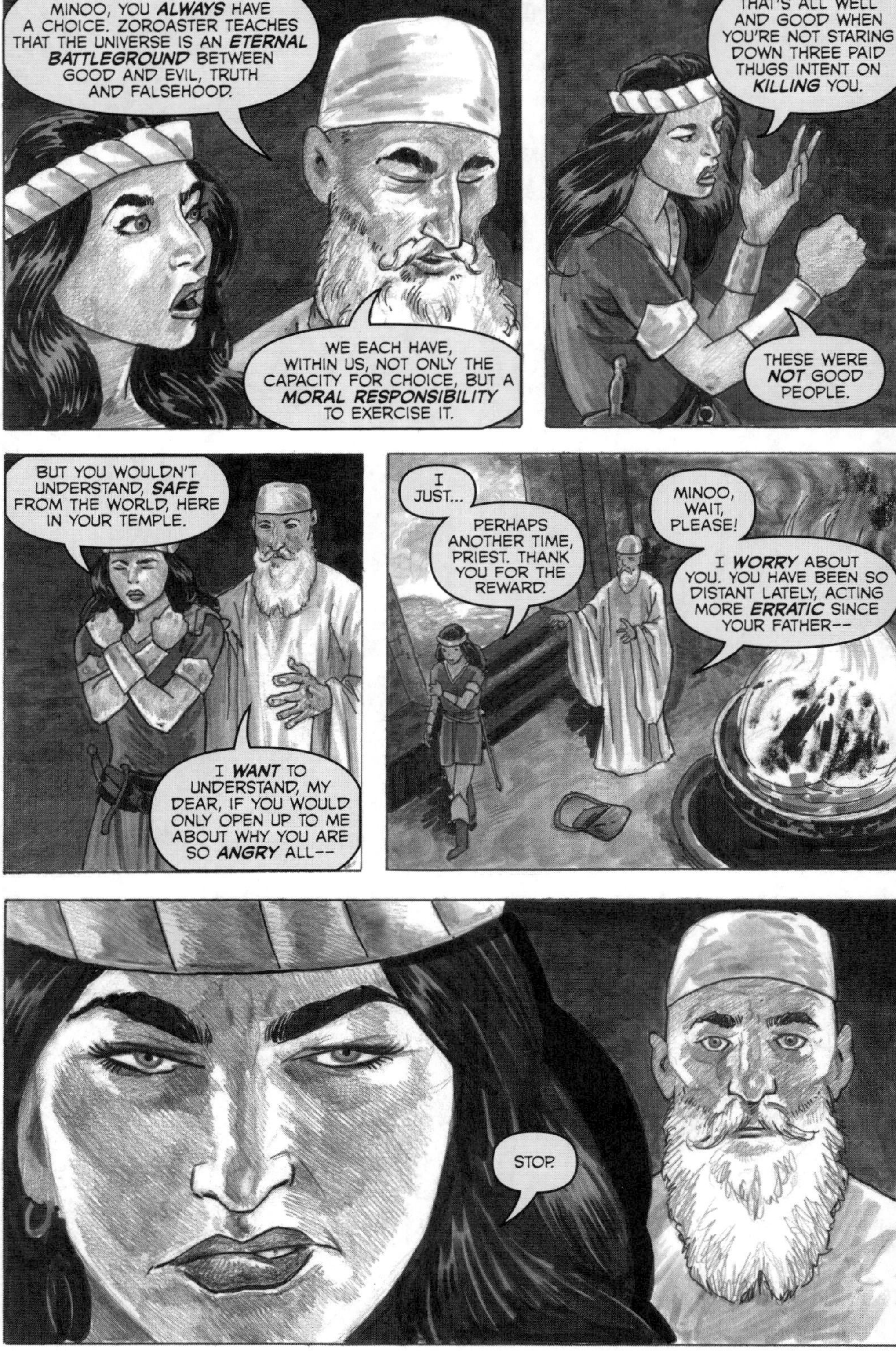
MINOO, YOU ALWAYS HAVE A CHOICE. ZOROASTER TEACHES THAT THE UNIVERSE IS AN ETERNAL BATTLEGROUND BETWEEN GOOD AND EVIL, TRUTH AND FALSEHOOD.
WE EACH HAVE, WITHIN US, NOT ONLY THE CAPACITY FOR CHOICE, BUT A MORAL RESPONSIBILITY TO EXERCISE IT.
THAT'S ALL WELL AND GOOD WHEN YOU'RE NOT STARING DOWN THREE PAID THUGS INTENT ON KILLING YOU.
THESE WERE NOT GOOD PEOPLE.
BUT YOU WOULDN'T UNDERSTAND, SAFE FROM THE WORLD, HERE IN YOUR TEMPLE.
I WANT TO UNDERSTAND, MY DEAR, IF YOU WOULD ONLY OPEN UP TO ME ABOUT WHY YOU ARE SO ANGRY ALL--
I JUST...
PERHAPS ANOTHER TIME, PRIEST. THANK YOU FOR THE REWARD.
MINOO, WAIT, PLEASE!
I WORRY ABOUT YOU. YOU HAVE BEEN SO DISTANT LATELY, ACTING MORE ERRATIC SINCE YOUR FATHER--
STOP.

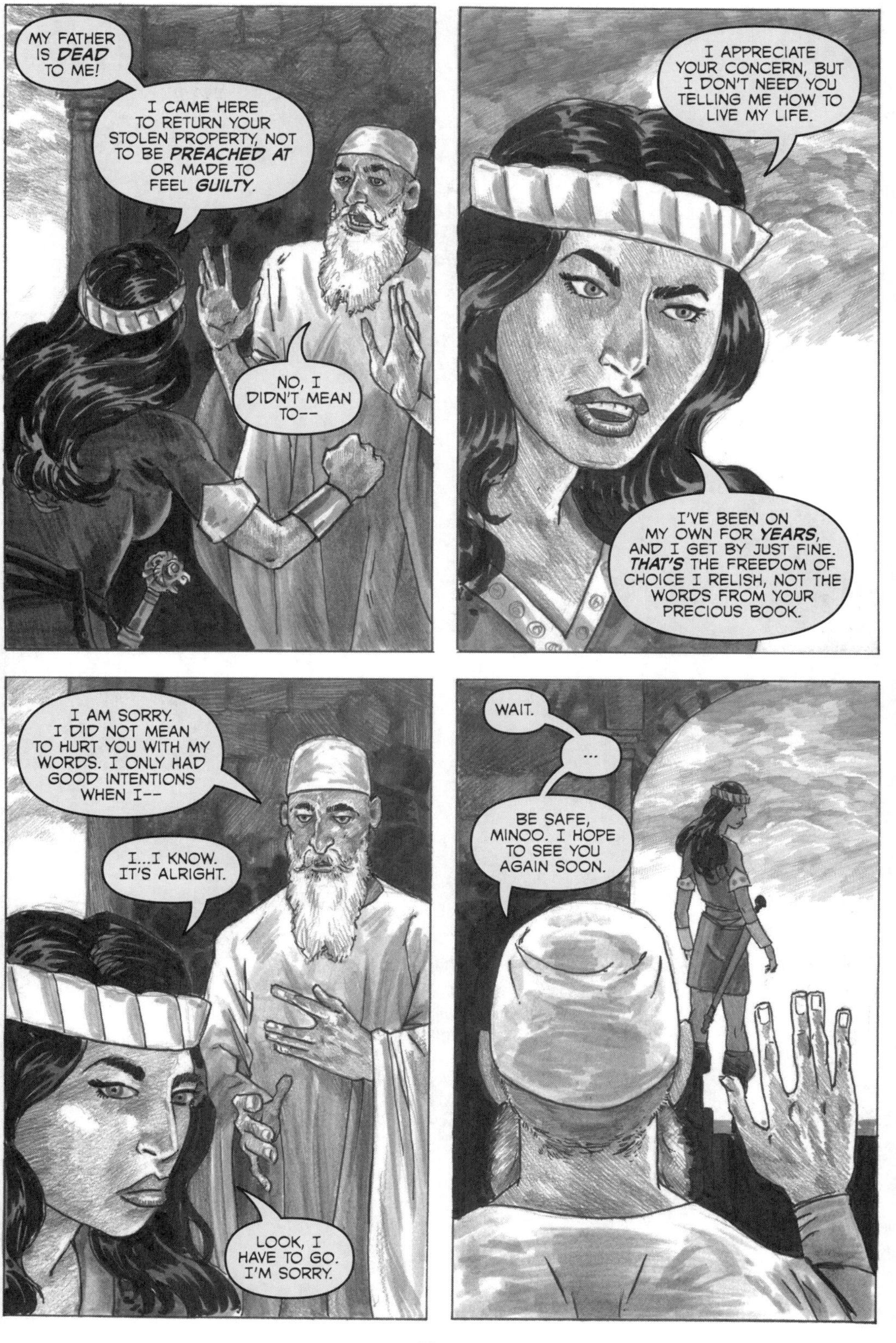

MY FATHER IS DEAD TO ME!
I CAME HERE TO RETURN YOUR STOLEN PROPERTY, NOT TO BE PREACHED AT OR MADE TO FEEL GUILTY.
NO, I DIDN'T MEAN TO--
I APPRECIATE YOUR CONCERN, BUT I DON'T NEED YOU TELLING ME HOW TO LIVE MY LIFE.
I'VE BEEN ON MY OWN FOR YEARS, AND I GET BY JUST FINE. THAT'S THE FREEDOM OF CHOICE I RELISH, NOT THE WORDS FROM YOUR PRECIOUS BOOK.
I AM SORRY. I DID NOT MEAN TO HURT YOU WITH MY WORDS. I ONLY HAD GOOD INTENTIONS WHEN I--
I...I KNOW. IT'S ALRIGHT.
LOOK, I HAVE TO GO. I'M SORRY.
WAIT.
...
BE SAFE, MINOO. I HOPE TO SEE YOU AGAIN SOON.

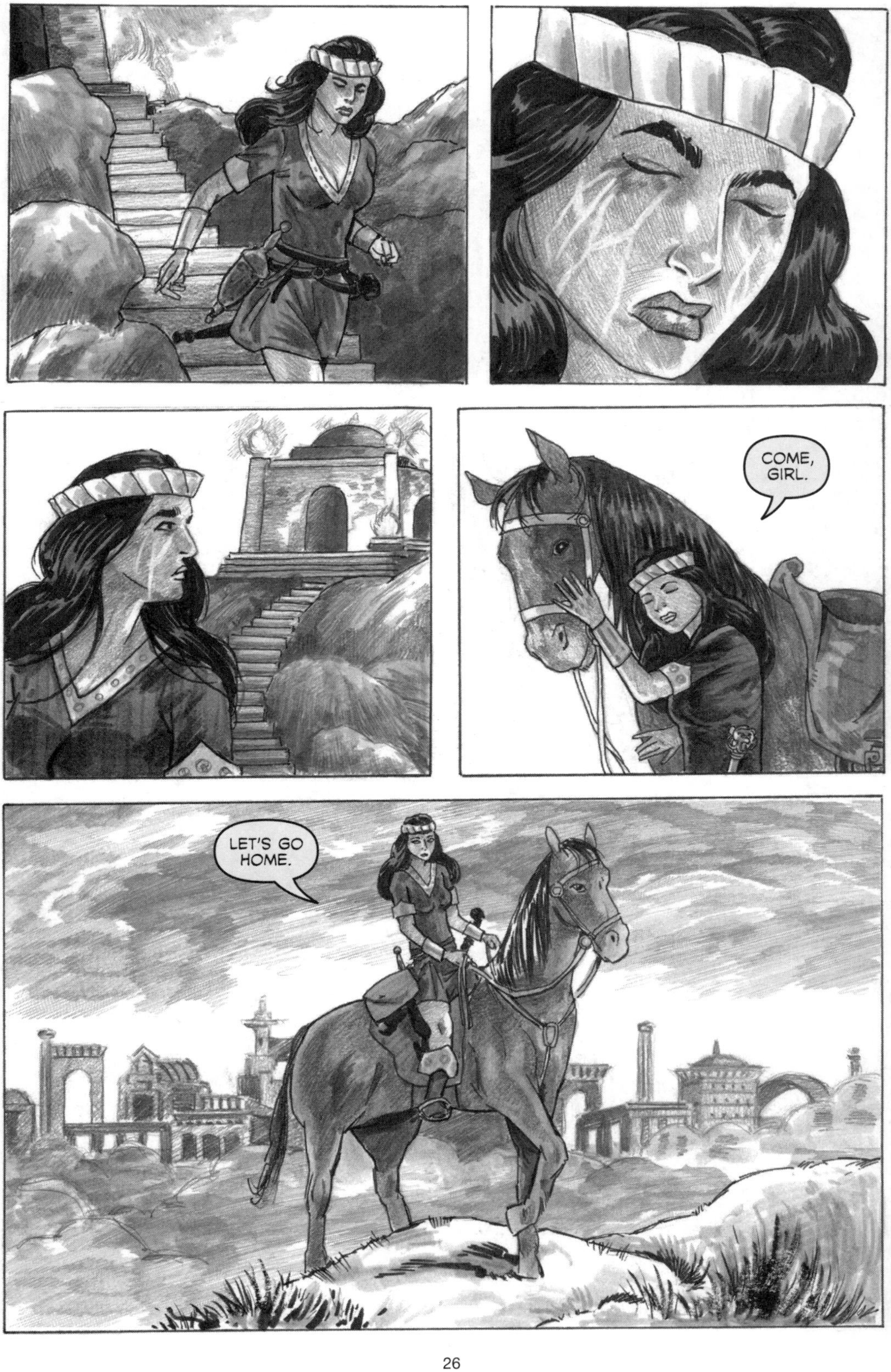
COME, GIRL.
LET'S GO HOME.

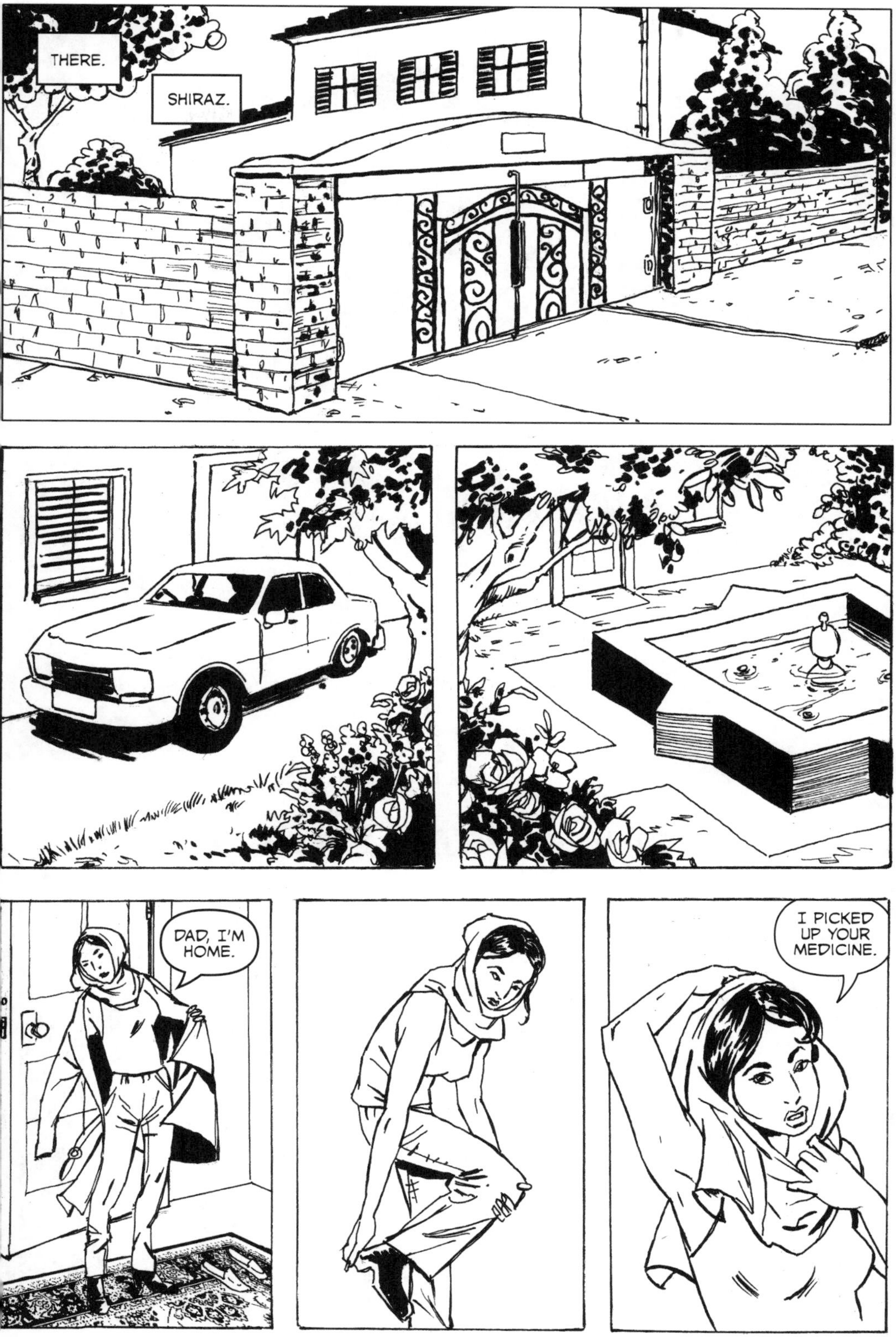
THERE.
SHIRAZ.
DAD, I'M HOME.
I PICKED UP YOUR MEDICINE.

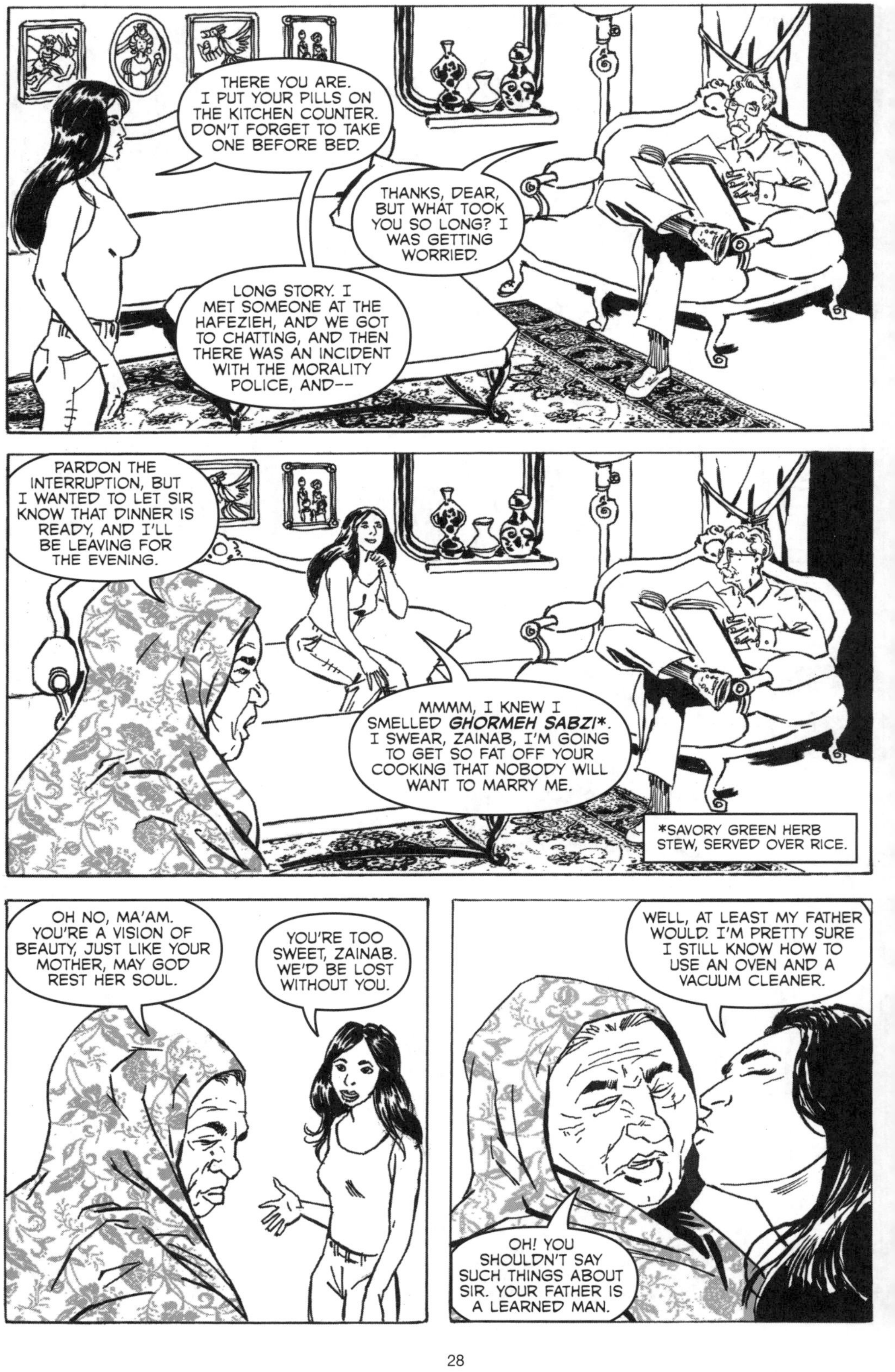
THERE YOU ARE. I PUT YOUR PILLS ON THE KITCHEN COUNTER. DON'T FORGET TO TAKE ONE BEFORE BED.
THANKS, DEAR, BUT WHAT TOOK YOU SO LONG? I WAS GETTING WORRIED.
LONG STORY. I MET SOMEONE AT THE HAFEZIEH, AND WE GOT TO CHATTING, AND THEN THERE WAS AN INCIDENT WITH THE MORALITY POLICE, AND--
PARDON THE INTERRUPTION, BUT I WANTED TO LET SIR KNOW THAT DINNER IS READY, AND I'LL BE LEAVING FOR THE EVENING.
MMMM, I KNEW I SMELLED ***GHORMEH SABZI****. I SWEAR, ZAINAB, I'M GOING TO GET SO FAT OFF YOUR COOKING THAT NOBODY WILL WANT TO MARRY ME.
*SAVORY GREEN HERB STEW, SERVED OVER RICE.
OH NO, MA'AM. YOU'RE A VISION OF BEAUTY, JUST LIKE YOUR MOTHER, MAY GOD REST HER SOUL.
YOU'RE TOO SWEET, ZAINAB. WE'D BE LOST WITHOUT YOU.
WELL, AT LEAST MY FATHER WOULD. I'M PRETTY SURE I STILL KNOW HOW TO USE AN OVEN AND A VACUUM CLEANER.
OH! YOU SHOULDN'T SAY SUCH THINGS ABOUT SIR. YOUR FATHER IS A LEARNED MAN.

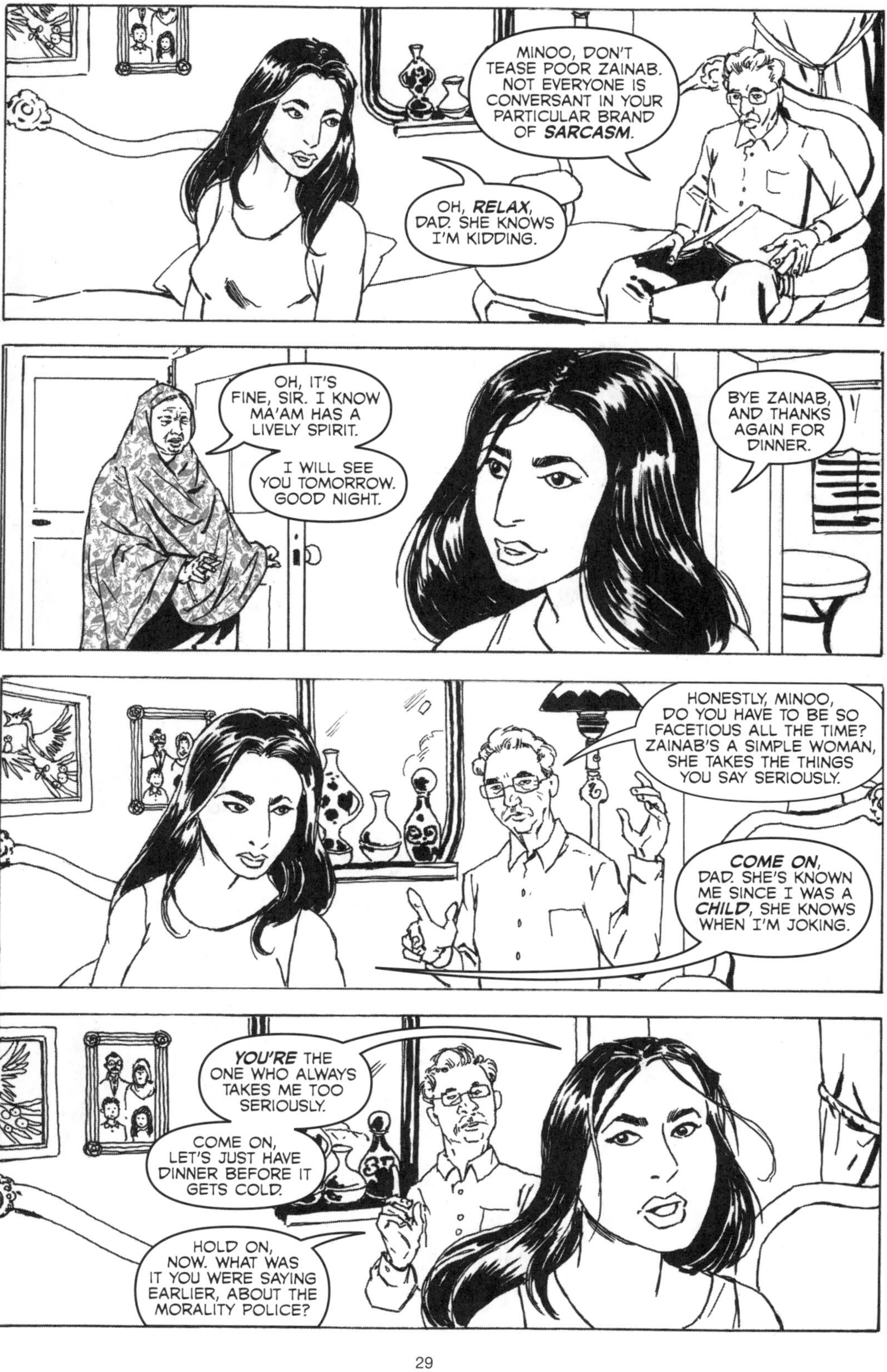
MINOO, DON'T TEASE POOR ZAINAB. NOT EVERYONE IS CONVERSANT IN YOUR PARTICULAR BRAND OF SARCASM.
OH, RELAX, DAD. SHE KNOWS I'M KIDDING.
OH, IT'S FINE, SIR. I KNOW MA'AM HAS A LIVELY SPIRIT.
I WILL SEE YOU TOMORROW. GOOD NIGHT.
BYE ZAINAB, AND THANKS AGAIN FOR DINNER.
HONESTLY, MINOO, DO YOU HAVE TO BE SO FACETIOUS ALL THE TIME? ZAINAB'S A SIMPLE WOMAN, SHE TAKES THE THINGS YOU SAY SERIOUSLY.
COME ON, DAD. SHE'S KNOWN ME SINCE I WAS A CHILD, SHE KNOWS WHEN I'M JOKING.
YOU'RE THE ONE WHO ALWAYS TAKES ME TOO SERIOUSLY.
COME ON, LET'S JUST HAVE DINNER BEFORE IT GETS COLD.
HOLD ON, NOW. WHAT WAS IT YOU WERE SAYING EARLIER, ABOUT THE MORALITY POLICE?

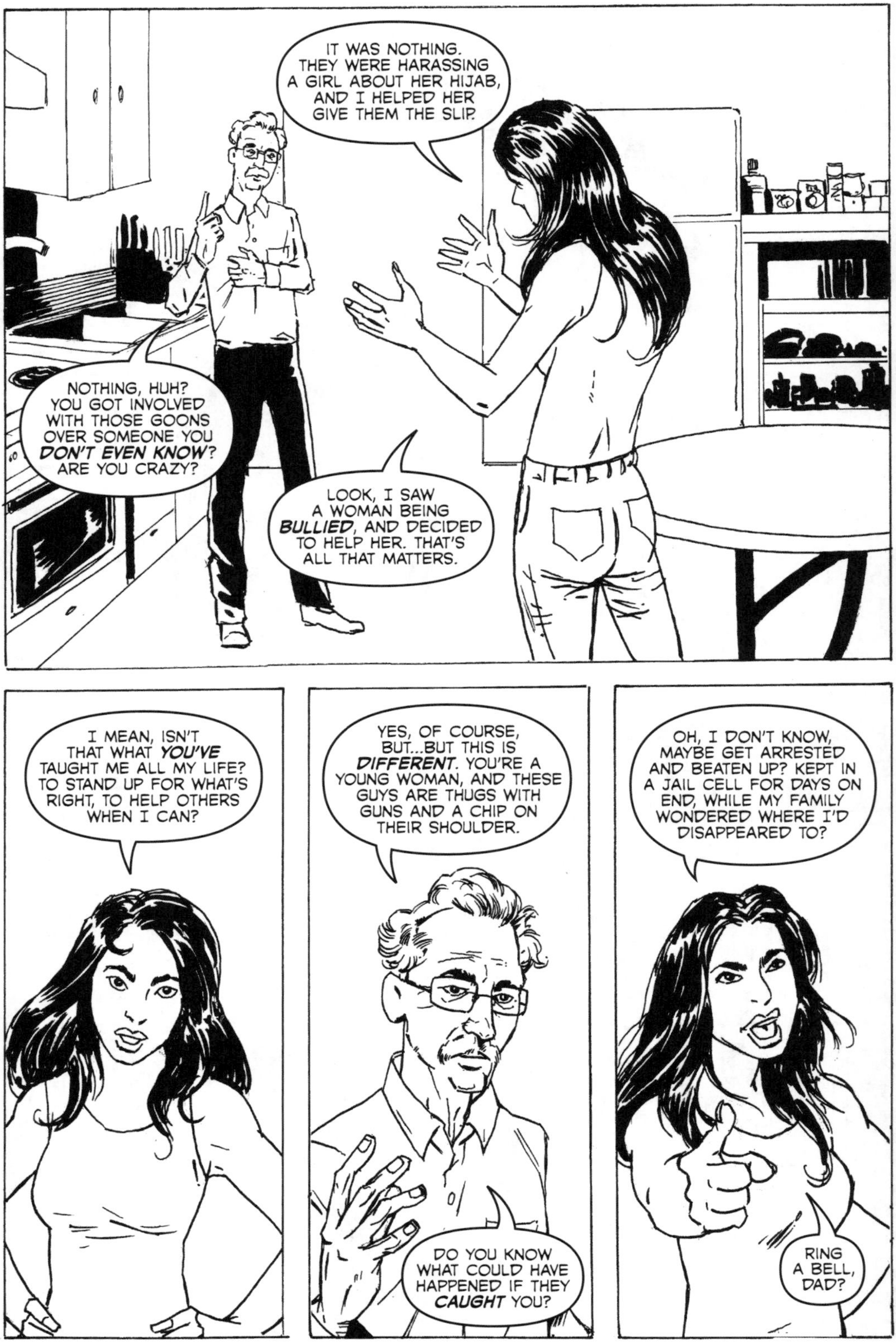
IT WAS NOTHING. THEY WERE HARASSING A GIRL ABOUT HER HIJAB, AND I HELPED HER GIVE THEM THE SLIP.
NOTHING, HUH? YOU GOT INVOLVED WITH THOSE GOONS OVER SOMEONE YOU DON'T EVEN KNOW? ARE YOU CRAZY?
LOOK, I SAW A WOMAN BEING BULLIED, AND DECIDED TO HELP HER. THAT'S ALL THAT MATTERS.
I MEAN, ISN'T THAT WHAT YOU'VE TAUGHT ME ALL MY LIFE? TO STAND UP FOR WHAT'S RIGHT, TO HELP OTHERS WHEN I CAN?
YES, OF COURSE, BUT...BUT THIS IS DIFFERENT. YOU'RE A YOUNG WOMAN, AND THESE GUYS ARE THUGS WITH GUNS AND A CHIP ON THEIR SHOULDER.
DO YOU KNOW WHAT COULD HAVE HAPPENED IF THEY CAUGHT YOU?
OH, I DON'T KNOW, MAYBE GET ARRESTED AND BEATEN UP? KEPT IN A JAIL CELL FOR DAYS ON END, WHILE MY FAMILY WONDERED WHERE I'D DISAPPEARED TO?
RING A BELL, DAD?

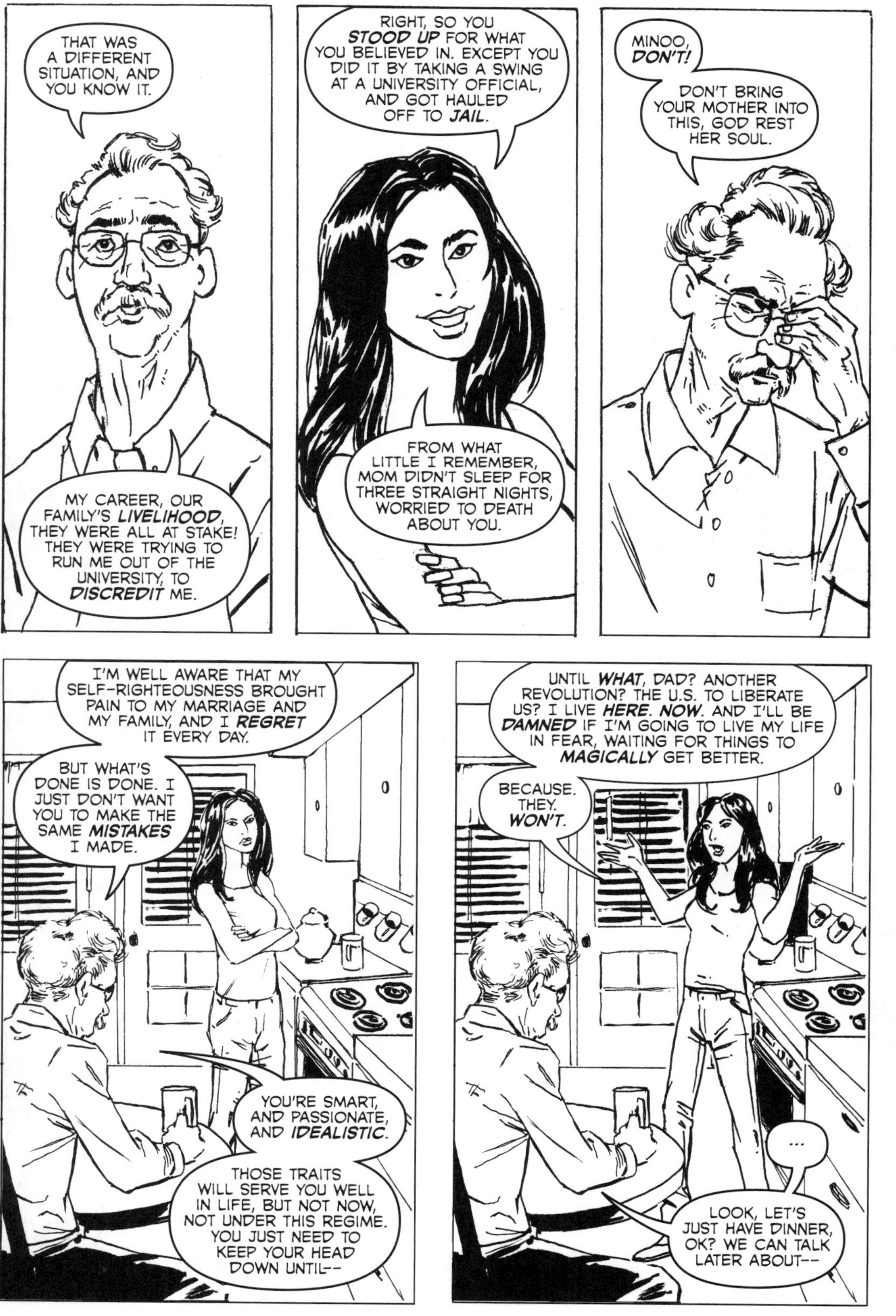
THAT WAS A DIFFERENT SITUATION, AND YOU KNOW IT.
MY CAREER, OUR FAMILY'S LIVELIHOOD, THEY WERE ALL AT STAKE! THEY WERE TRYING TO RUN ME OUT OF THE UNIVERSITY, TO DISCREDIT ME.
RIGHT, SO YOU STOOD UP FOR WHAT YOU BELIEVED IN. EXCEPT YOU DID IT BY TAKING A SWING AT A UNIVERSITY OFFICIAL, AND GOT HAULED OFF TO JAIL.
FROM WHAT LITTLE I REMEMBER, MOM DIDN'T SLEEP FOR THREE STRAIGHT NIGHTS, WORRIED TO DEATH ABOUT YOU.
MINOO, DON'T!
DON'T BRING YOUR MOTHER INTO THIS, GOD REST HER SOUL.
I'M WELL AWARE THAT MY SELF-RIGHTEOUSNESS BROUGHT PAIN TO MY MARRIAGE AND MY FAMILY, AND I REGRET IT EVERY DAY.
BUT WHAT'S DONE IS DONE. I JUST DON'T WANT YOU TO MAKE THE SAME MISTAKES I MADE.
YOU'RE SMART, AND PASSIONATE, AND IDEALISTIC.
THOSE TRAITS WILL SERVE YOU WELL IN LIFE, BUT NOT NOW, NOT UNDER THIS REGIME. YOU JUST NEED TO KEEP YOUR HEAD DOWN UNTIL--
UNTIL WHAT, DAD? ANOTHER REVOLUTION? THE U.S. TO LIBERATE US? I LIVE HERE. NOW. AND I'LL BE DAMNED IF I'M GOING TO LIVE MY LIFE IN FEAR, WAITING FOR THINGS TO MAGICALLY GET BETTER.
BECAUSE. THEY. WON'T.
...
LOOK, LET'S JUST HAVE DINNER, OK? WE CAN TALK LATER ABOUT--

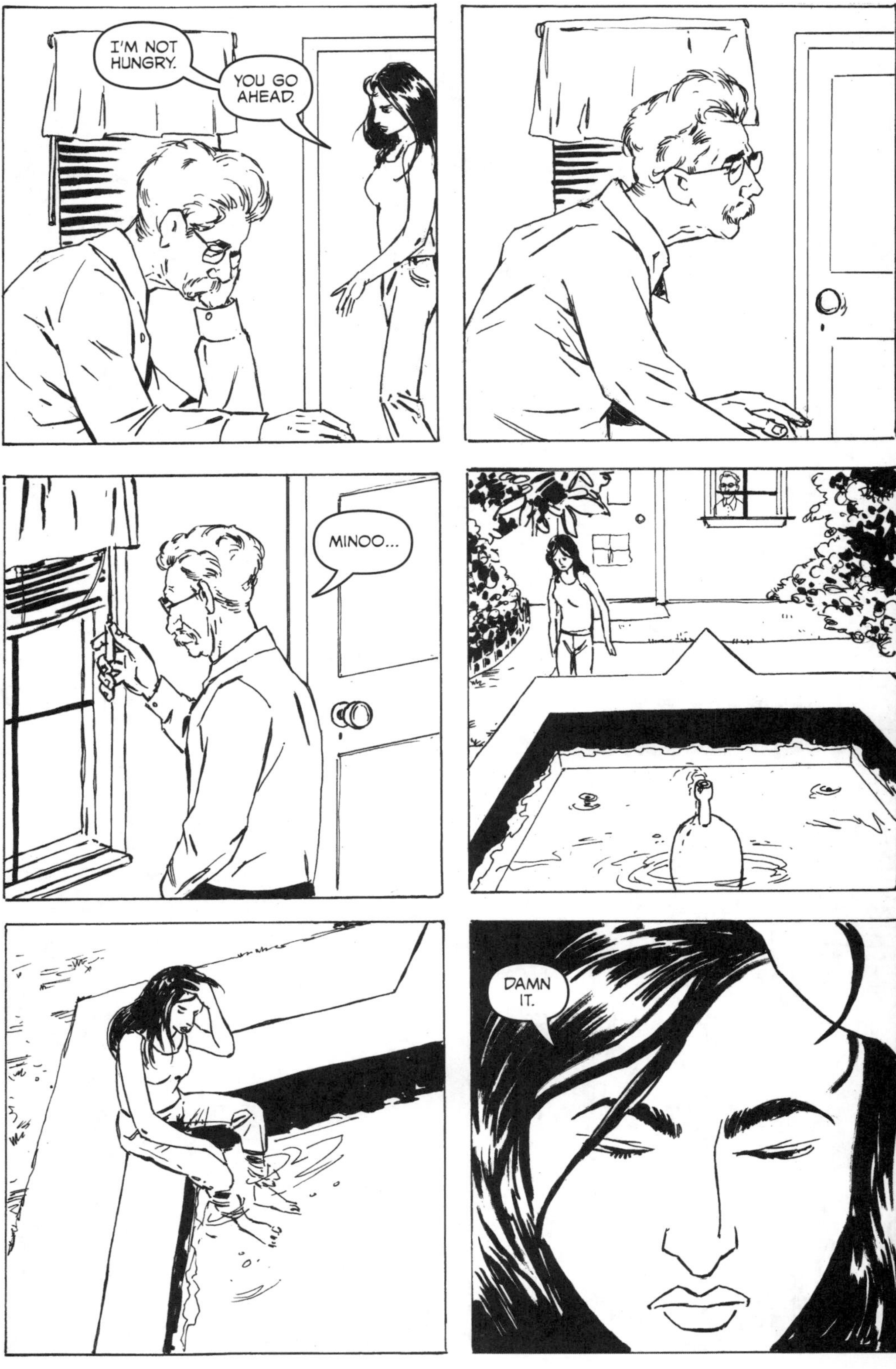
I'M NOT HUNGRY.
YOU GO AHEAD.
MINOO...
DAMN IT.

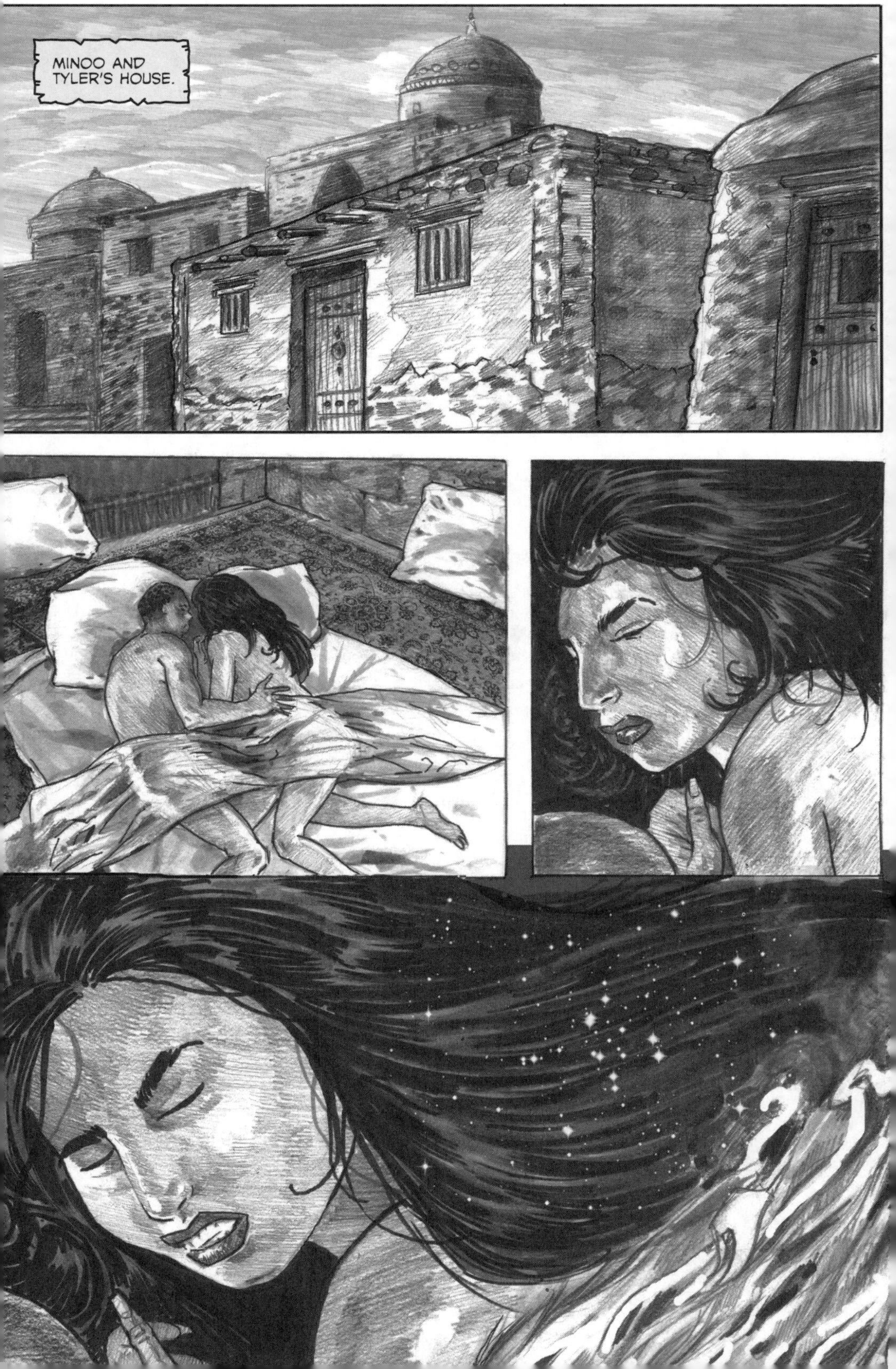
MINOO AND TYLER'S HOUSE.

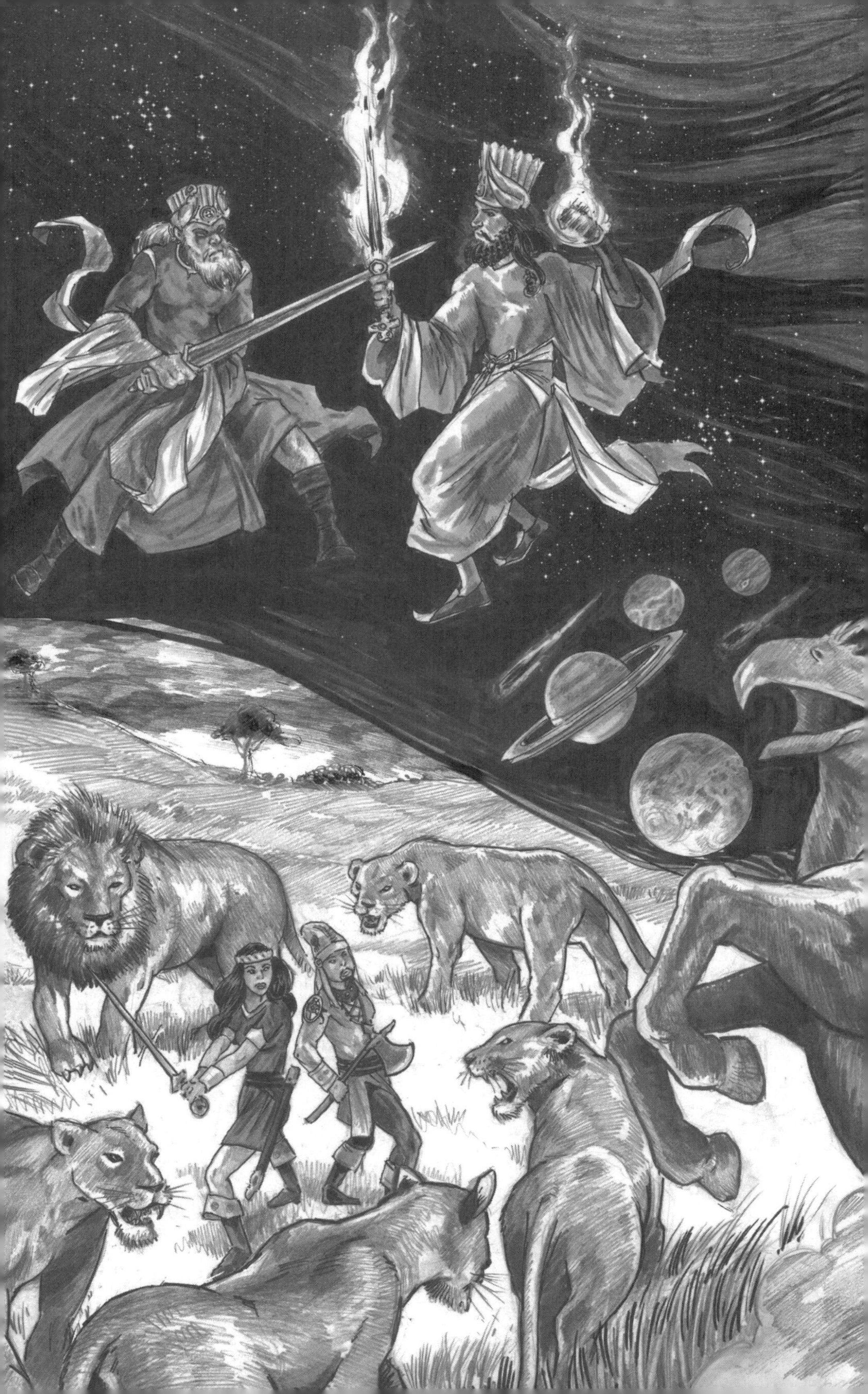

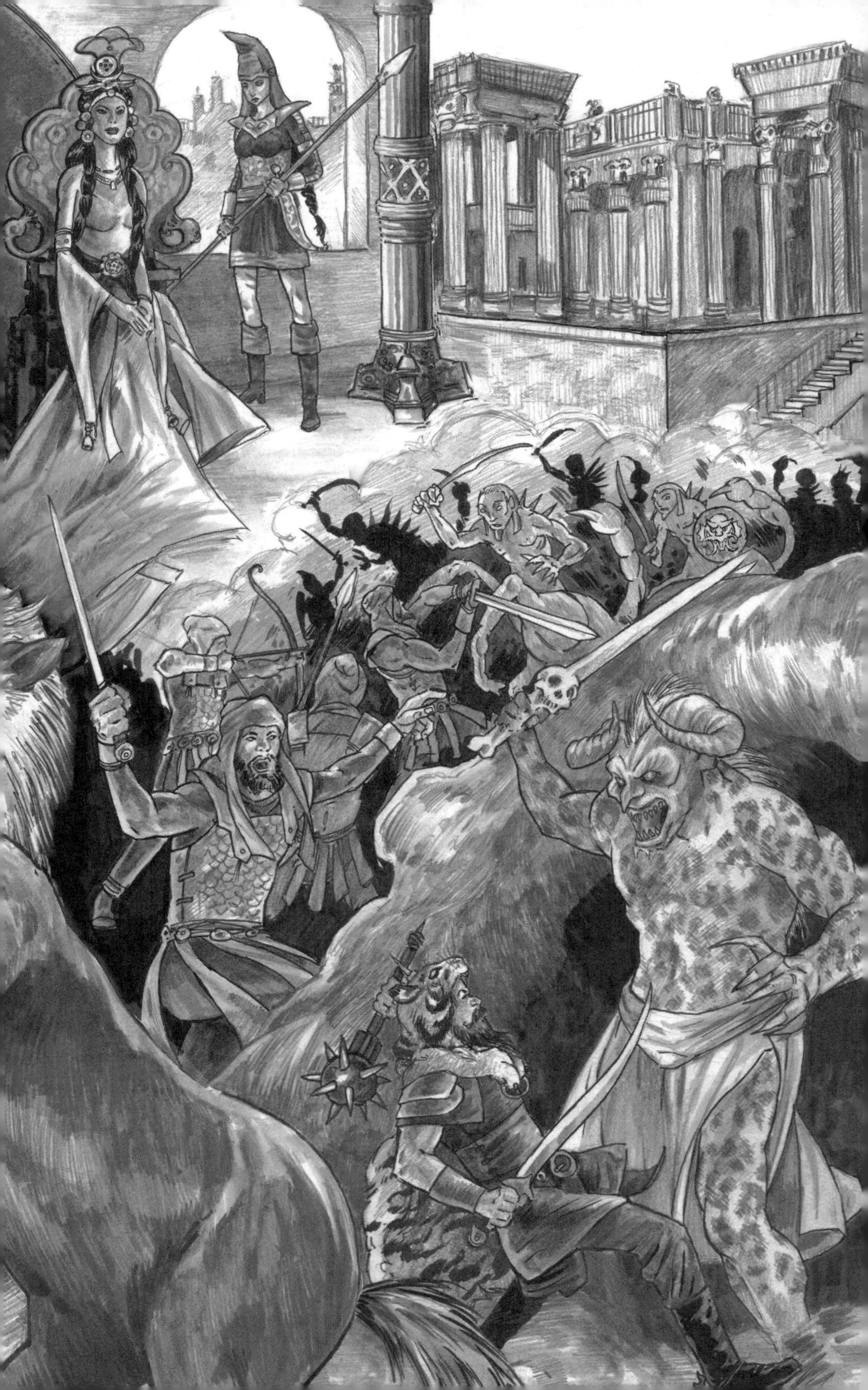

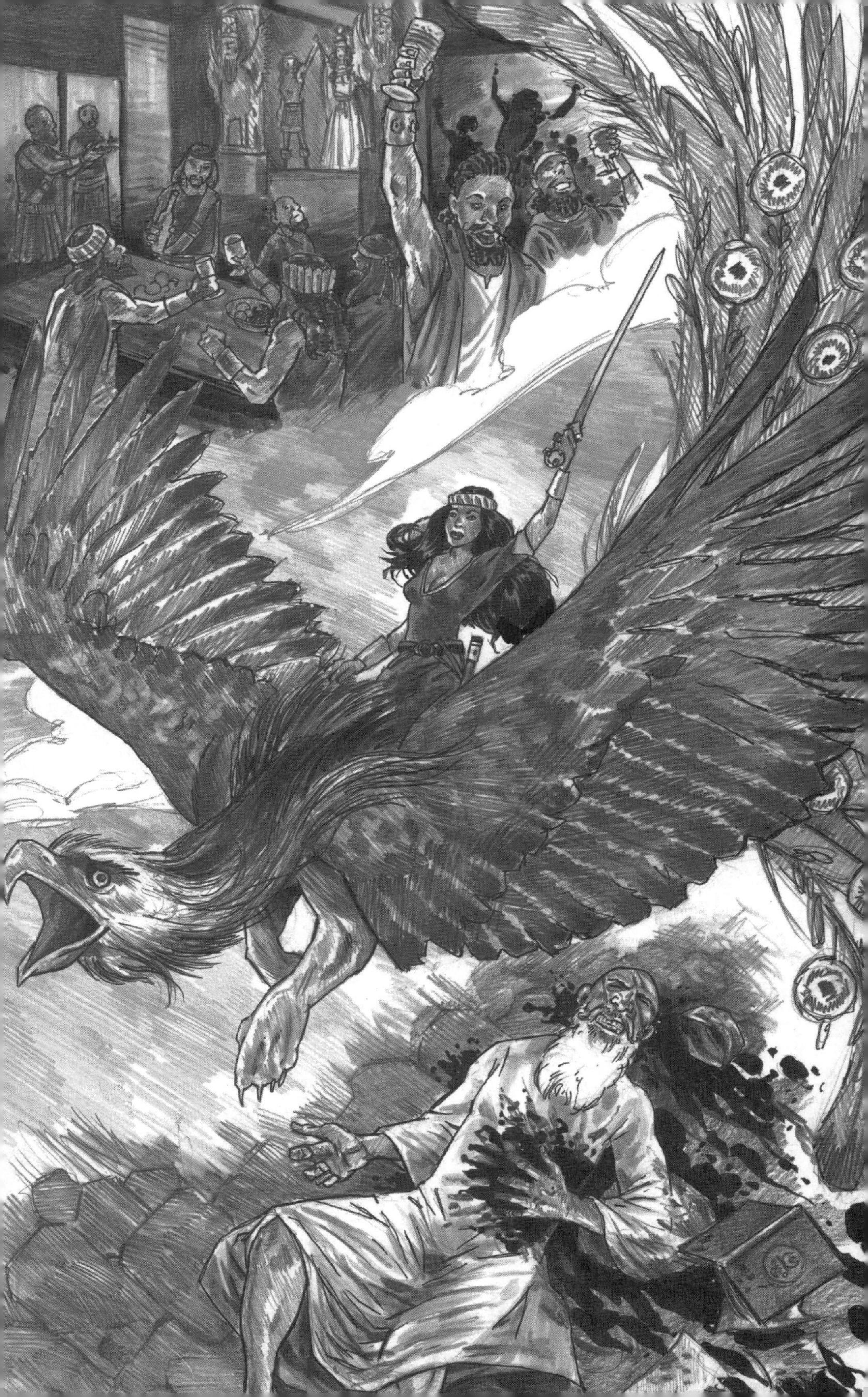

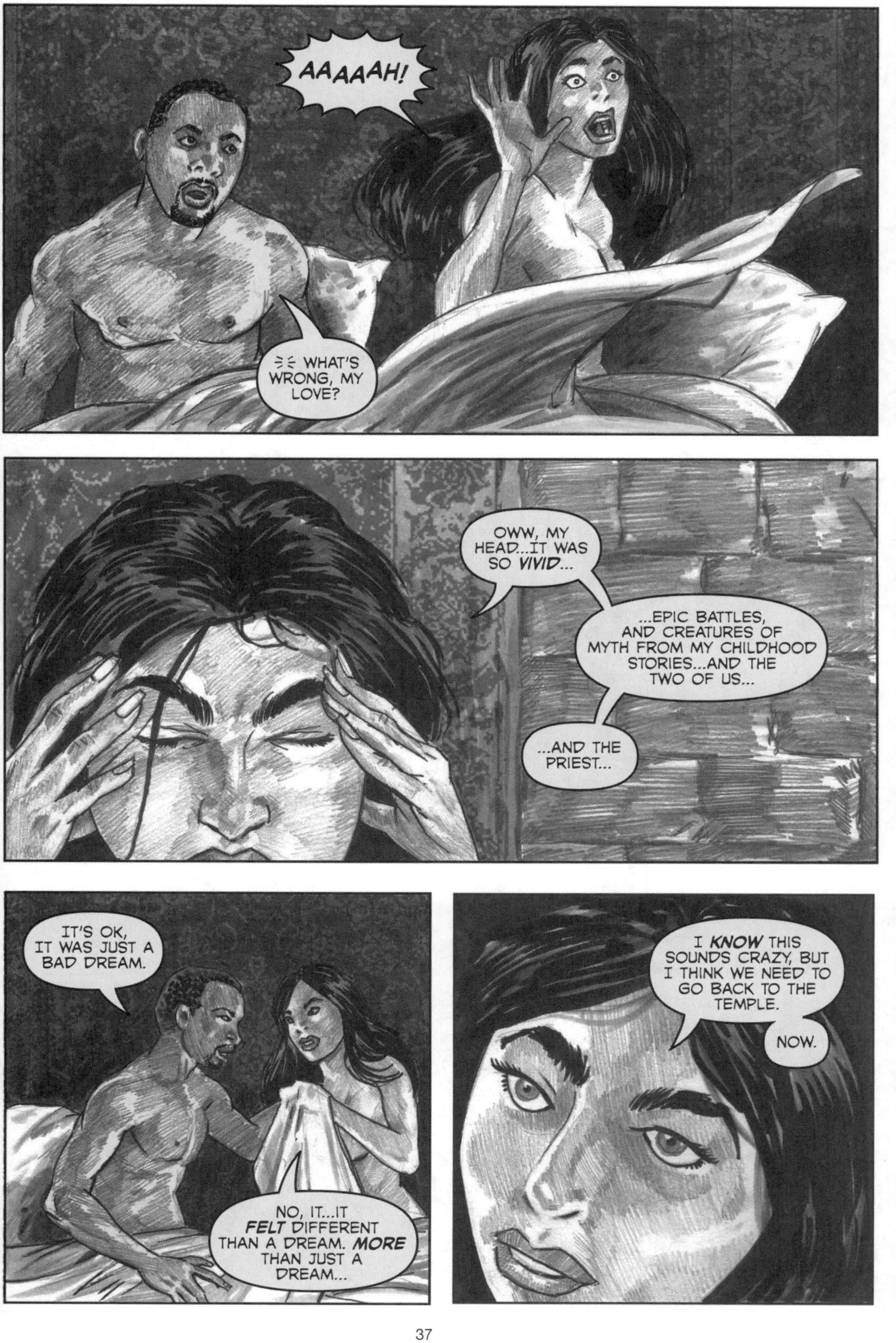
AAAAAH!
WHAT'S WRONG, MY LOVE?
OWW, MY HEAD...IT WAS SO VIVID...
...EPIC BATTLES, AND CREATURES OF MYTH FROM MY CHILDHOOD STORIES...AND THE TWO OF US...
...AND THE PRIEST...
IT'S OK, IT WAS JUST A BAD DREAM.
NO, IT...IT FELT DIFFERENT THAN A DREAM. MORE THAN JUST A DREAM...
I KNOW THIS SOUNDS CRAZY, BUT I THINK WE NEED TO GO BACK TO THE TEMPLE.
NOW.

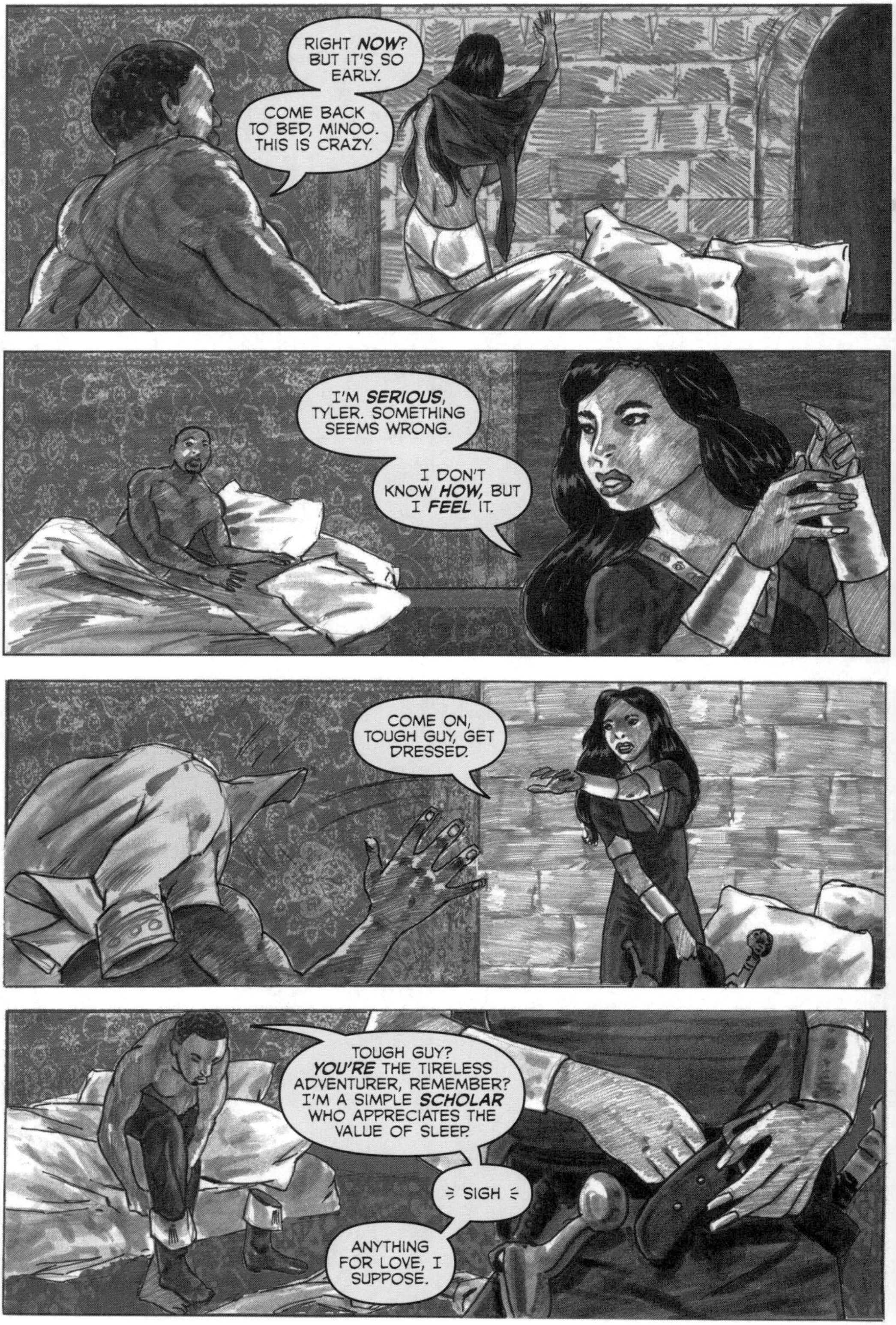
RIGHT NOW? BUT IT'S SO EARLY.
COME BACK TO BED, MINOO. THIS IS CRAZY.
I'M SERIOUS, TYLER. SOMETHING SEEMS WRONG.
I DON'T KNOW HOW, BUT I FEEL IT.
COME ON, TOUGH GUY, GET DRESSED.
TOUGH GUY? YOU'RE THE TIRELESS ADVENTURER, REMEMBER? I'M A SIMPLE SCHOLAR WHO APPRECIATES THE VALUE OF SLEEP.
SIGH
ANYTHING FOR LOVE, I SUPPOSE.

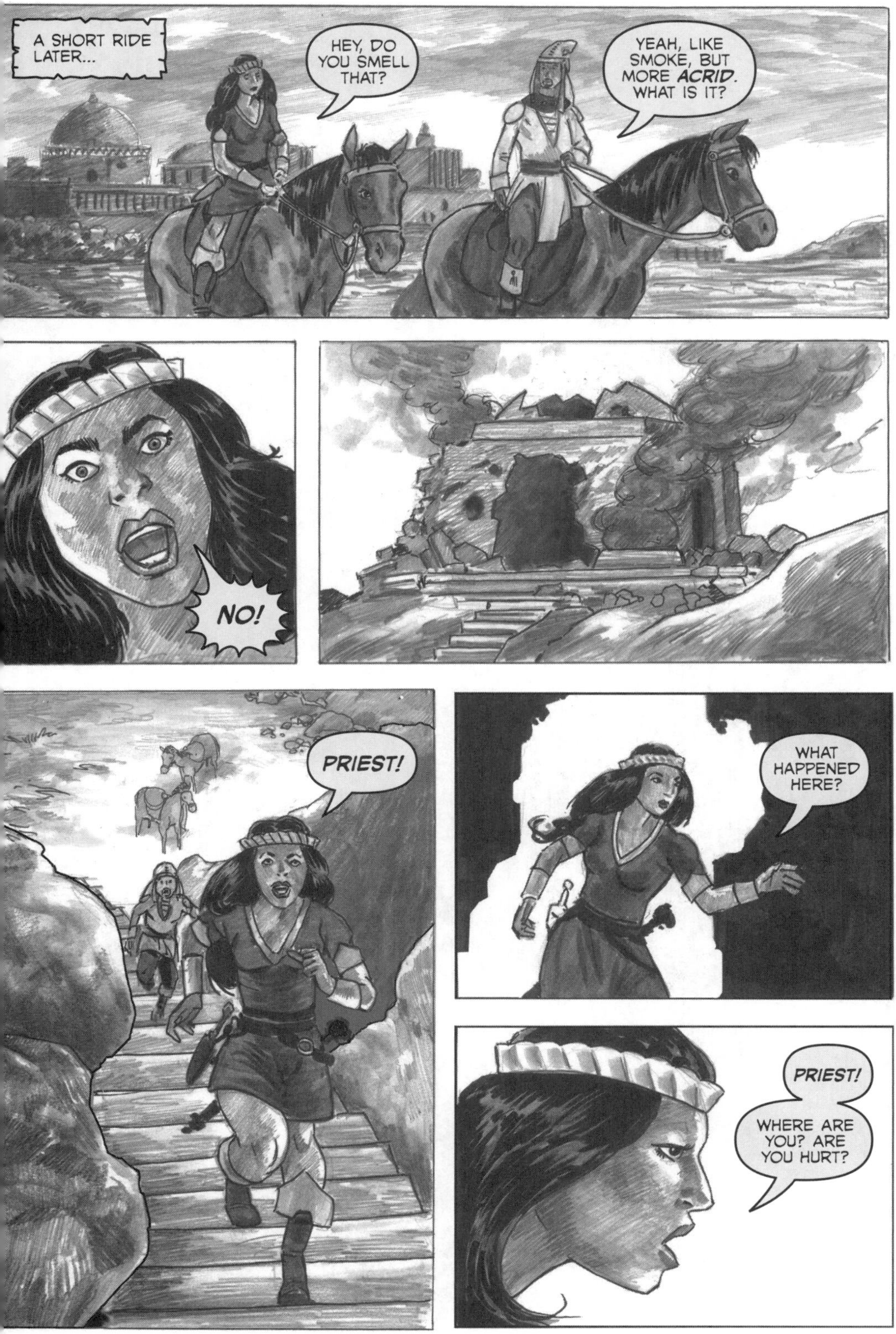
A SHORT RIDE LATER...
HEY, DO YOU SMELL THAT?
YEAH, LIKE SMOKE, BUT MORE *ACRID*. WHAT IS IT?
NO!
PRIEST!
WHAT HAPPENED HERE?
PRIEST!
WHERE ARE YOU? ARE YOU HURT?

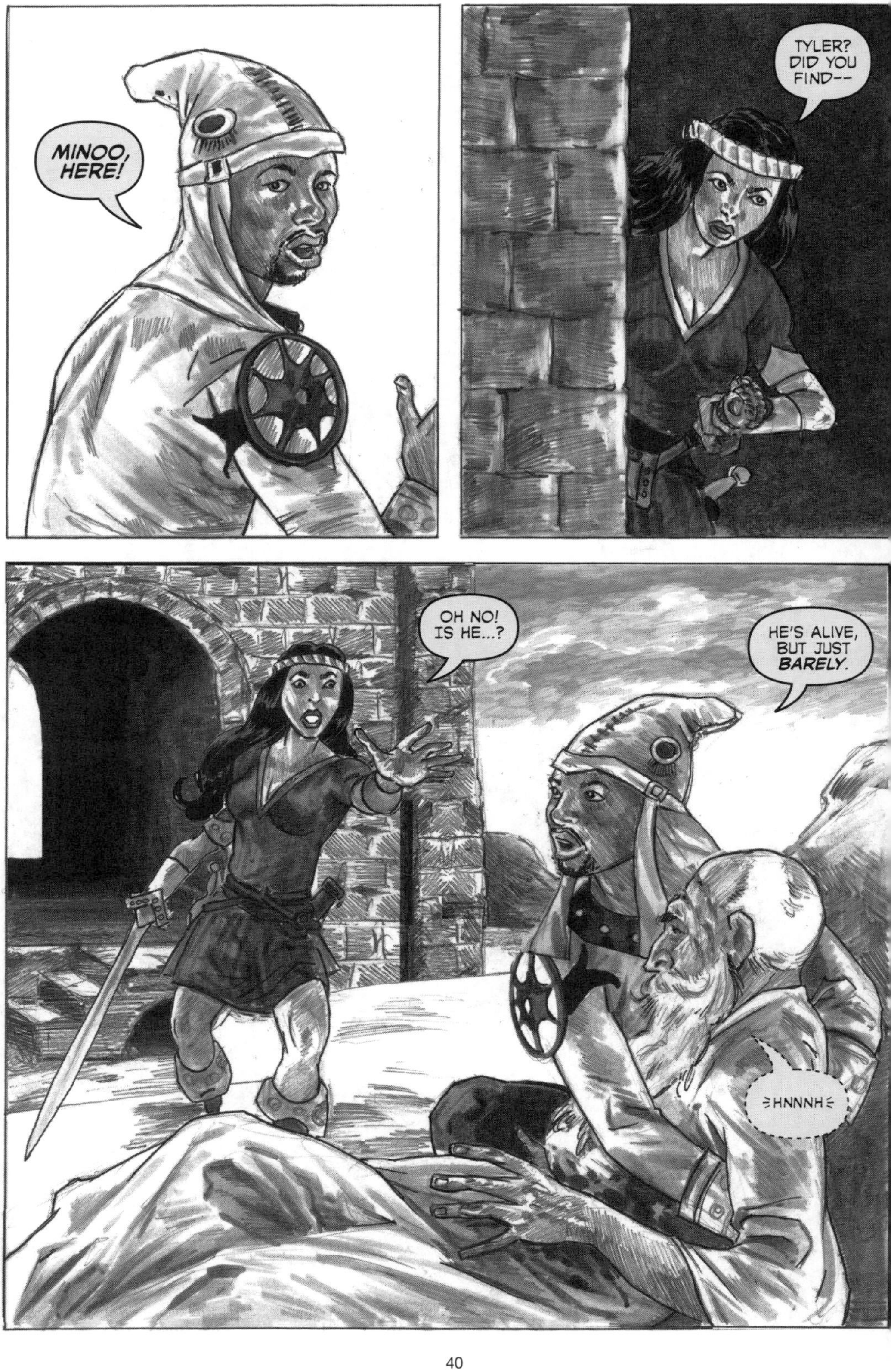
MINOO, HERE!
TYLER? DID YOU FIND--
OH NO! IS HE...?
HE'S ALIVE, BUT JUST BARELY.
HNNNH

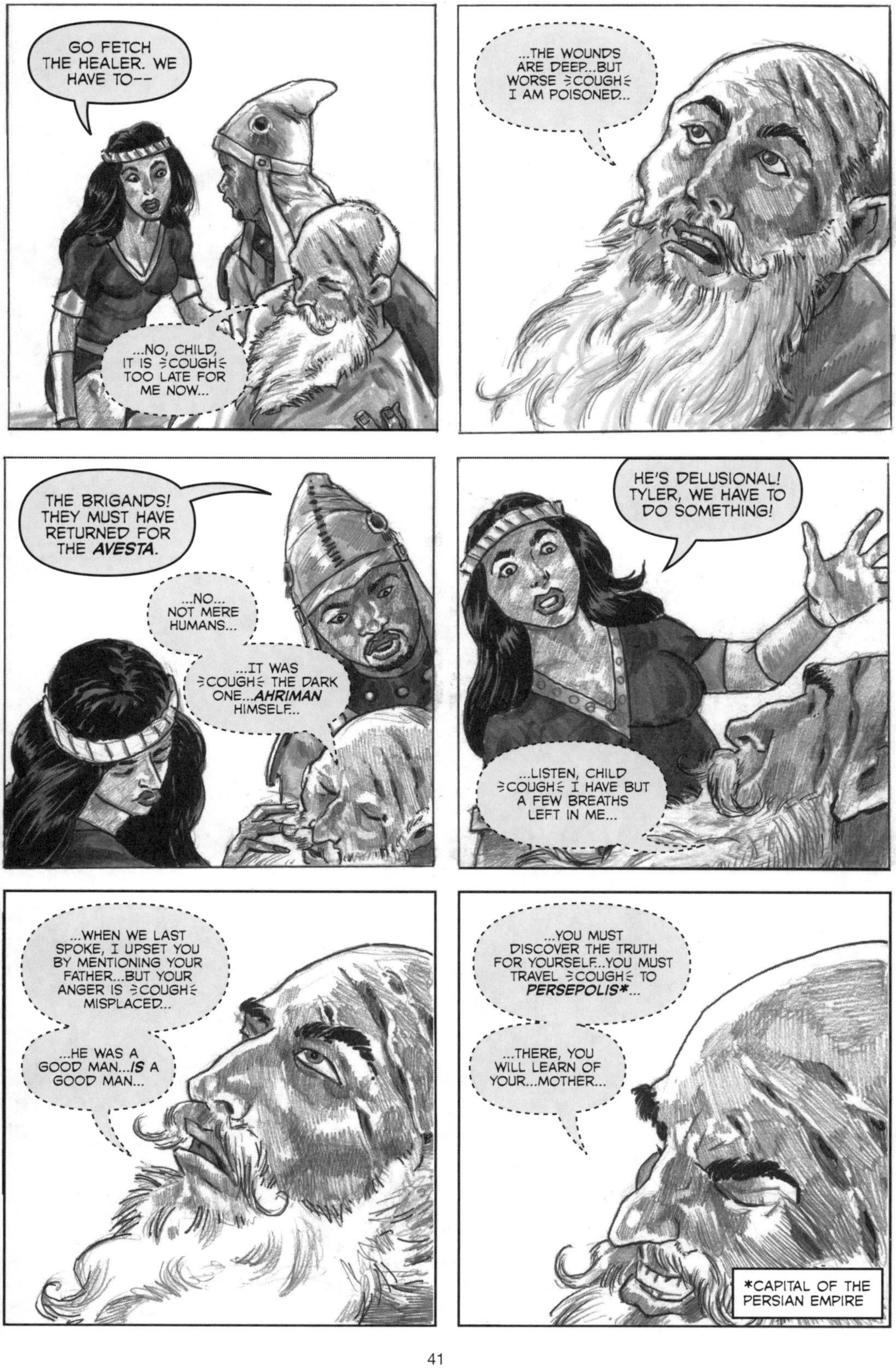
GO FETCH THE HEALER. WE HAVE TO--
...NO, CHILD, IT IS ≶COUGH≶ TOO LATE FOR ME NOW...
...THE WOUNDS ARE DEEP...BUT WORSE ≶COUGH≶ I AM POISONED...
THE BRIGANDS! THEY MUST HAVE RETURNED FOR THE *AVESTA*.
...NO... NOT MERE HUMANS...
...IT WAS ≶COUGH≶ THE DARK ONE...*AHRIMAN* HIMSELF...
HE'S DELUSIONAL! TYLER, WE HAVE TO DO SOMETHING!
...LISTEN, CHILD ≶COUGH≶ I HAVE BUT A FEW BREATHS LEFT IN ME...
...WHEN WE LAST SPOKE, I UPSET YOU BY MENTIONING YOUR FATHER...BUT YOUR ANGER IS ≶COUGH≶ MISPLACED...
...HE WAS A GOOD MAN...*IS* A GOOD MAN...
...YOU MUST DISCOVER THE TRUTH FOR YOURSELF...YOU MUST TRAVEL ≶COUGH≶ TO *PERSEPOLIS**...
...THERE, YOU WILL LEARN OF YOUR...MOTHER...
*CAPITAL OF THE PERSIAN EMPIRE

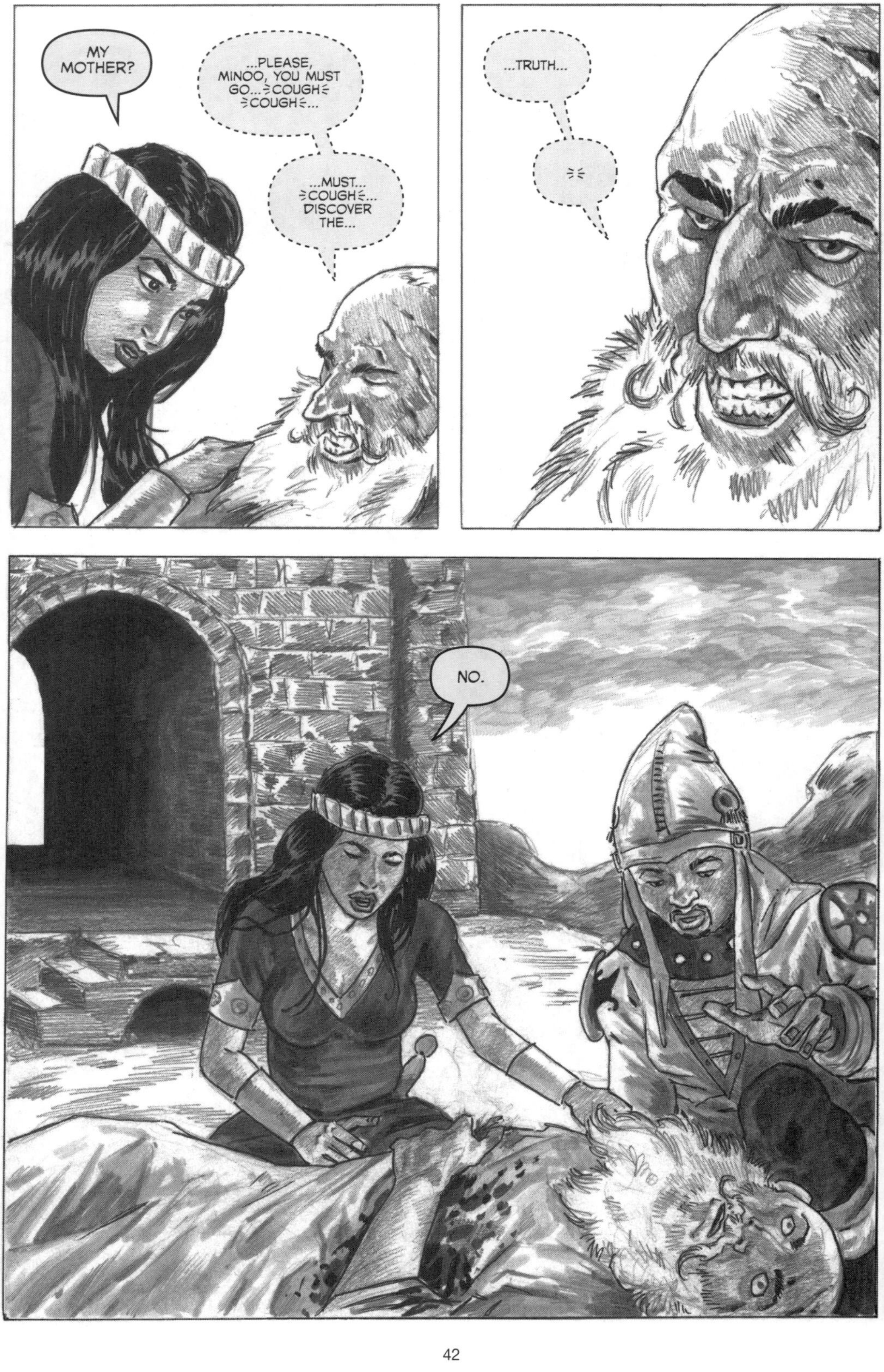
MY MOTHER?
...PLEASE, MINOO, YOU MUST GO... ⋛COUGH⋚ ⋛COUGH⋚...
...MUST... ⋛COUGH⋚... DISCOVER THE...
...TRUTH...
NO.

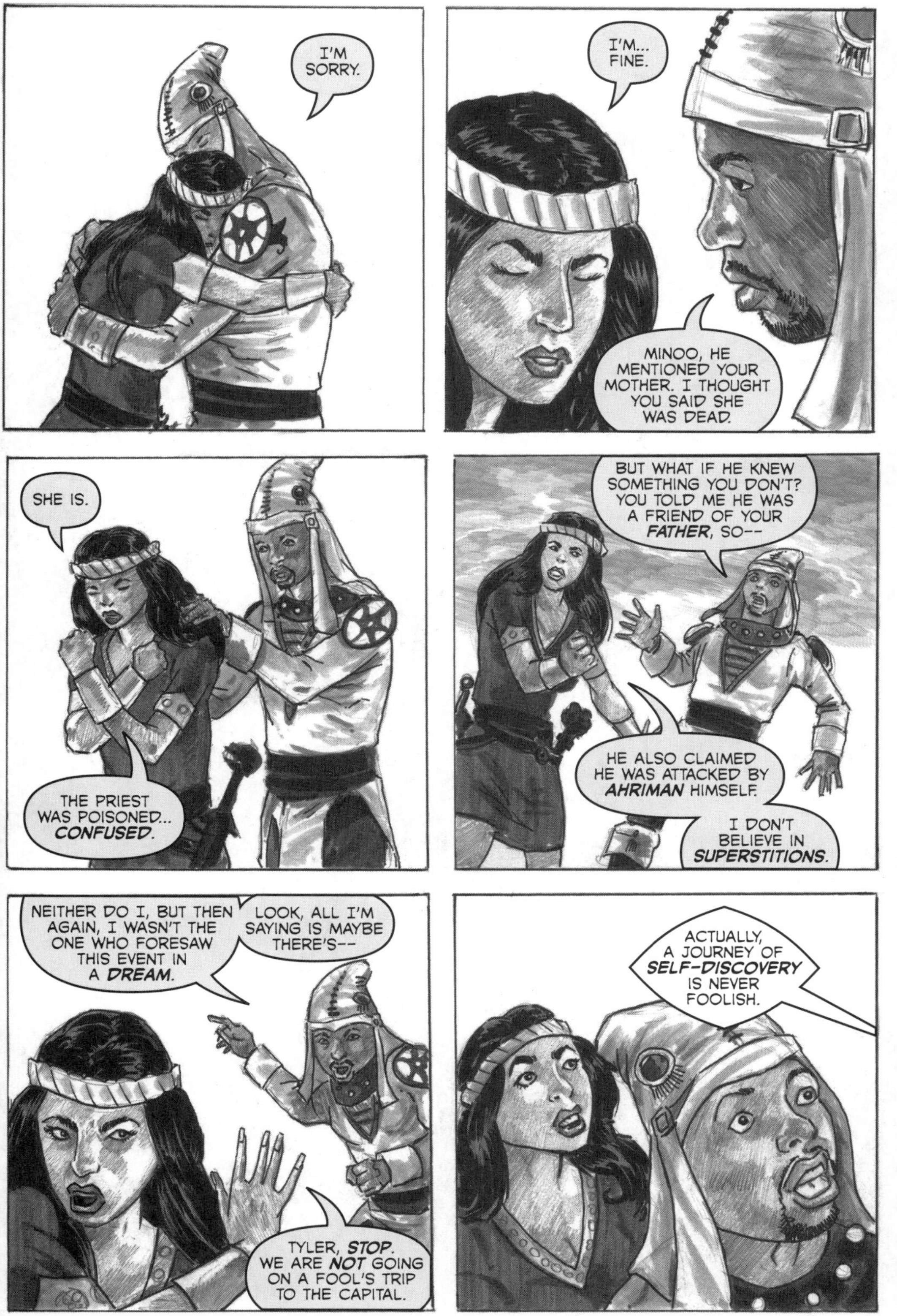
I'M SORRY.
I'M... FINE.
MINOO, HE MENTIONED YOUR MOTHER. I THOUGHT YOU SAID SHE WAS DEAD.
SHE IS.
THE PRIEST WAS POISONED... CONFUSED.
BUT WHAT IF HE KNEW SOMETHING YOU DON'T? YOU TOLD ME HE WAS A FRIEND OF YOUR FATHER, SO--
HE ALSO CLAIMED HE WAS ATTACKED BY AHRIMAN HIMSELF.
I DON'T BELIEVE IN SUPERSTITIONS.
NEITHER DO I, BUT THEN AGAIN, I WASN'T THE ONE WHO FORESAW THIS EVENT IN A DREAM.
LOOK, ALL I'M SAYING IS MAYBE THERE'S--
TYLER, STOP. WE ARE NOT GOING ON A FOOL'S TRIP TO THE CAPITAL.
ACTUALLY, A JOURNEY OF SELF-DISCOVERY IS NEVER FOOLISH.

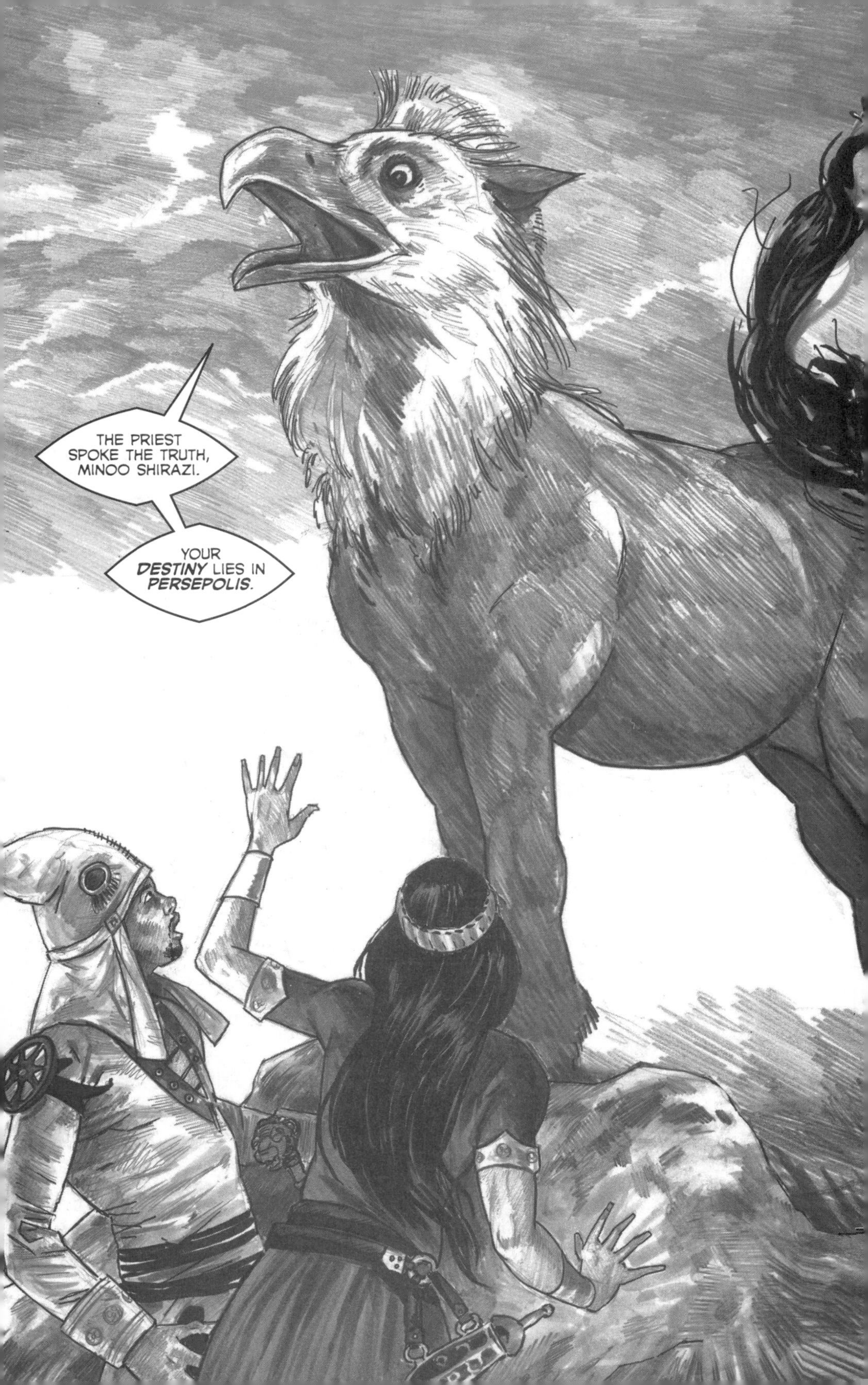
THE PRIEST SPOKE THE TRUTH, MINOO SHIRAZI.
YOUR **DESTINY** LIES IN **PERSEPOLIS**.

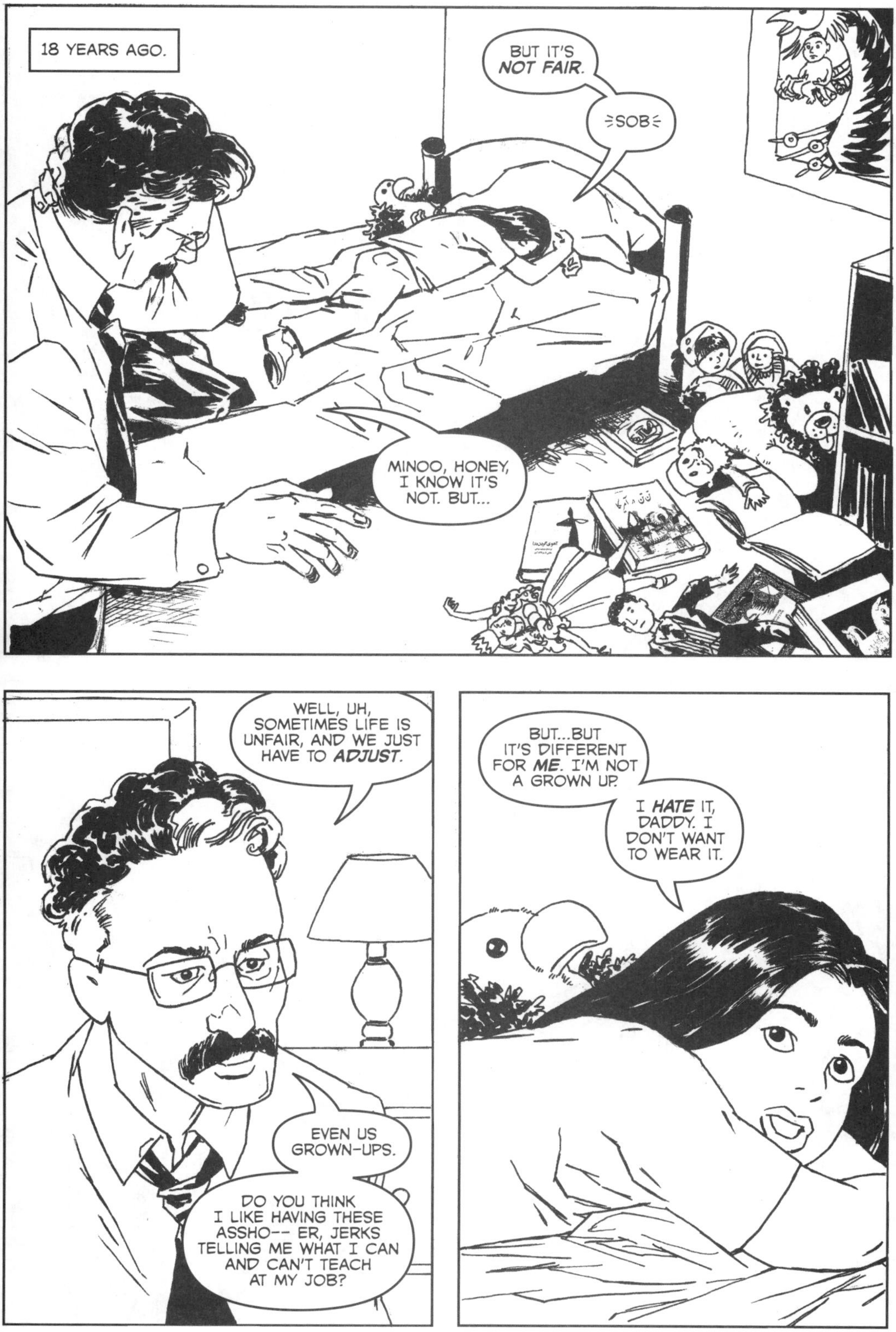
18 YEARS AGO.
BUT IT'S NOT FAIR.
SOB
MINOO, HONEY, I KNOW IT'S NOT. BUT...
WELL, UH, SOMETIMES LIFE IS UNFAIR, AND WE JUST HAVE TO ADJUST.
EVEN US GROWN-UPS.
DO YOU THINK I LIKE HAVING THESE ASSHO-- ER, JERKS TELLING ME WHAT I CAN AND CAN'T TEACH AT MY JOB?
BUT...BUT IT'S DIFFERENT FOR ME. I'M NOT A GROWN UP.
I HATE IT, DADDY. I DON'T WANT TO WEAR IT.

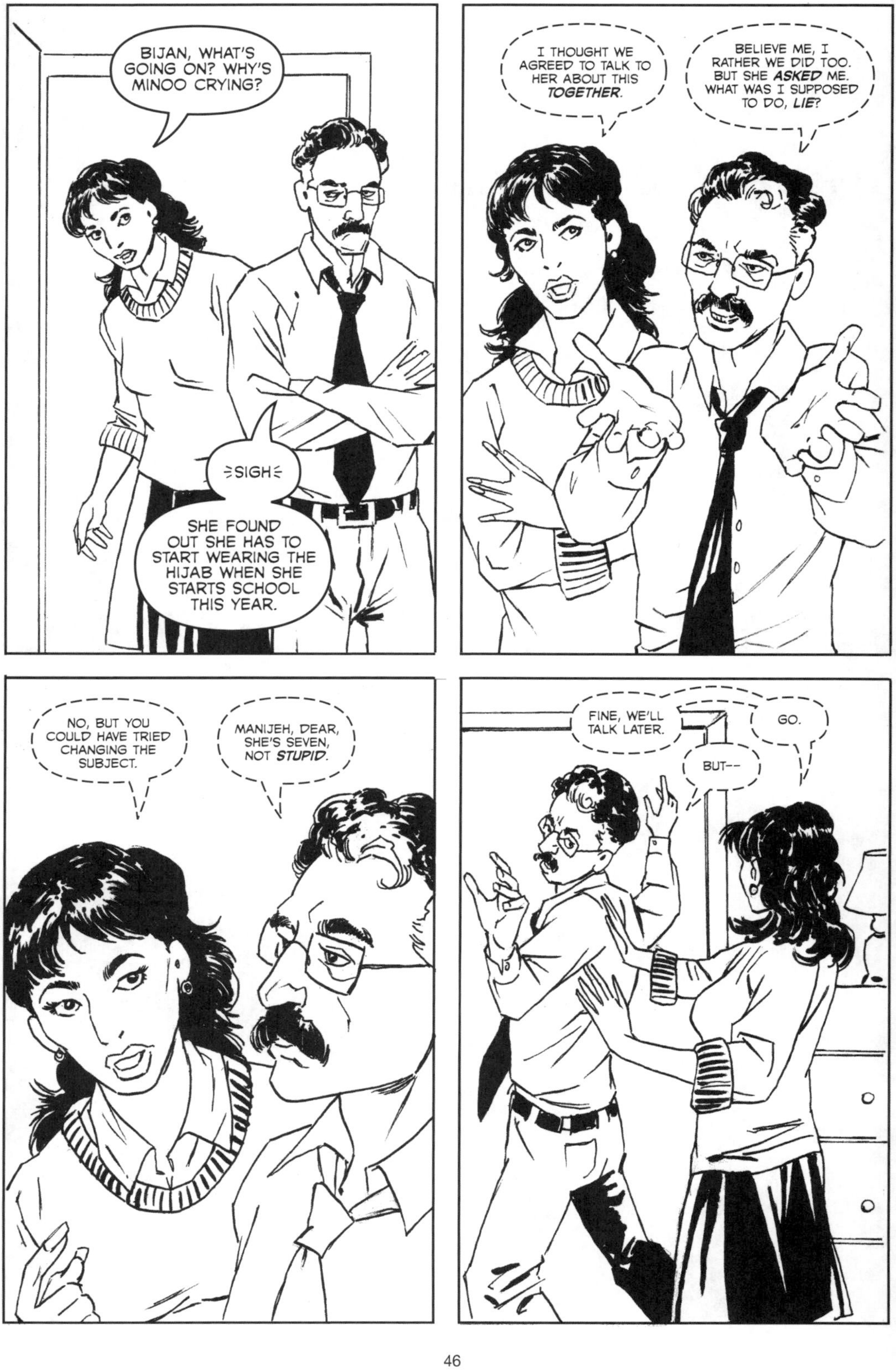
BIJAN, WHAT'S GOING ON? WHY'S MINOO CRYING?
≡SIGH≡
SHE FOUND OUT SHE HAS TO START WEARING THE HIJAB WHEN SHE STARTS SCHOOL THIS YEAR.
I THOUGHT WE AGREED TO TALK TO HER ABOUT THIS *TOGETHER*.
BELIEVE ME, I RATHER WE DID TOO. BUT SHE *ASKED* ME. WHAT WAS I SUPPOSED TO DO, *LIE*?
NO, BUT YOU COULD HAVE TRIED CHANGING THE SUBJECT.
MANIJEH, DEAR, SHE'S SEVEN, NOT *STUPID*.
FINE, WE'LL TALK LATER.
BUT--
GO.

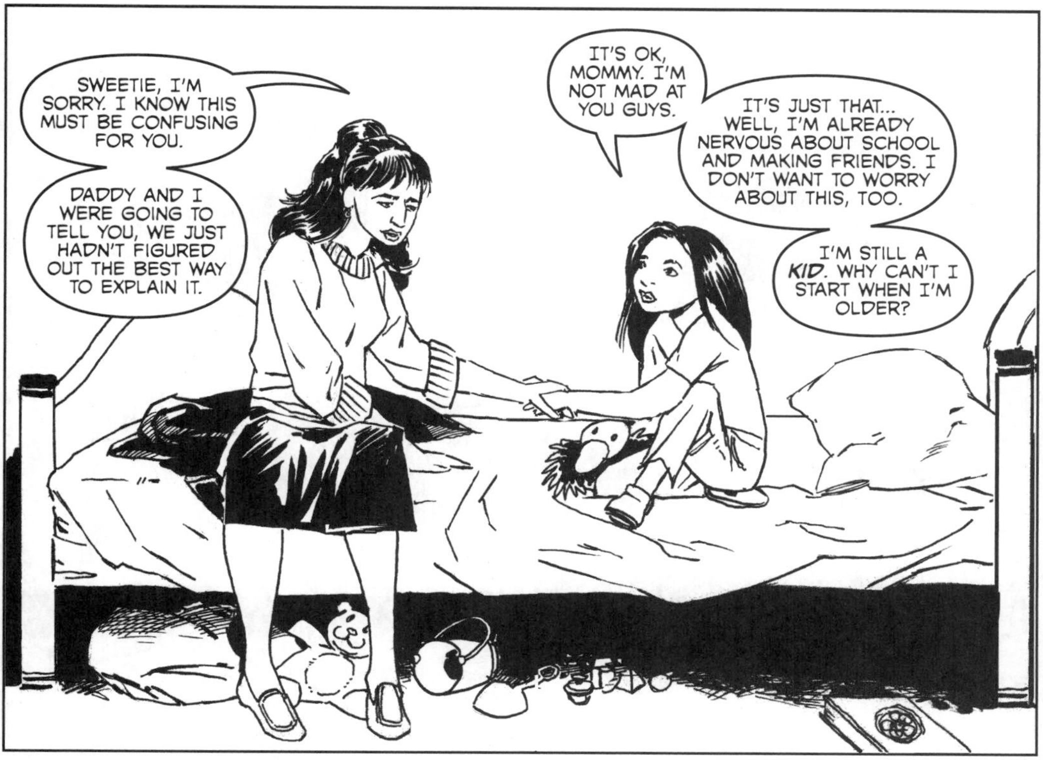
SWEETIE, I'M SORRY. I KNOW THIS MUST BE CONFUSING FOR YOU.
DADDY AND I WERE GOING TO TELL YOU, WE JUST HADN'T FIGURED OUT THE BEST WAY TO EXPLAIN IT.
IT'S OK, MOMMY. I'M NOT MAD AT YOU GUYS.
IT'S JUST THAT... WELL, I'M ALREADY NERVOUS ABOUT SCHOOL AND MAKING FRIENDS. I DON'T WANT TO WORRY ABOUT THIS, TOO.
I'M STILL A ***KID***. WHY CAN'T I START WHEN I'M OLDER?

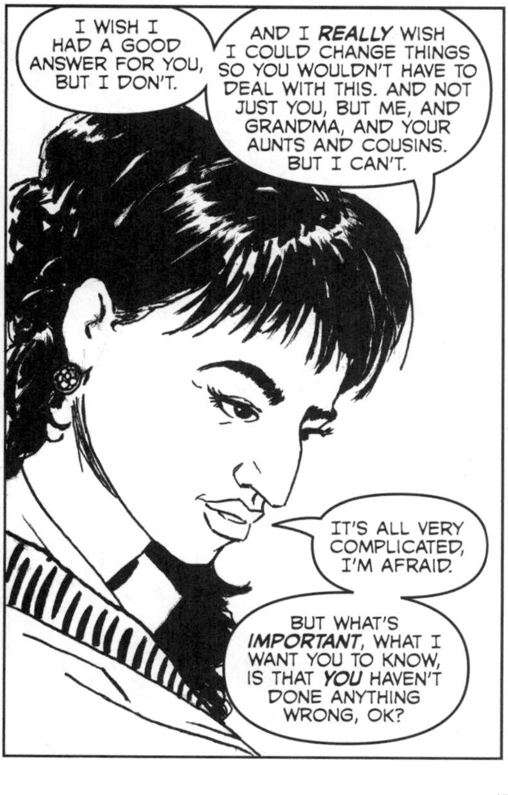
I WISH I HAD A GOOD ANSWER FOR YOU, BUT I DON'T.
AND I ***REALLY*** WISH I COULD CHANGE THINGS SO YOU WOULDN'T HAVE TO DEAL WITH THIS. AND NOT JUST YOU, BUT ME, AND GRANDMA, AND YOUR AUNTS AND COUSINS. BUT I CAN'T.
IT'S ALL VERY COMPLICATED, I'M AFRAID.
BUT WHAT'S ***IMPORTANT***, WHAT I WANT YOU TO KNOW, IS THAT ***YOU*** HAVEN'T DONE ANYTHING WRONG, OK?

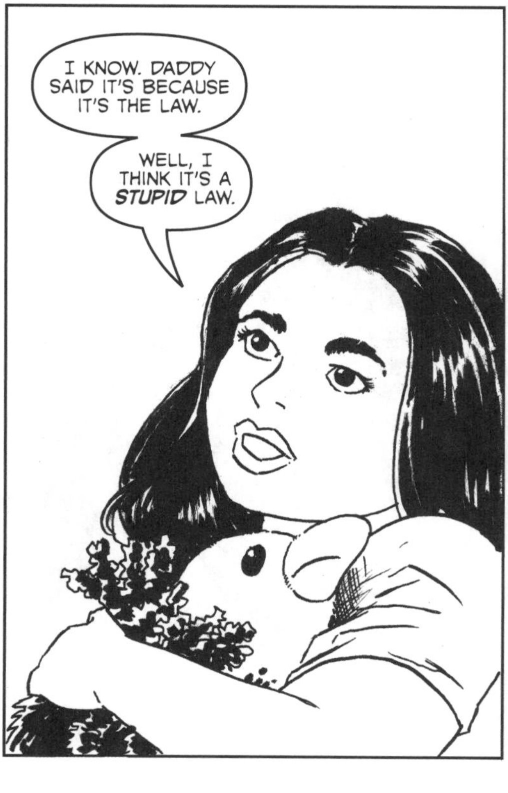
I KNOW. DADDY SAID IT'S BECAUSE IT'S THE LAW.
WELL, I THINK IT'S A ***STUPID*** LAW.

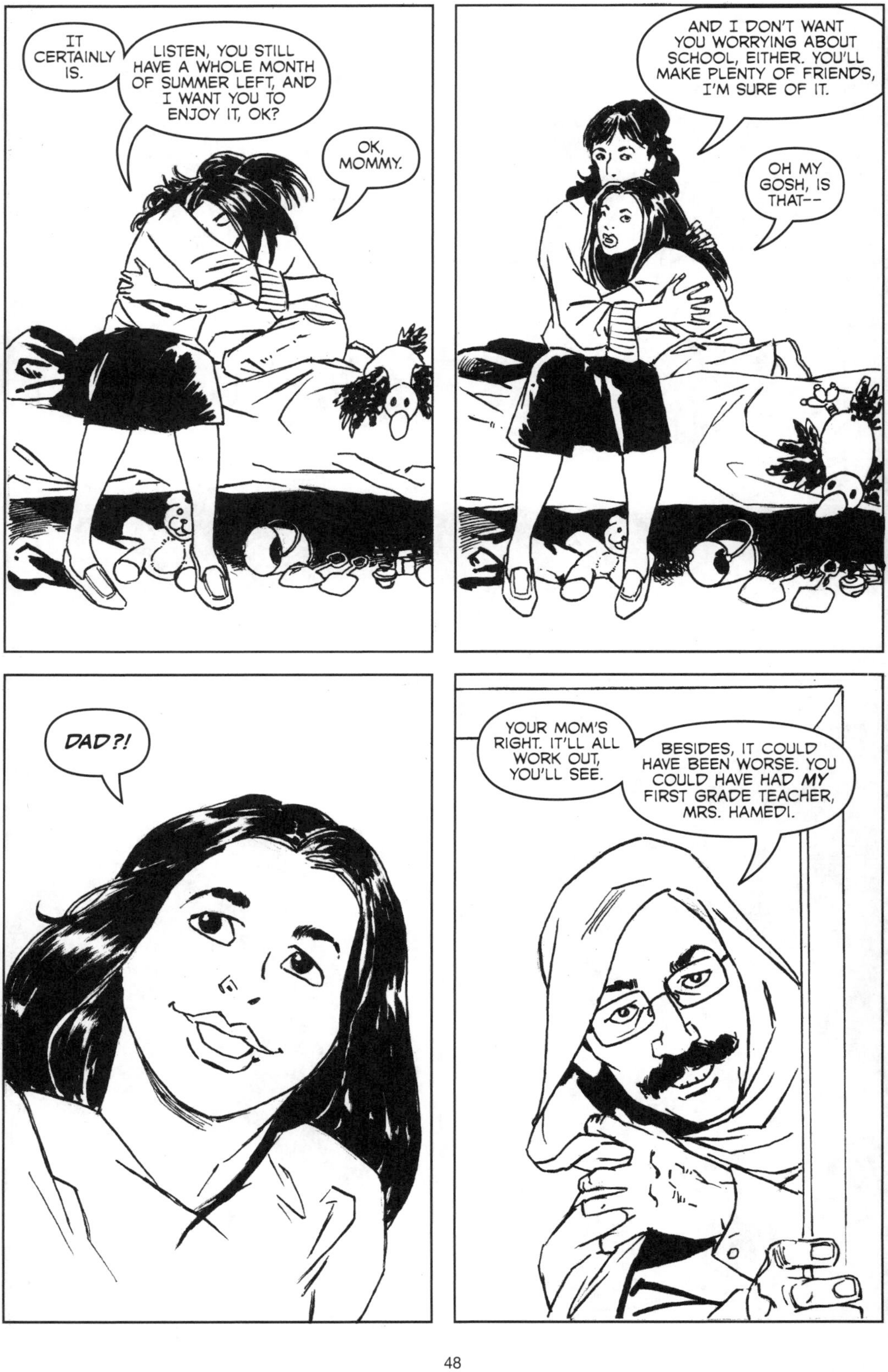
IT CERTAINLY IS.
LISTEN, YOU STILL HAVE A WHOLE MONTH OF SUMMER LEFT, AND I WANT YOU TO ENJOY IT, OK?
OK, MOMMY.
AND I DON'T WANT YOU WORRYING ABOUT SCHOOL, EITHER. YOU'LL MAKE PLENTY OF FRIENDS, I'M SURE OF IT.
OH MY GOSH, IS THAT--
DAD?!
YOUR MOM'S RIGHT. IT'LL ALL WORK OUT, YOU'LL SEE.
BESIDES, IT COULD HAVE BEEN WORSE. YOU COULD HAVE HAD MY FIRST GRADE TEACHER, MRS. HAMEDI.

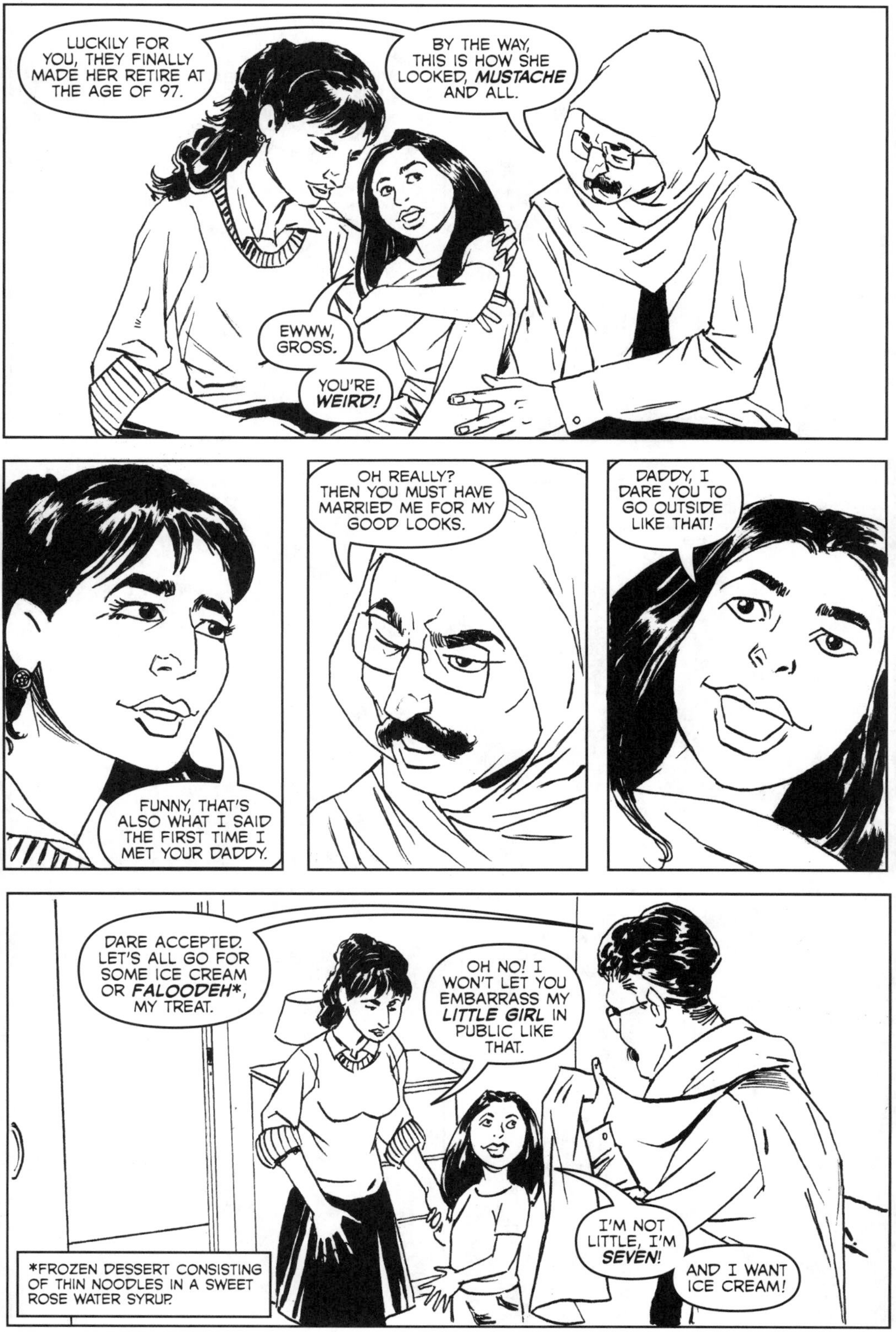
LUCKILY FOR YOU, THEY FINALLY MADE HER RETIRE AT THE AGE OF 97.
BY THE WAY, THIS IS HOW SHE LOOKED, ***MUSTACHE*** AND ALL.
EWWW, GROSS.
YOU'RE ***WEIRD!***
FUNNY, THAT'S ALSO WHAT I SAID THE FIRST TIME I MET YOUR DADDY.
OH REALLY? THEN YOU MUST HAVE MARRIED ME FOR MY GOOD LOOKS.
DADDY, I DARE YOU TO GO OUTSIDE LIKE THAT!
DARE ACCEPTED. LET'S ALL GO FOR SOME ICE CREAM OR ***FALOODEH****, MY TREAT.
OH NO! I WON'T LET YOU EMBARRASS MY ***LITTLE GIRL*** IN PUBLIC LIKE THAT.
I'M NOT LITTLE, I'M ***SEVEN***!
AND I WANT ICE CREAM!
*FROZEN DESSERT CONSISTING OF THIN NOODLES IN A SWEET ROSE WATER SYRUP.

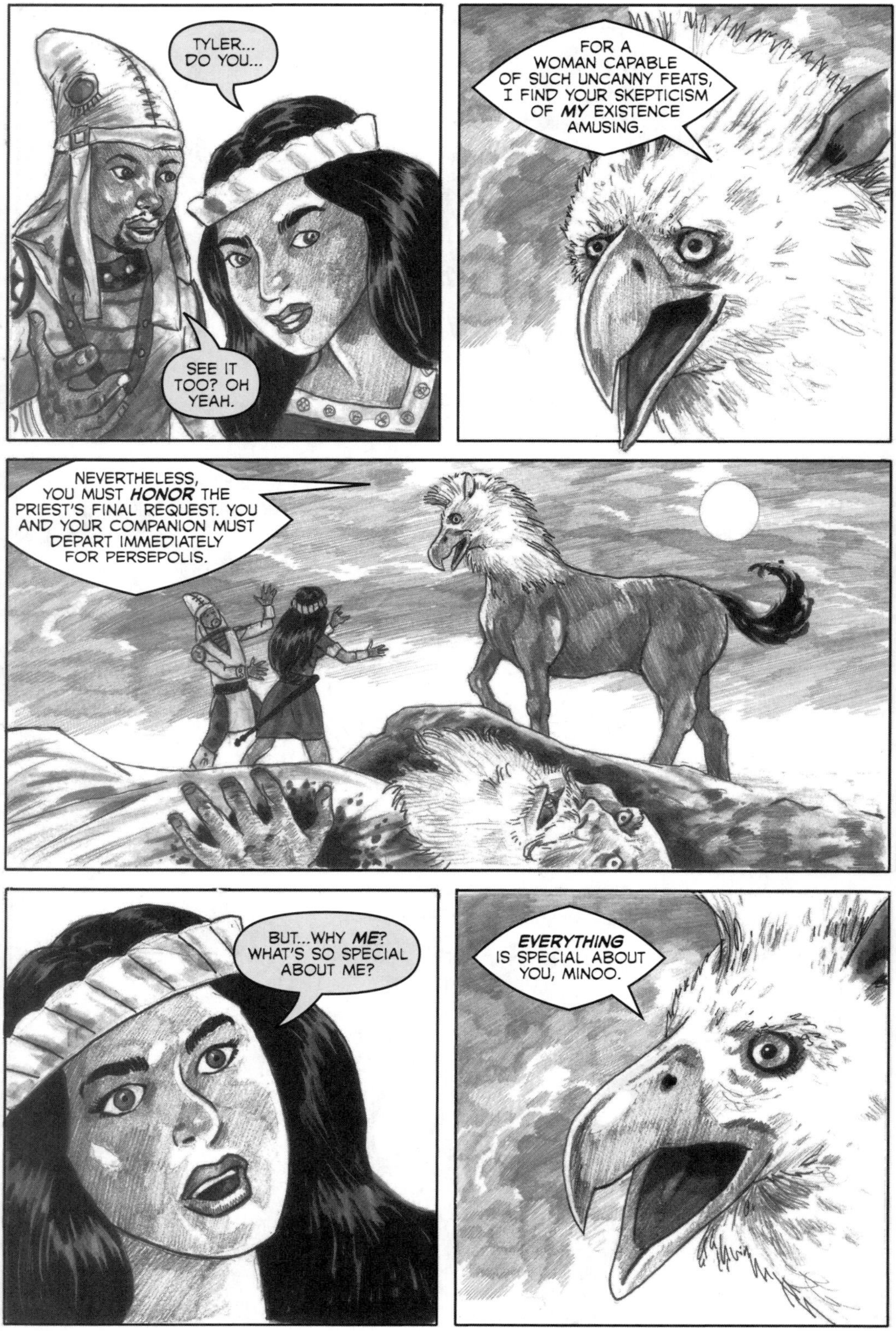
TYLER... DO YOU...
SEE IT TOO? OH YEAH.
FOR A WOMAN CAPABLE OF SUCH UNCANNY FEATS, I FIND YOUR SKEPTICISM OF *MY* EXISTENCE AMUSING.
NEVERTHELESS, YOU MUST *HONOR* THE PRIEST'S FINAL REQUEST. YOU AND YOUR COMPANION MUST DEPART IMMEDIATELY FOR PERSEPOLIS.
BUT...WHY *ME*? WHAT'S SO SPECIAL ABOUT ME?
EVERYTHING IS SPECIAL ABOUT YOU, MINOO.

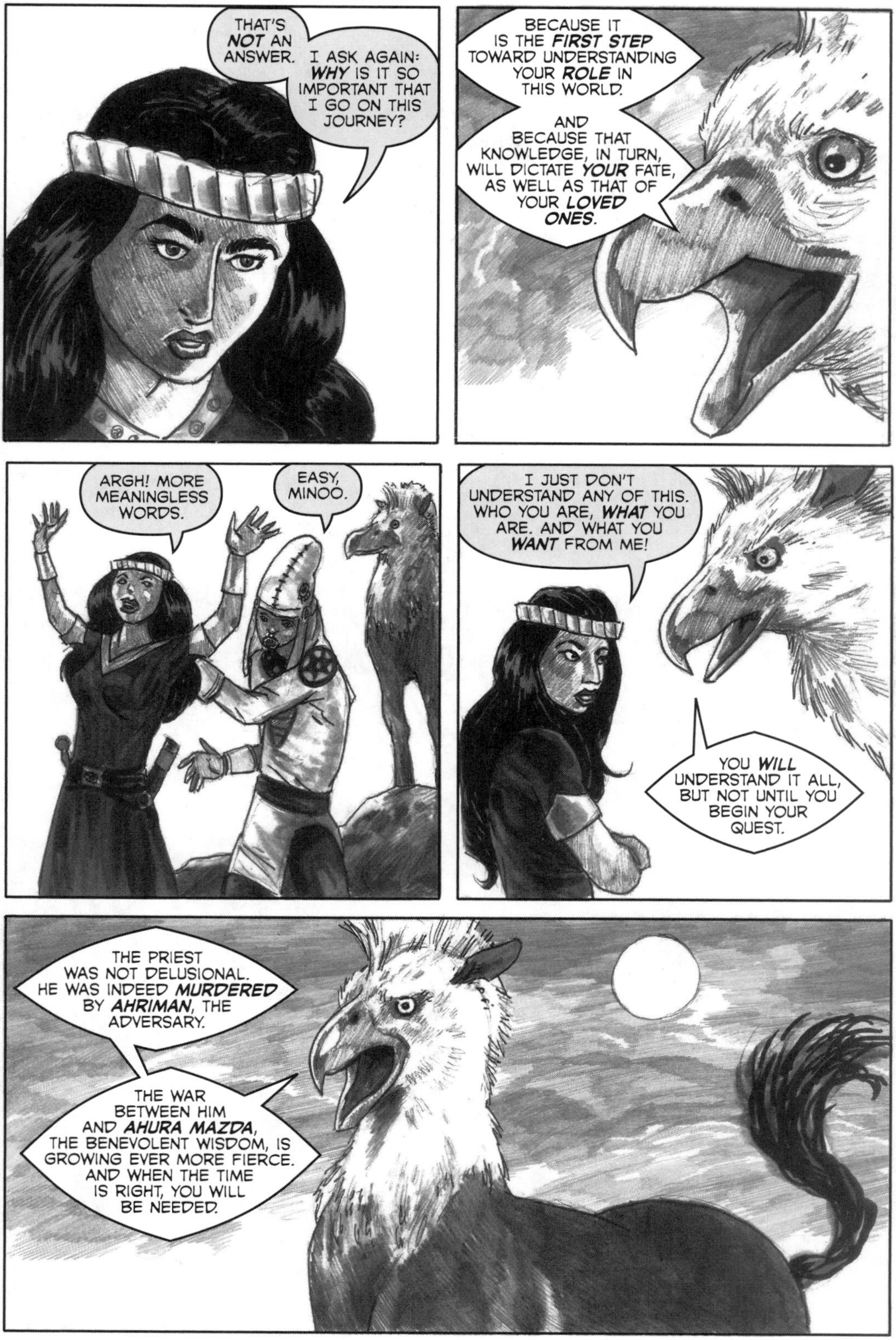
THAT'S NOT AN ANSWER.
I ASK AGAIN: WHY IS IT SO IMPORTANT THAT I GO ON THIS JOURNEY?
BECAUSE IT IS THE FIRST STEP TOWARD UNDERSTANDING YOUR ROLE IN THIS WORLD.
AND BECAUSE THAT KNOWLEDGE, IN TURN, WILL DICTATE YOUR FATE, AS WELL AS THAT OF YOUR LOVED ONES.
ARGH! MORE MEANINGLESS WORDS.
EASY, MINOO.
I JUST DON'T UNDERSTAND ANY OF THIS. WHO YOU ARE, WHAT YOU ARE. AND WHAT YOU WANT FROM ME!
YOU WILL UNDERSTAND IT ALL, BUT NOT UNTIL YOU BEGIN YOUR QUEST.
THE PRIEST WAS NOT DELUSIONAL. HE WAS INDEED MURDERED BY AHRIMAN, THE ADVERSARY.
THE WAR BETWEEN HIM AND AHURA MAZDA, THE BENEVOLENT WISDOM, IS GROWING EVER MORE FIERCE. AND WHEN THE TIME IS RIGHT, YOU WILL BE NEEDED.

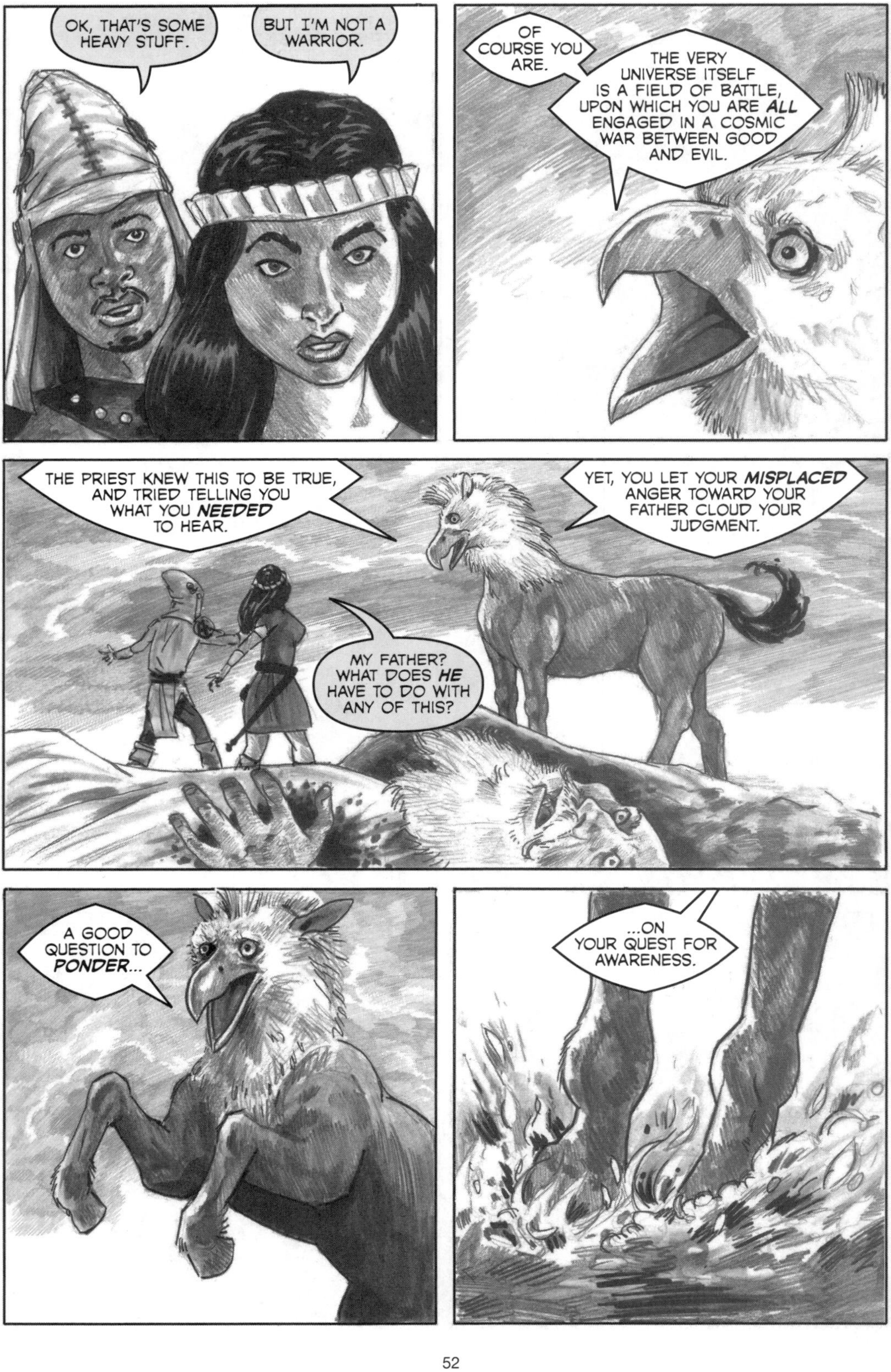
OK, THAT'S SOME HEAVY STUFF.
BUT I'M NOT A WARRIOR.
OF COURSE YOU ARE.
THE VERY UNIVERSE ITSELF IS A FIELD OF BATTLE, UPON WHICH YOU ARE ALL ENGAGED IN A COSMIC WAR BETWEEN GOOD AND EVIL.
THE PRIEST KNEW THIS TO BE TRUE, AND TRIED TELLING YOU WHAT YOU NEEDED TO HEAR.
YET, YOU LET YOUR MISPLACED ANGER TOWARD YOUR FATHER CLOUD YOUR JUDGMENT.
MY FATHER? WHAT DOES HE HAVE TO DO WITH ANY OF THIS?
A GOOD QUESTION TO PONDER...
...ON YOUR QUEST FOR AWARENESS.

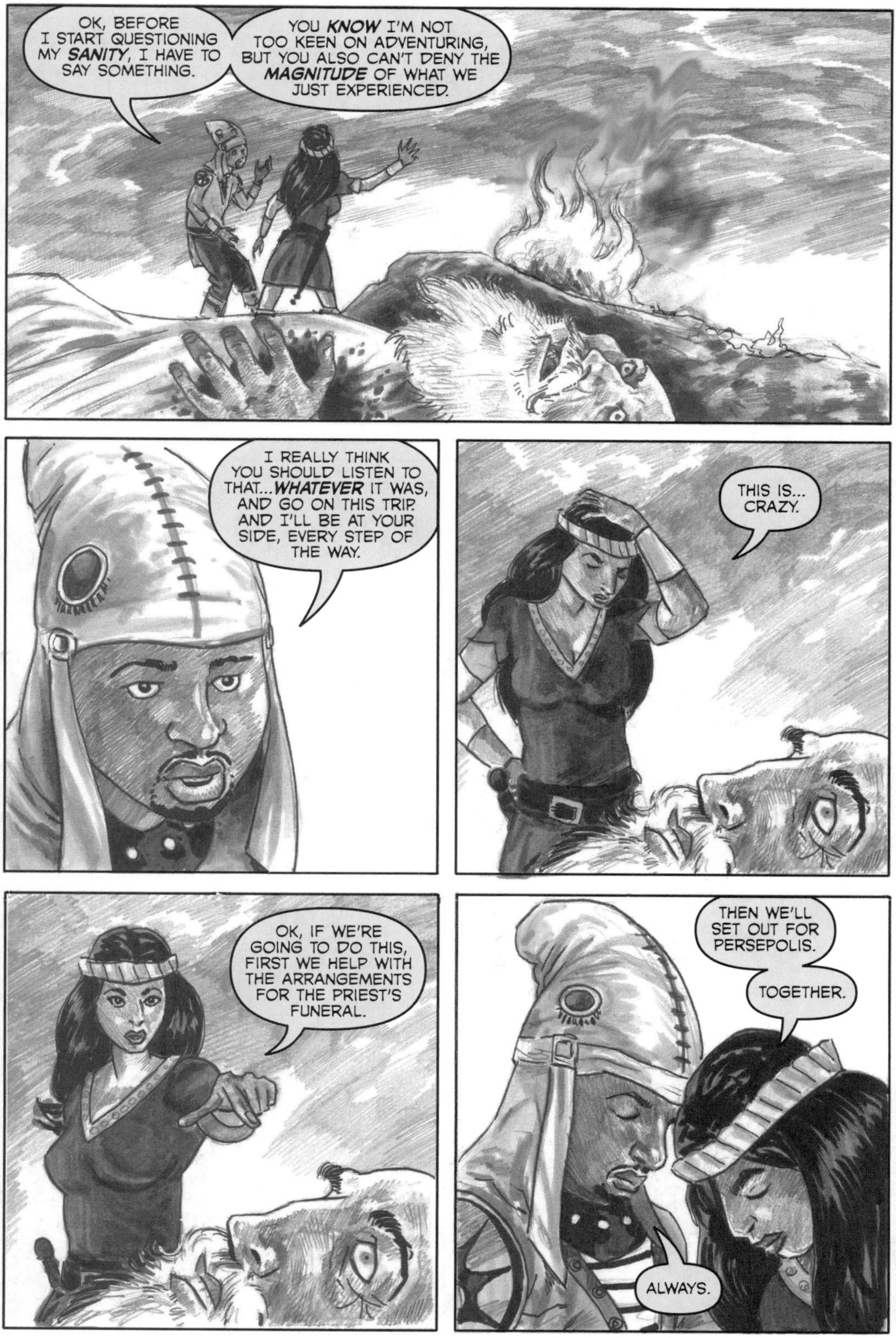
OK, BEFORE I START QUESTIONING MY SANITY, I HAVE TO SAY SOMETHING.
YOU KNOW I'M NOT TOO KEEN ON ADVENTURING, BUT YOU ALSO CAN'T DENY THE MAGNITUDE OF WHAT WE JUST EXPERIENCED.
I REALLY THINK YOU SHOULD LISTEN TO THAT...WHATEVER IT WAS, AND GO ON THIS TRIP. AND I'LL BE AT YOUR SIDE, EVERY STEP OF THE WAY.
THIS IS... CRAZY.
OK, IF WE'RE GOING TO DO THIS, FIRST WE HELP WITH THE ARRANGEMENTS FOR THE PRIEST'S FUNERAL.
THEN WE'LL SET OUT FOR PERSEPOLIS.
TOGETHER.
ALWAYS.

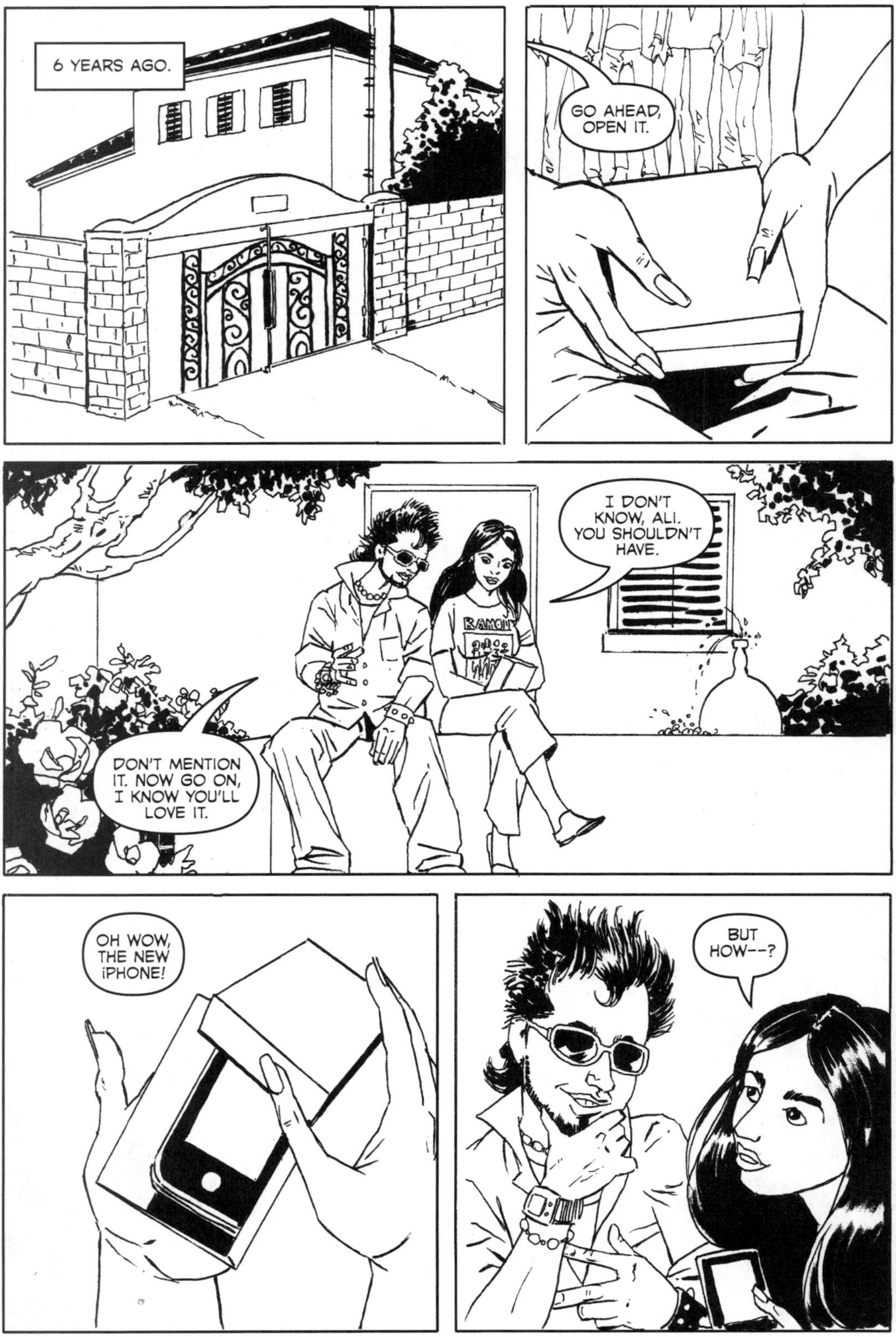
6 YEARS AGO.
GO AHEAD, OPEN IT.
I DON'T KNOW, ALI. YOU SHOULDN'T HAVE.
DON'T MENTION IT. NOW GO ON, I KNOW YOU'LL LOVE IT.
OH WOW, THE NEW iPHONE!
BUT HOW--?

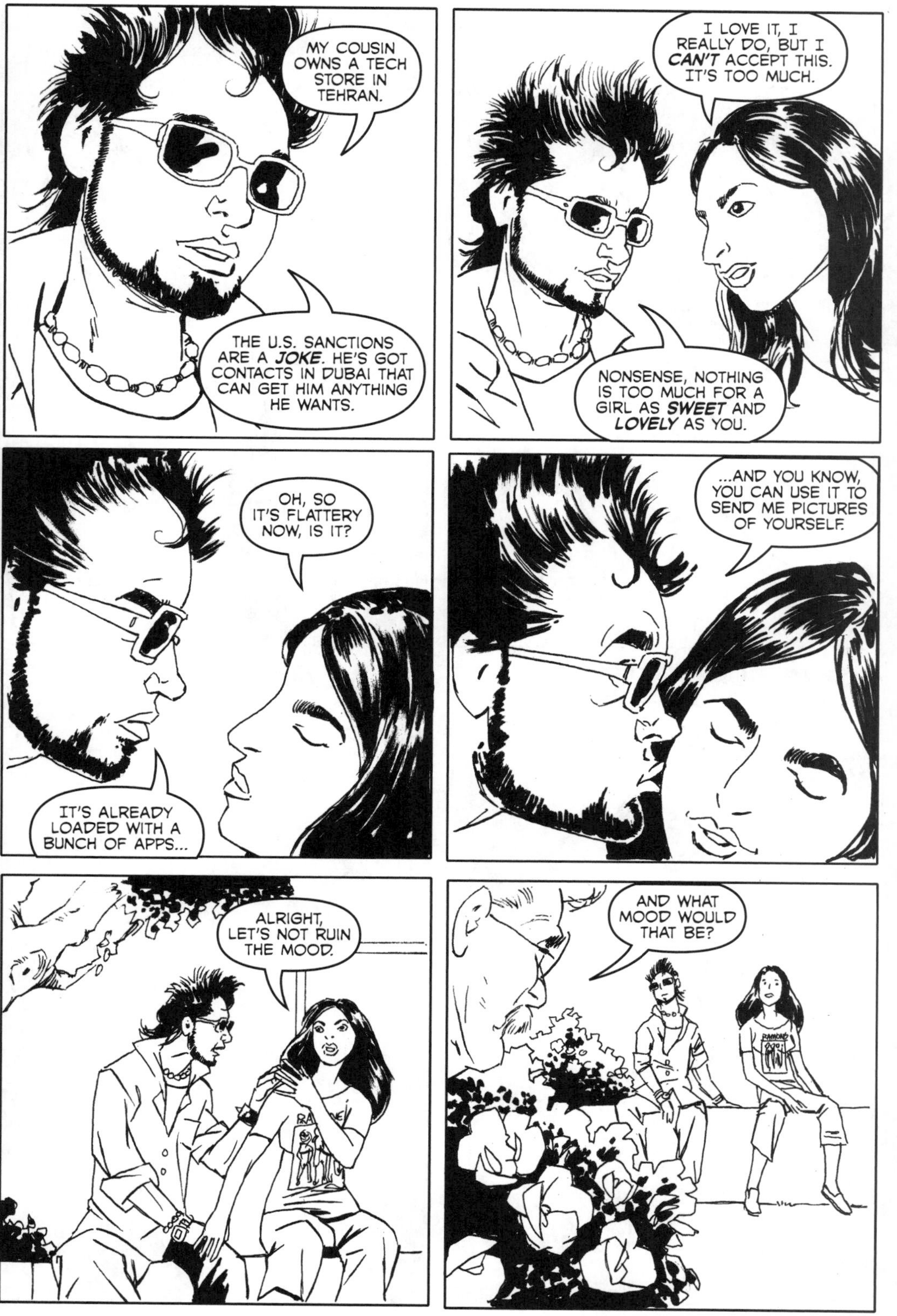
MY COUSIN OWNS A TECH STORE IN TEHRAN.
THE U.S. SANCTIONS ARE A JOKE. HE'S GOT CONTACTS IN DUBAI THAT CAN GET HIM ANYTHING HE WANTS.
I LOVE IT, I REALLY DO, BUT I CAN'T ACCEPT THIS. IT'S TOO MUCH.
NONSENSE, NOTHING IS TOO MUCH FOR A GIRL AS SWEET AND LOVELY AS YOU.
OH, SO IT'S FLATTERY NOW, IS IT?
IT'S ALREADY LOADED WITH A BUNCH OF APPS...
...AND YOU KNOW, YOU CAN USE IT TO SEND ME PICTURES OF YOURSELF.
ALRIGHT, LET'S NOT RUIN THE MOOD.
AND WHAT MOOD WOULD THAT BE?

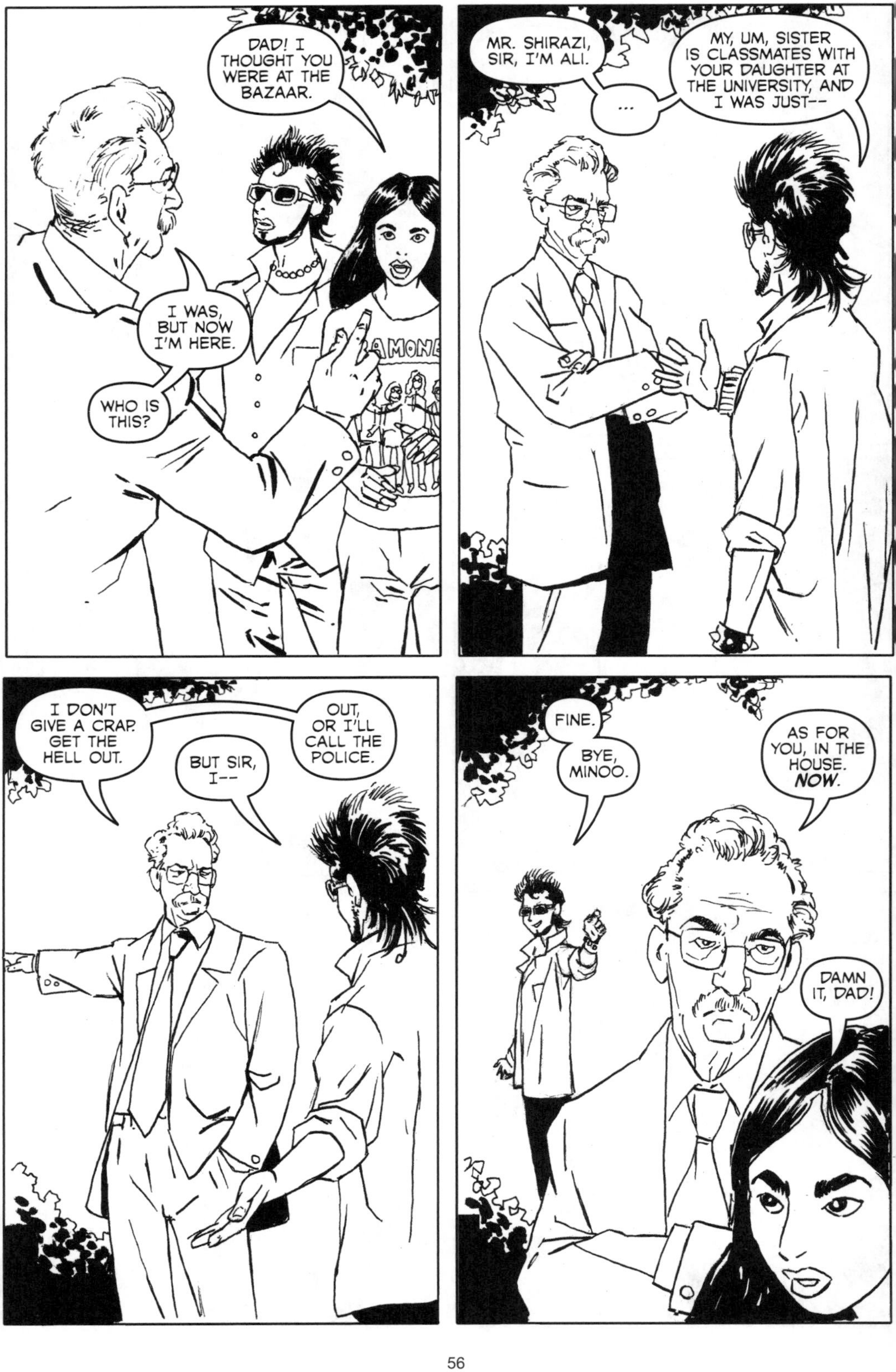
DAD! I THOUGHT YOU WERE AT THE BAZAAR.
I WAS, BUT NOW I'M HERE.
WHO IS THIS?
MR. SHIRAZI, SIR, I'M ALI.
...
MY, UM, SISTER IS CLASSMATES WITH YOUR DAUGHTER AT THE UNIVERSITY, AND I WAS JUST--
I DON'T GIVE A CRAP. GET THE HELL OUT.
BUT SIR, I--
OUT, OR I'LL CALL THE POLICE.
FINE.
BYE, MINOO.
AS FOR YOU, IN THE HOUSE. *NOW*.
DAMN IT, DAD!

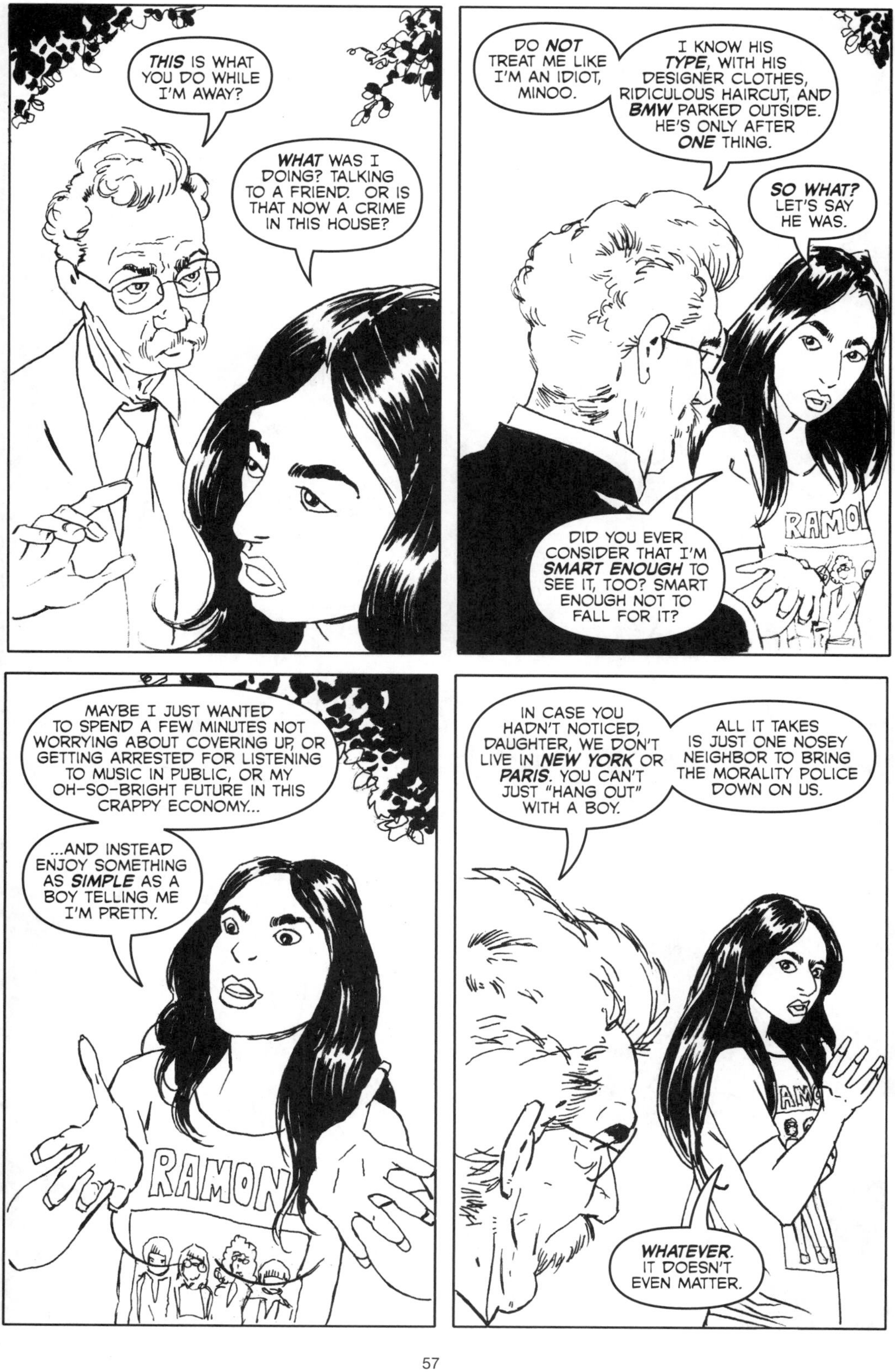
THIS IS WHAT YOU DO WHILE I'M AWAY?
WHAT WAS I DOING? TALKING TO A FRIEND. OR IS THAT NOW A CRIME IN THIS HOUSE?
DO NOT TREAT ME LIKE I'M AN IDIOT, MINOO.
I KNOW HIS TYPE, WITH HIS DESIGNER CLOTHES, RIDICULOUS HAIRCUT, AND BMW PARKED OUTSIDE. HE'S ONLY AFTER ONE THING.
SO WHAT? LET'S SAY HE WAS.
DID YOU EVER CONSIDER THAT I'M SMART ENOUGH TO SEE IT, TOO? SMART ENOUGH NOT TO FALL FOR IT?
MAYBE I JUST WANTED TO SPEND A FEW MINUTES NOT WORRYING ABOUT COVERING UP, OR GETTING ARRESTED FOR LISTENING TO MUSIC IN PUBLIC, OR MY OH-SO-BRIGHT FUTURE IN THIS CRAPPY ECONOMY...
...AND INSTEAD ENJOY SOMETHING AS SIMPLE AS A BOY TELLING ME I'M PRETTY.
RAMON
IN CASE YOU HADN'T NOTICED, DAUGHTER, WE DON'T LIVE IN NEW YORK OR PARIS. YOU CAN'T JUST "HANG OUT" WITH A BOY.
ALL IT TAKES IS JUST ONE NOSEY NEIGHBOR TO BRING THE MORALITY POLICE DOWN ON US.
WHATEVER. IT DOESN'T EVEN MATTER.

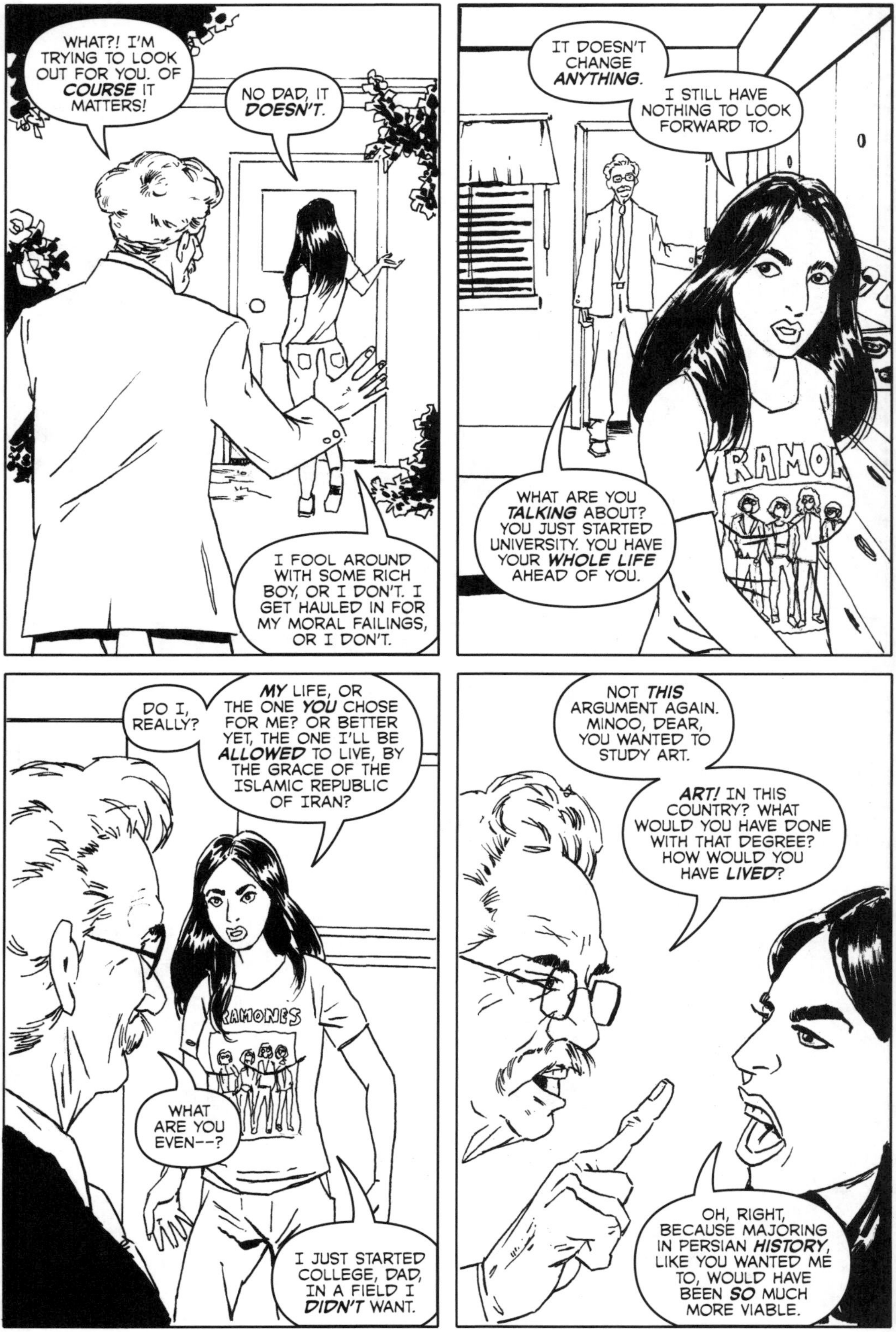
WHAT?! I'M TRYING TO LOOK OUT FOR YOU. OF *COURSE* IT MATTERS!
NO DAD, IT *DOESN'T*.
I FOOL AROUND WITH SOME RICH BOY, OR I DON'T. I GET HAULED IN FOR MY MORAL FAILINGS, OR I DON'T.
IT DOESN'T CHANGE *ANYTHING*.
I STILL HAVE NOTHING TO LOOK FORWARD TO.
RAMON
WHAT ARE YOU *TALKING* ABOUT? YOU JUST STARTED UNIVERSITY. YOU HAVE YOUR *WHOLE LIFE* AHEAD OF YOU.
DO I, REALLY?
MY LIFE, OR THE ONE *YOU* CHOSE FOR ME? OR BETTER YET, THE ONE I'LL BE *ALLOWED* TO LIVE, BY THE GRACE OF THE ISLAMIC REPUBLIC OF IRAN?
RAMONES
WHAT ARE YOU EVEN--?
I JUST STARTED COLLEGE, DAD, IN A FIELD I *DIDN'T* WANT.
NOT *THIS* ARGUMENT AGAIN. MINOO, DEAR, YOU WANTED TO STUDY ART.
ART! IN THIS COUNTRY? WHAT WOULD YOU HAVE DONE WITH THAT DEGREE? HOW WOULD YOU HAVE *LIVED*?
OH, RIGHT, BECAUSE MAJORING IN PERSIAN *HISTORY*, LIKE YOU WANTED ME TO, WOULD HAVE BEEN *SO* MUCH MORE VIABLE.

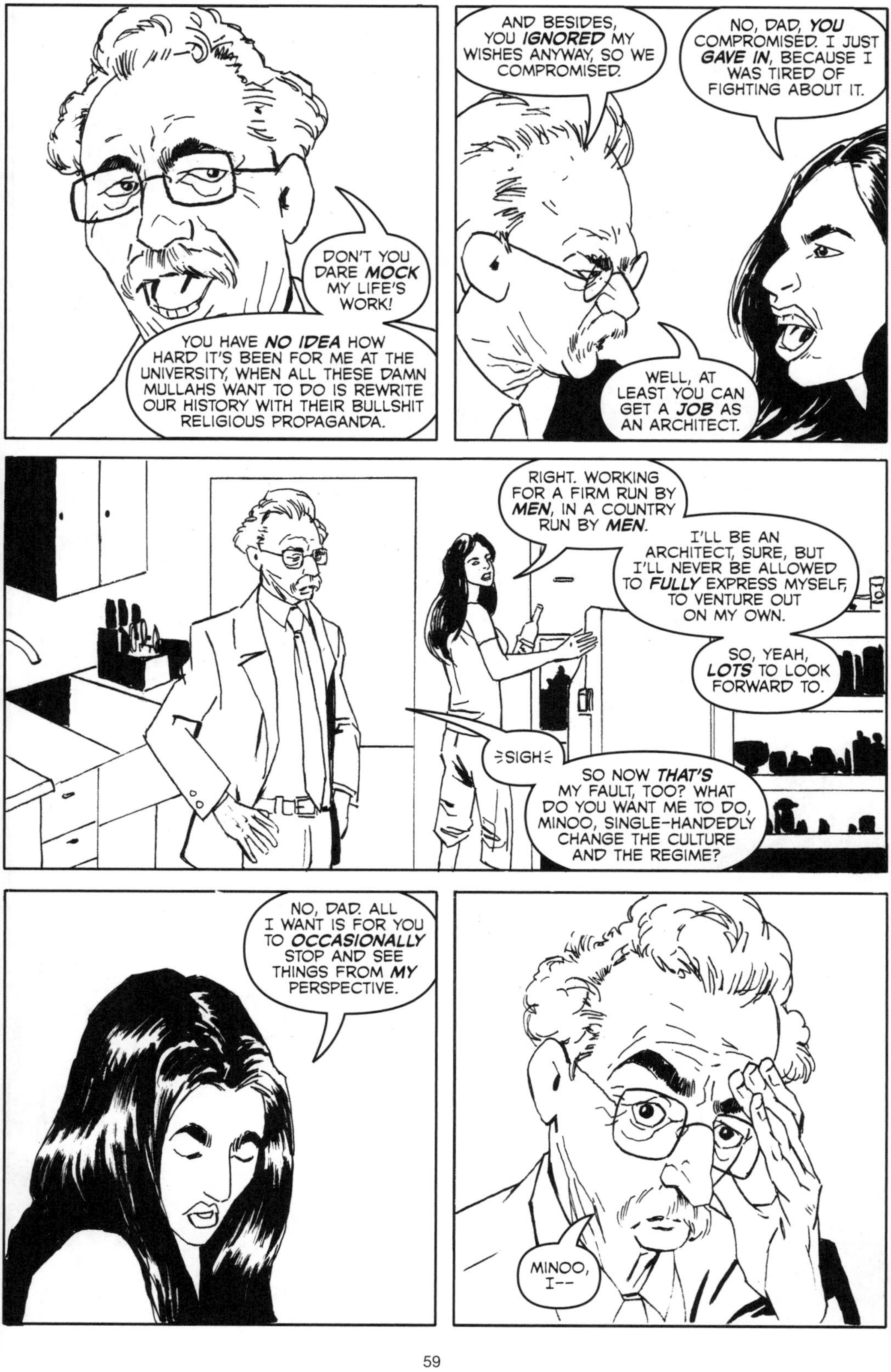
DON'T YOU DARE MOCK MY LIFE'S WORK!
YOU HAVE NO IDEA HOW HARD IT'S BEEN FOR ME AT THE UNIVERSITY, WHEN ALL THESE DAMN MULLAHS WANT TO DO IS REWRITE OUR HISTORY WITH THEIR BULLSHIT RELIGIOUS PROPAGANDA.
AND BESIDES, YOU IGNORED MY WISHES ANYWAY, SO WE COMPROMISED.
NO, DAD, YOU COMPROMISED. I JUST GAVE IN, BECAUSE I WAS TIRED OF FIGHTING ABOUT IT.
WELL, AT LEAST YOU CAN GET A JOB AS AN ARCHITECT.
RIGHT. WORKING FOR A FIRM RUN BY MEN, IN A COUNTRY RUN BY MEN.
I'LL BE AN ARCHITECT, SURE, BUT I'LL NEVER BE ALLOWED TO FULLY EXPRESS MYSELF, TO VENTURE OUT ON MY OWN.
SO, YEAH, LOTS TO LOOK FORWARD TO.
SIGH
SO NOW THAT'S MY FAULT, TOO? WHAT DO YOU WANT ME TO DO, MINOO, SINGLE-HANDEDLY CHANGE THE CULTURE AND THE REGIME?
NO, DAD. ALL I WANT IS FOR YOU TO OCCASIONALLY STOP AND SEE THINGS FROM MY PERSPECTIVE.
MINOO, I--

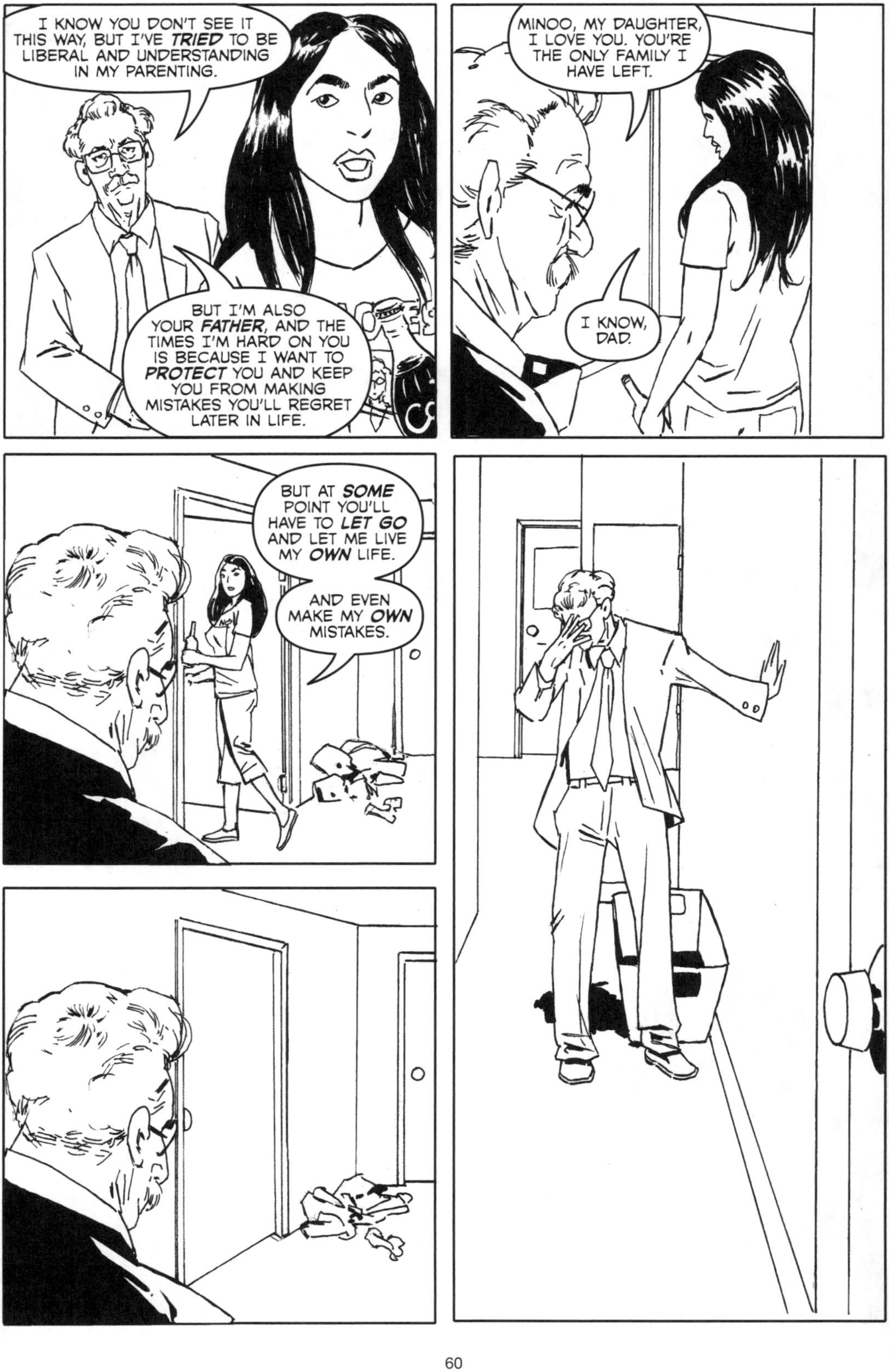
I KNOW YOU DON'T SEE IT THIS WAY, BUT I'VE *TRIED* TO BE LIBERAL AND UNDERSTANDING IN MY PARENTING.
BUT I'M ALSO YOUR *FATHER*, AND THE TIMES I'M HARD ON YOU IS BECAUSE I WANT TO *PROTECT* YOU AND KEEP YOU FROM MAKING MISTAKES YOU'LL REGRET LATER IN LIFE.
MINOO, MY DAUGHTER, I LOVE YOU. YOU'RE THE ONLY FAMILY I HAVE LEFT.
I KNOW, DAD.
BUT AT *SOME* POINT YOU'LL HAVE TO *LET GO* AND LET ME LIVE MY *OWN* LIFE.
AND EVEN MAKE MY *OWN* MISTAKES.

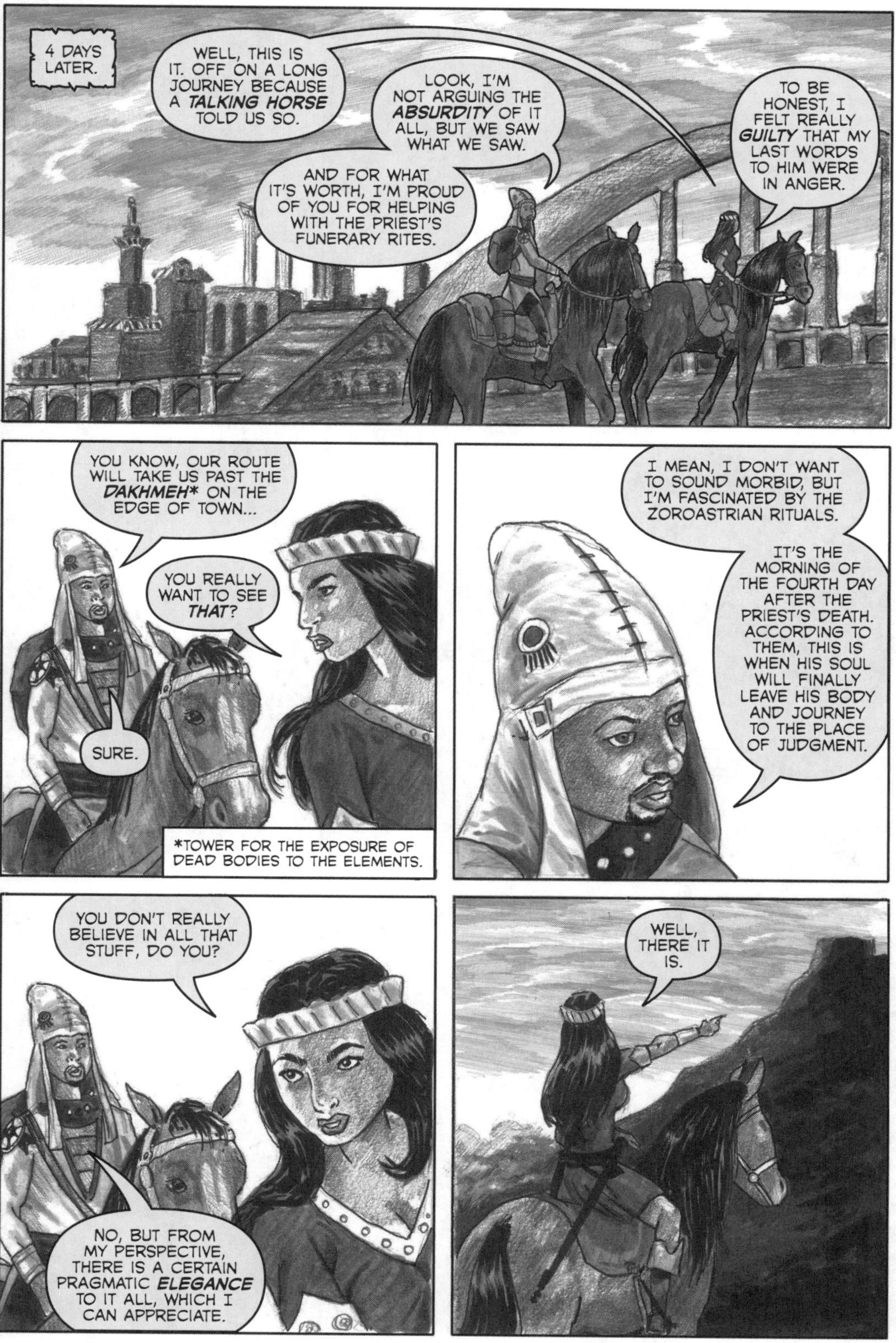
4 DAYS LATER.
WELL, THIS IS IT. OFF ON A LONG JOURNEY BECAUSE A TALKING HORSE TOLD US SO.
LOOK, I'M NOT ARGUING THE ABSURDITY OF IT ALL, BUT WE SAW WHAT WE SAW.
AND FOR WHAT IT'S WORTH, I'M PROUD OF YOU FOR HELPING WITH THE PRIEST'S FUNERARY RITES.
TO BE HONEST, I FELT REALLY GUILTY THAT MY LAST WORDS TO HIM WERE IN ANGER.
YOU KNOW, OUR ROUTE WILL TAKE US PAST THE DAKHMEH* ON THE EDGE OF TOWN...
YOU REALLY WANT TO SEE THAT?
SURE.
*TOWER FOR THE EXPOSURE OF DEAD BODIES TO THE ELEMENTS.
I MEAN, I DON'T WANT TO SOUND MORBID, BUT I'M FASCINATED BY THE ZOROASTRIAN RITUALS.
IT'S THE MORNING OF THE FOURTH DAY AFTER THE PRIEST'S DEATH. ACCORDING TO THEM, THIS IS WHEN HIS SOUL WILL FINALLY LEAVE HIS BODY AND JOURNEY TO THE PLACE OF JUDGMENT.
YOU DON'T REALLY BELIEVE IN ALL THAT STUFF, DO YOU?
NO, BUT FROM MY PERSPECTIVE, THERE IS A CERTAIN PRAGMATIC ELEGANCE TO IT ALL, WHICH I CAN APPRECIATE.
WELL, THERE IT IS.

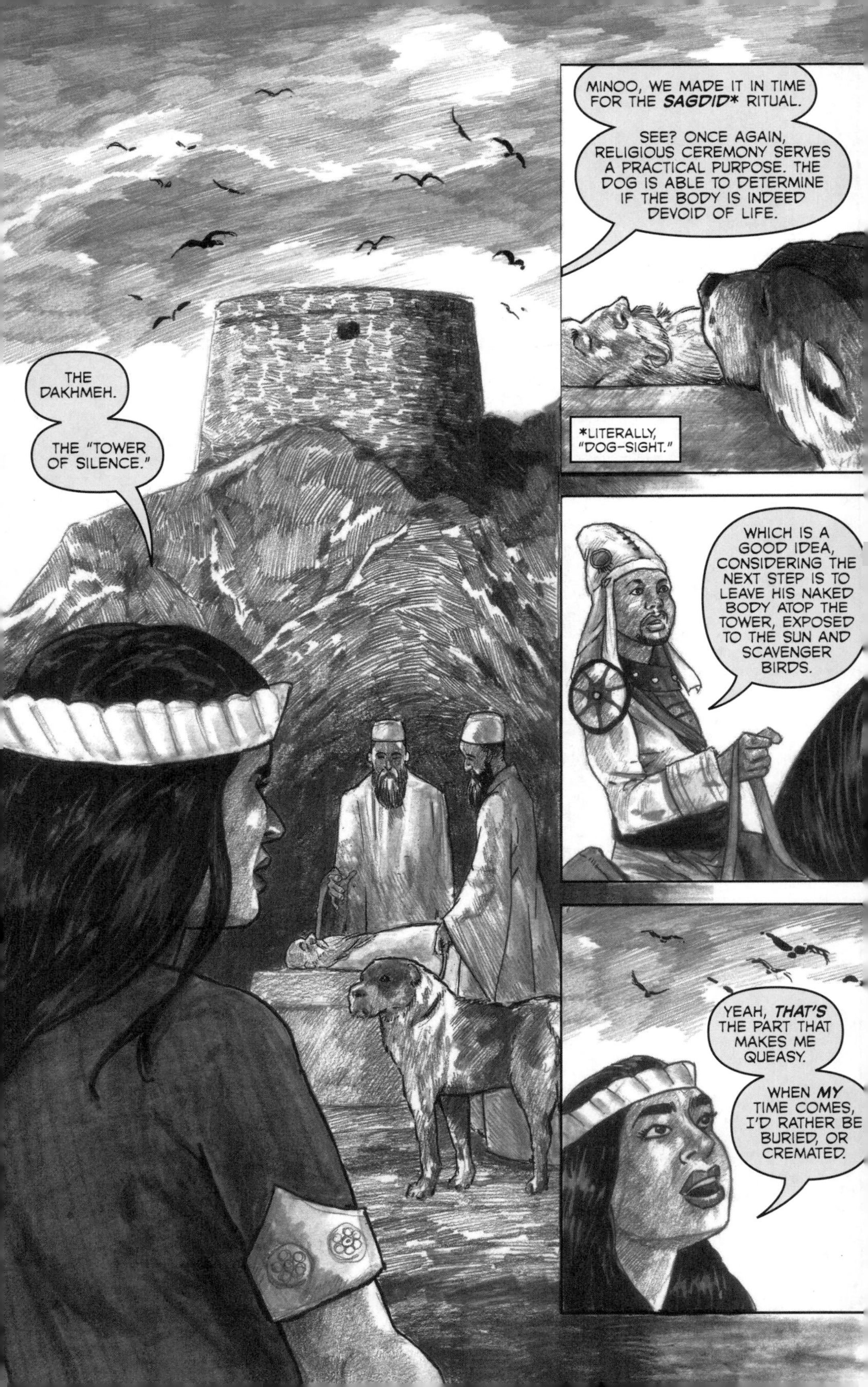
THE DAKHMEH.
THE "TOWER OF SILENCE."
MINOO, WE MADE IT IN TIME FOR THE SAGDID* RITUAL.
SEE? ONCE AGAIN, RELIGIOUS CEREMONY SERVES A PRACTICAL PURPOSE. THE DOG IS ABLE TO DETERMINE IF THE BODY IS INDEED DEVOID OF LIFE.
*LITERALLY, "DOG-SIGHT."
WHICH IS A GOOD IDEA, CONSIDERING THE NEXT STEP IS TO LEAVE HIS NAKED BODY ATOP THE TOWER, EXPOSED TO THE SUN AND SCAVENGER BIRDS.
YEAH, THAT'S THE PART THAT MAKES ME QUEASY.
WHEN MY TIME COMES, I'D RATHER BE BURIED, OR CREMATED.

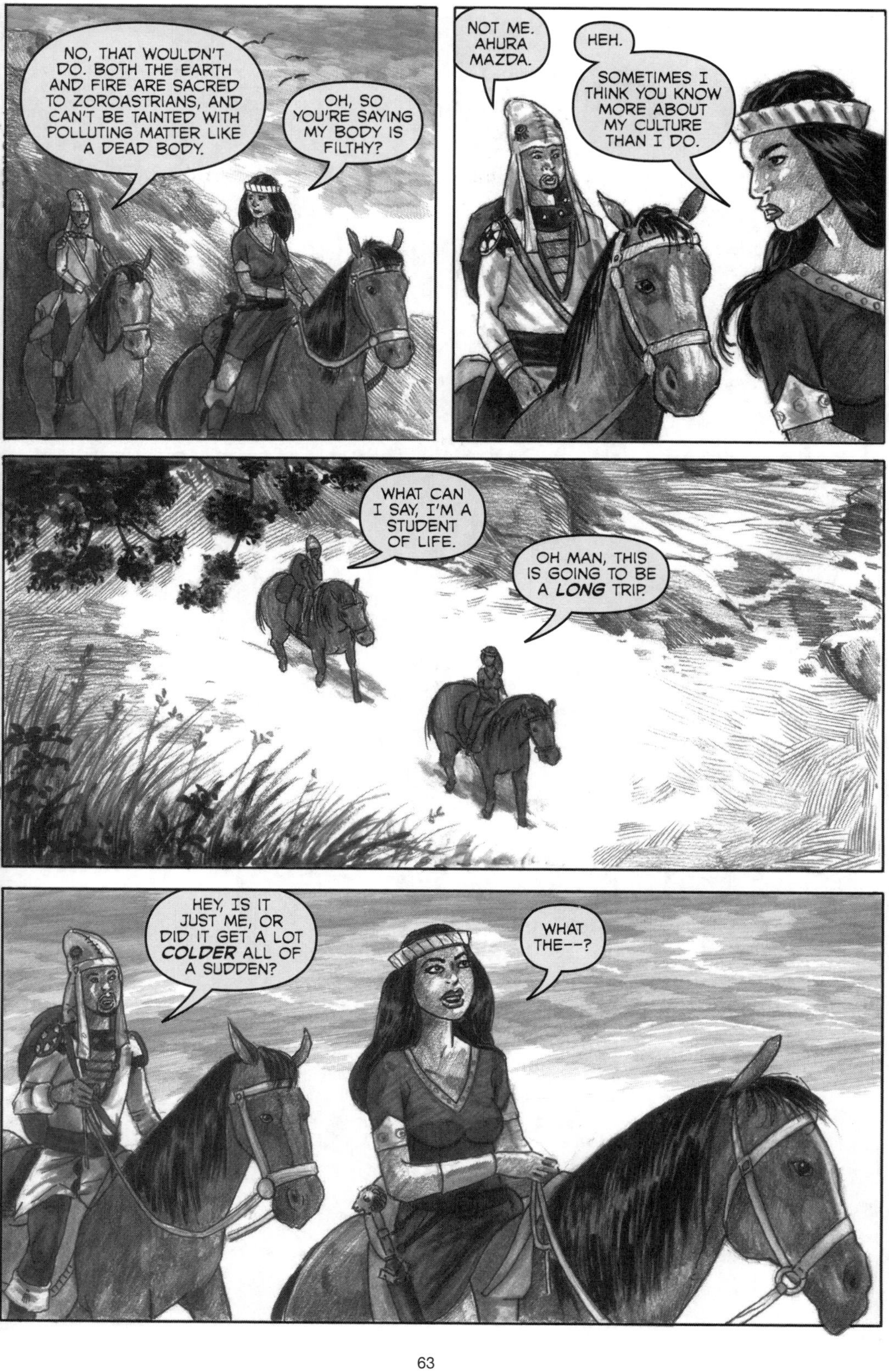
NO, THAT WOULDN'T DO. BOTH THE EARTH AND FIRE ARE SACRED TO ZOROASTRIANS, AND CAN'T BE TAINTED WITH POLLUTING MATTER LIKE A DEAD BODY.
OH, SO YOU'RE SAYING MY BODY IS FILTHY?
NOT ME. AHURA MAZDA.
HEH.
SOMETIMES I THINK YOU KNOW MORE ABOUT MY CULTURE THAN I DO.
WHAT CAN I SAY, I'M A STUDENT OF LIFE.
OH MAN, THIS IS GOING TO BE A ***LONG*** TRIP.
HEY, IS IT JUST ME, OR DID IT GET A LOT ***COLDER*** ALL OF A SUDDEN?
WHAT THE--?

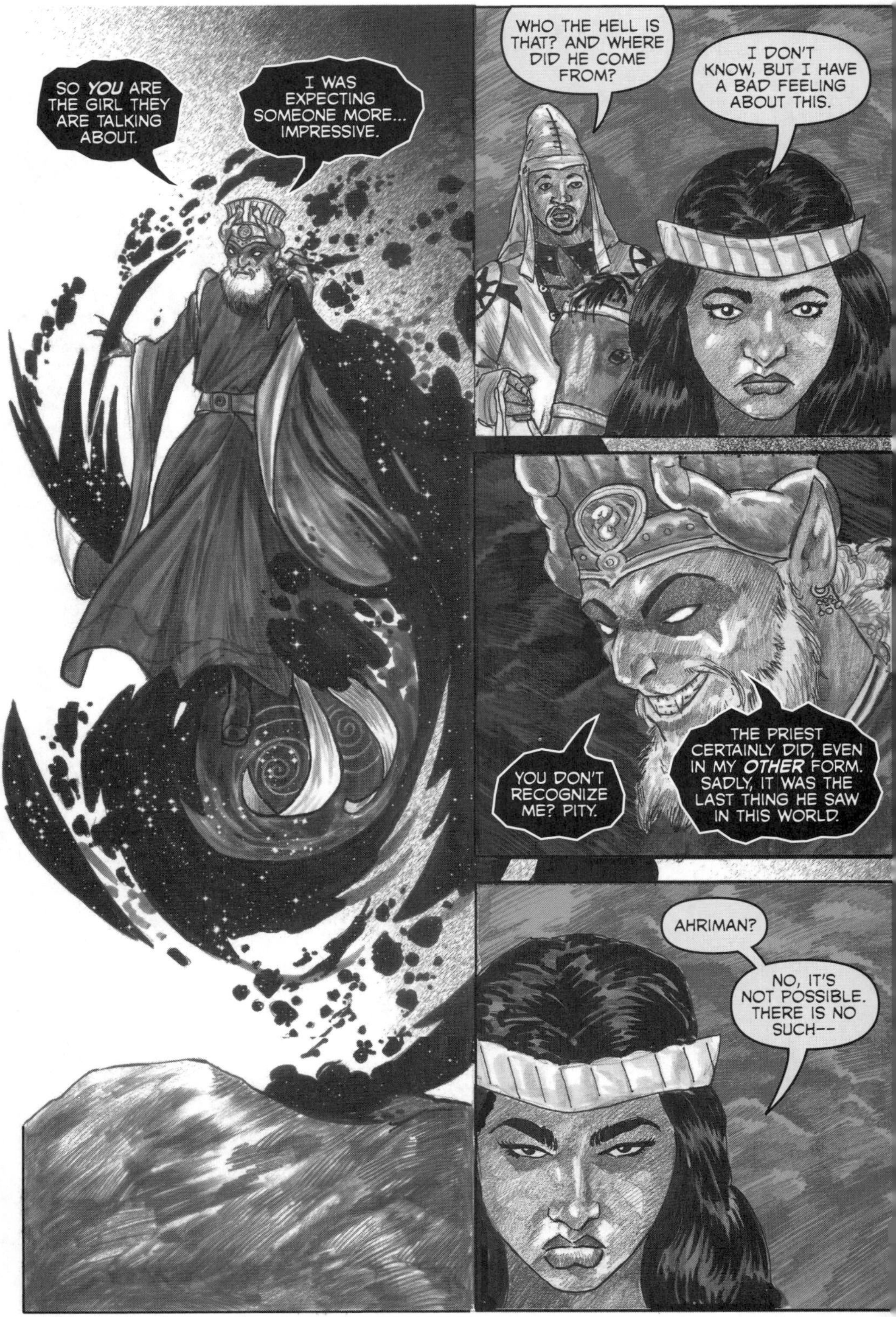
SO YOU ARE THE GIRL THEY ARE TALKING ABOUT.
I WAS EXPECTING SOMEONE MORE... IMPRESSIVE.
WHO THE HELL IS THAT? AND WHERE DID HE COME FROM?
I DON'T KNOW, BUT I HAVE A BAD FEELING ABOUT THIS.
YOU DON'T RECOGNIZE ME? PITY.
THE PRIEST CERTAINLY DID, EVEN IN MY OTHER FORM. SADLY, IT WAS THE LAST THING HE SAW IN THIS WORLD.
AHRIMAN?
NO, IT'S NOT POSSIBLE. THERE IS NO SUCH--

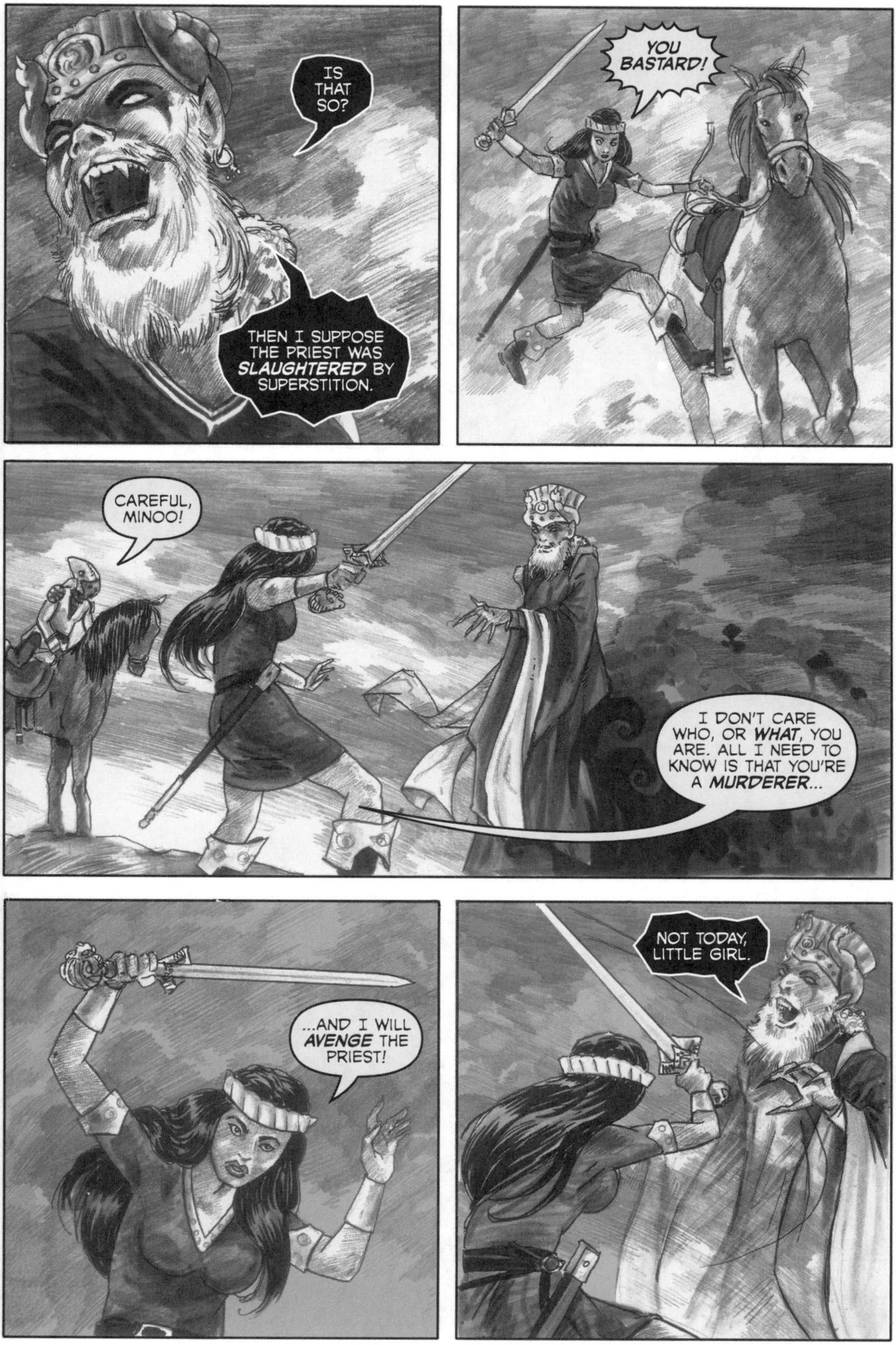
IS THAT SO?
THEN I SUPPOSE THE PRIEST WAS SLAUGHTERED BY SUPERSTITION.
YOU BASTARD!
CAREFUL, MINOO!
I DON'T CARE WHO, OR WHAT, YOU ARE. ALL I NEED TO KNOW IS THAT YOU'RE A MURDERER...
...AND I WILL AVENGE THE PRIEST!
NOT TODAY, LITTLE GIRL.

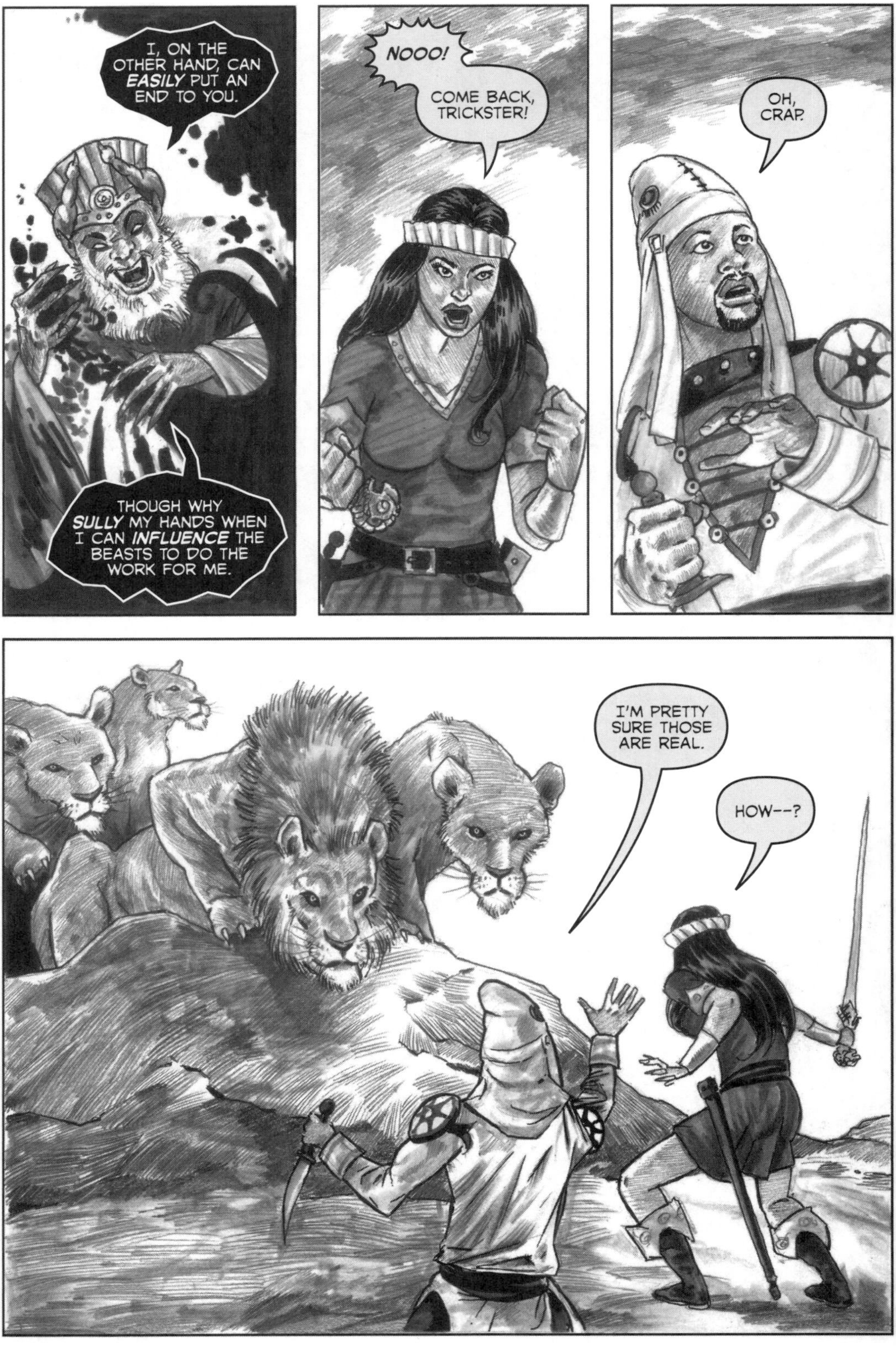
I, ON THE OTHER HAND, CAN *EASILY* PUT AN END TO YOU.
THOUGH WHY *SULLY* MY HANDS WHEN I CAN *INFLUENCE* THE BEASTS TO DO THE WORK FOR ME.
NOOO!
COME BACK, TRICKSTER!
OH, CRAP.
I'M PRETTY SURE THOSE ARE REAL.
HOW--?

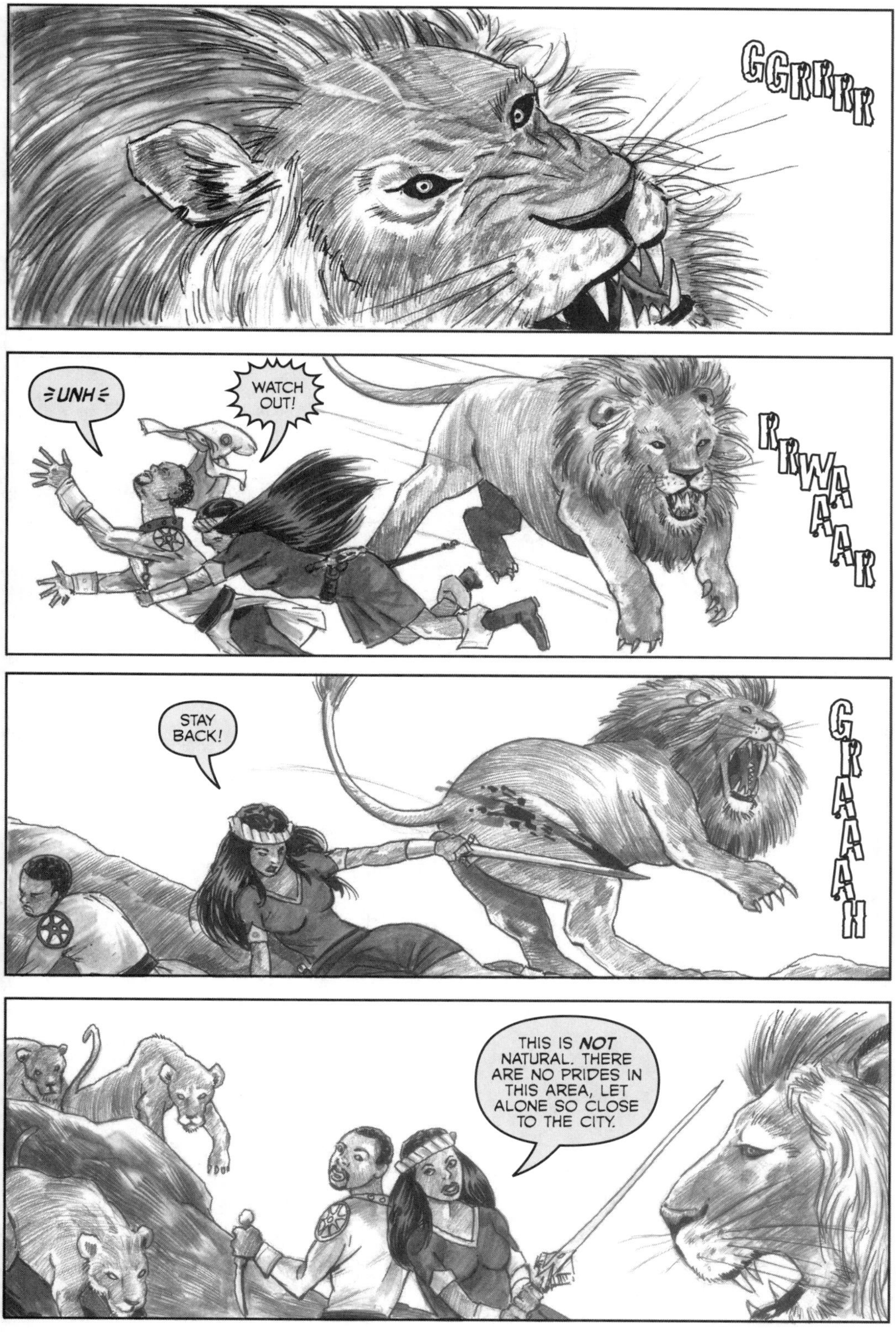
GGRRRRR
UNH
WATCH OUT!
RRWAAAAR
STAY BACK!
GRAAAAAH
THIS IS NOT NATURAL. THERE ARE NO PRIDES IN THIS AREA, LET ALONE SO CLOSE TO THE CITY.

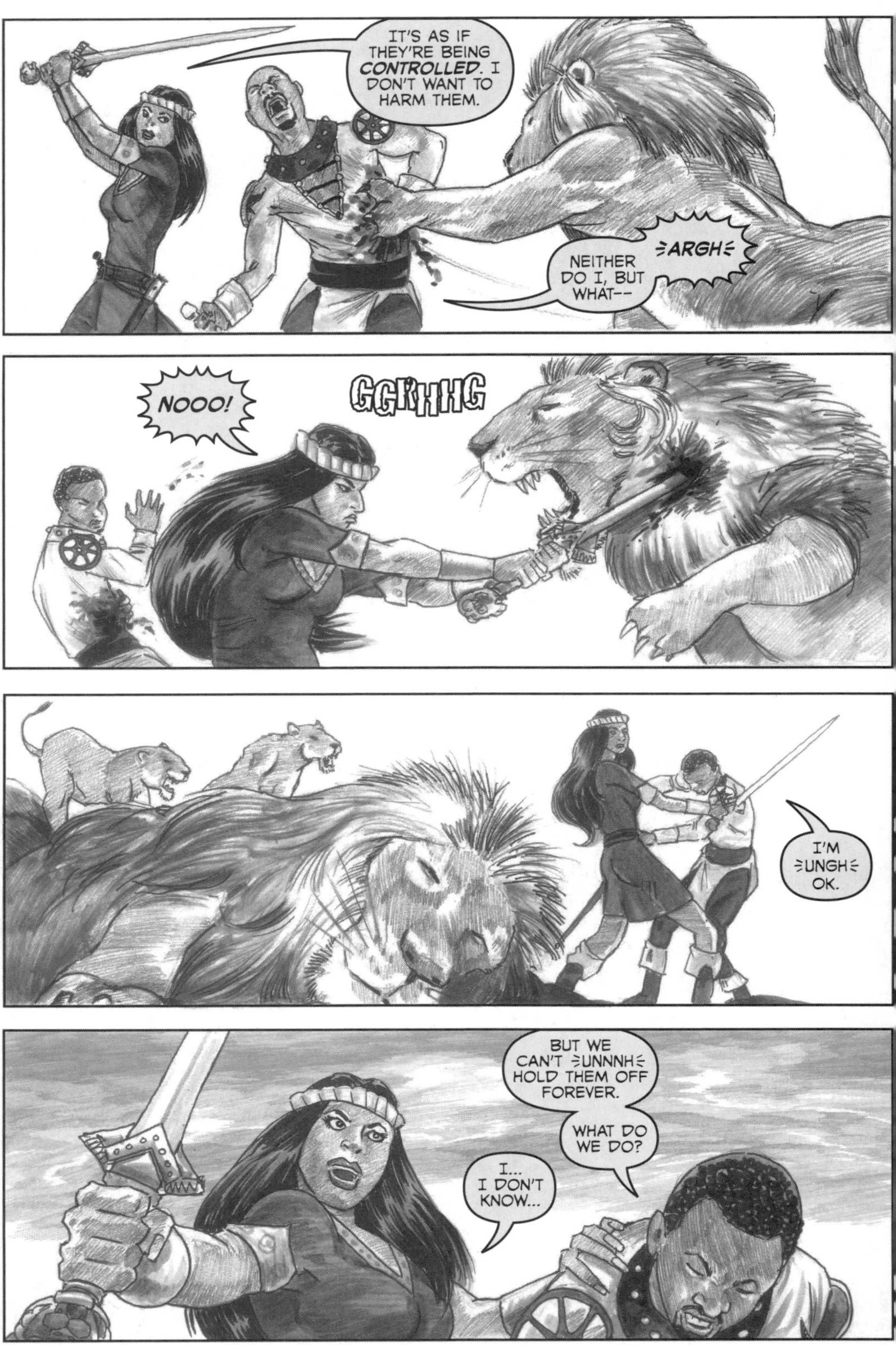

IT'S AS IF THEY'RE BEING ***CONTROLLED***. I DON'T WANT TO HARM THEM.
NEITHER DO I, BUT WHAT--
=ARGH=
NOOO!
GGRHHG
I'M =UNGH= OK.
BUT WE CAN'T =UNNNH= HOLD THEM OFF FOREVER.
WHAT DO WE DO?
I... I DON'T KNOW...

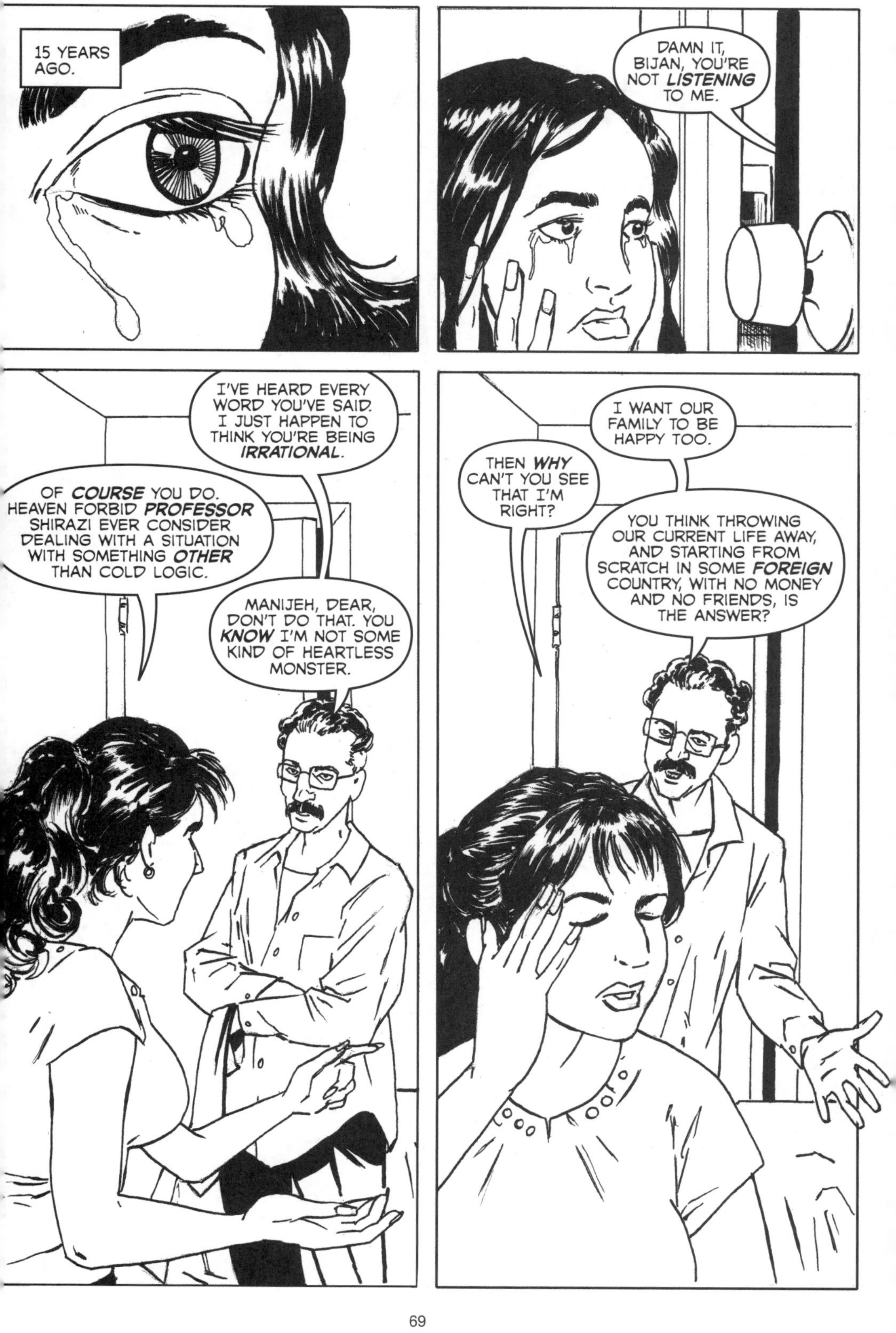
15 YEARS AGO.
DAMN IT, BIJAN, YOU'RE NOT LISTENING TO ME.
I'VE HEARD EVERY WORD YOU'VE SAID. I JUST HAPPEN TO THINK YOU'RE BEING IRRATIONAL.
OF COURSE YOU DO. HEAVEN FORBID PROFESSOR SHIRAZI EVER CONSIDER DEALING WITH A SITUATION WITH SOMETHING OTHER THAN COLD LOGIC.
MANIJEH, DEAR, DON'T DO THAT. YOU KNOW I'M NOT SOME KIND OF HEARTLESS MONSTER.
I WANT OUR FAMILY TO BE HAPPY TOO.
THEN WHY CAN'T YOU SEE THAT I'M RIGHT?
YOU THINK THROWING OUR CURRENT LIFE AWAY, AND STARTING FROM SCRATCH IN SOME FOREIGN COUNTRY, WITH NO MONEY AND NO FRIENDS, IS THE ANSWER?

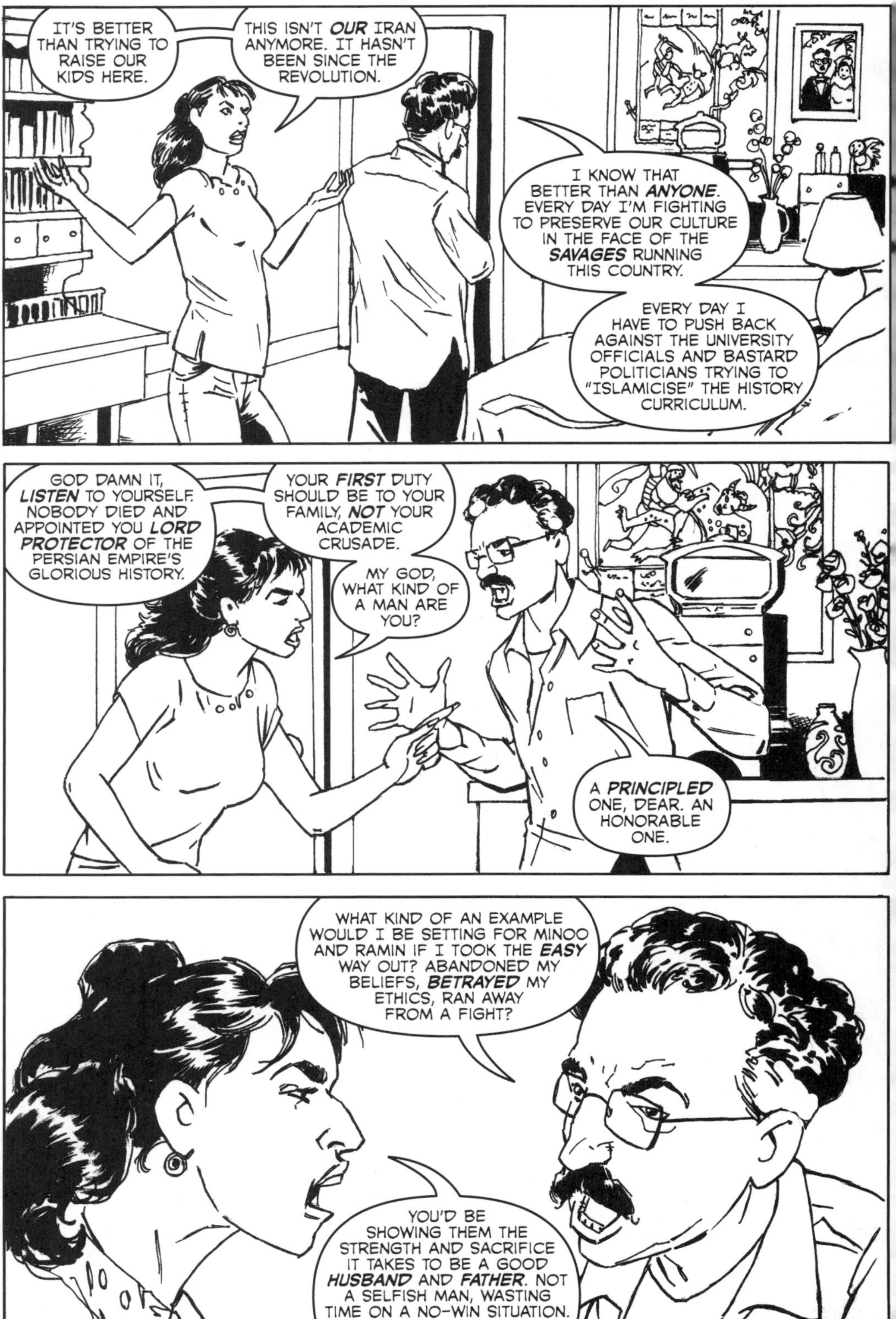

IT'S BETTER THAN TRYING TO RAISE OUR KIDS HERE.
THIS ISN'T OUR IRAN ANYMORE. IT HASN'T BEEN SINCE THE REVOLUTION.
I KNOW THAT BETTER THAN ANYONE. EVERY DAY I'M FIGHTING TO PRESERVE OUR CULTURE IN THE FACE OF THE SAVAGES RUNNING THIS COUNTRY.
EVERY DAY I HAVE TO PUSH BACK AGAINST THE UNIVERSITY OFFICIALS AND BASTARD POLITICIANS TRYING TO "ISLAMICISE" THE HISTORY CURRICULUM.
GOD DAMN IT, LISTEN TO YOURSELF. NOBODY DIED AND APPOINTED YOU LORD PROTECTOR OF THE PERSIAN EMPIRE'S GLORIOUS HISTORY.
YOUR FIRST DUTY SHOULD BE TO YOUR FAMILY, NOT YOUR ACADEMIC CRUSADE.
MY GOD, WHAT KIND OF A MAN ARE YOU?
A PRINCIPLED ONE, DEAR. AN HONORABLE ONE.
WHAT KIND OF AN EXAMPLE WOULD I BE SETTING FOR MINOO AND RAMIN IF I TOOK THE EASY WAY OUT? ABANDONED MY BELIEFS, BETRAYED MY ETHICS, RAN AWAY FROM A FIGHT?
YOU'D BE SHOWING THEM THE STRENGTH AND SACRIFICE IT TAKES TO BE A GOOD HUSBAND AND FATHER. NOT A SELFISH MAN, WASTING TIME ON A NO-WIN SITUATION.

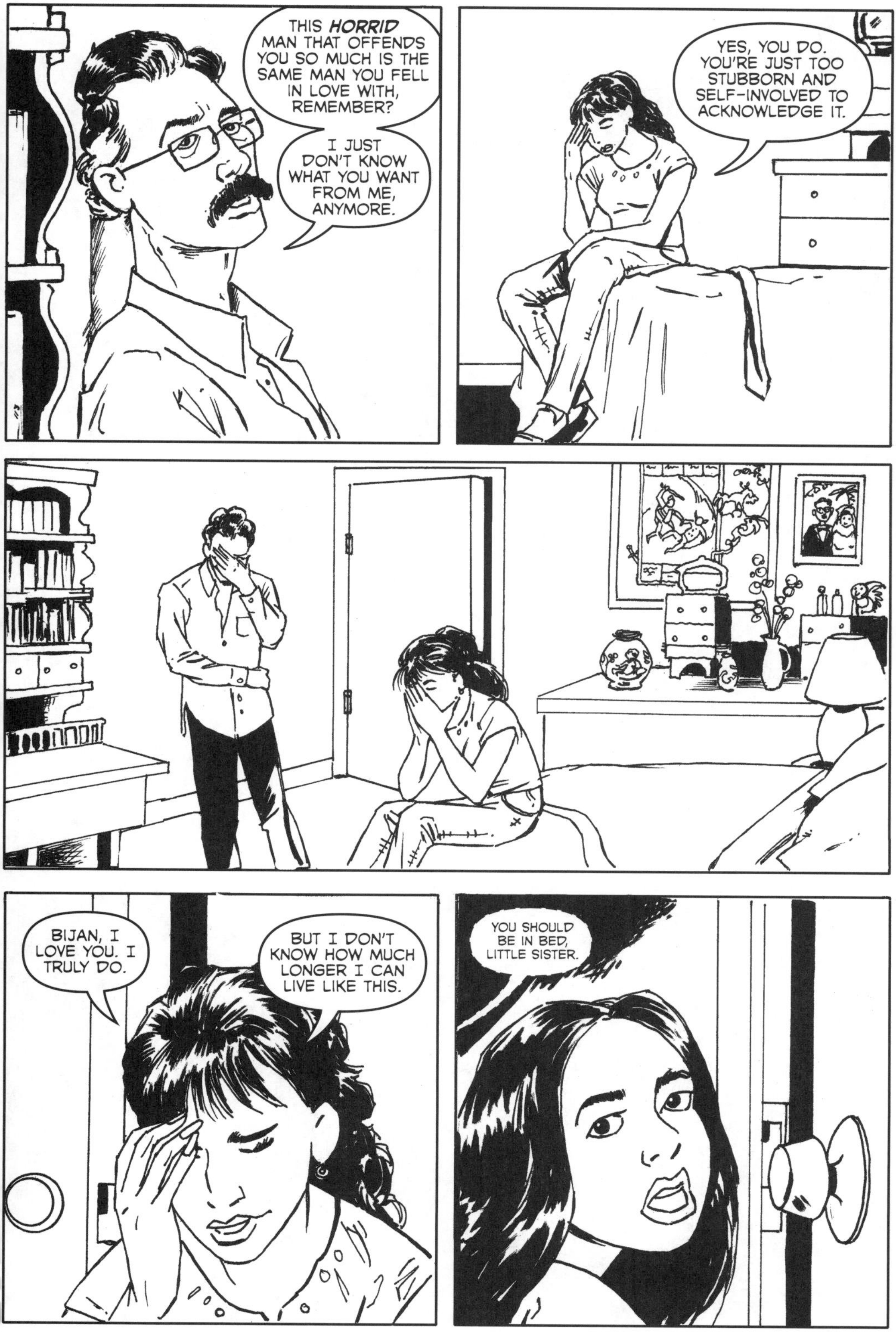
THIS **HORRID** MAN THAT OFFENDS YOU SO MUCH IS THE SAME MAN YOU FELL IN LOVE WITH, REMEMBER?
I JUST DON'T KNOW WHAT YOU WANT FROM ME, ANYMORE.
YES, YOU DO. YOU'RE JUST TOO STUBBORN AND SELF-INVOLVED TO ACKNOWLEDGE IT.
BIJAN, I LOVE YOU. I TRULY DO.
BUT I DON'T KNOW HOW MUCH LONGER I CAN LIVE LIKE THIS.
YOU SHOULD BE IN BED, LITTLE SISTER.

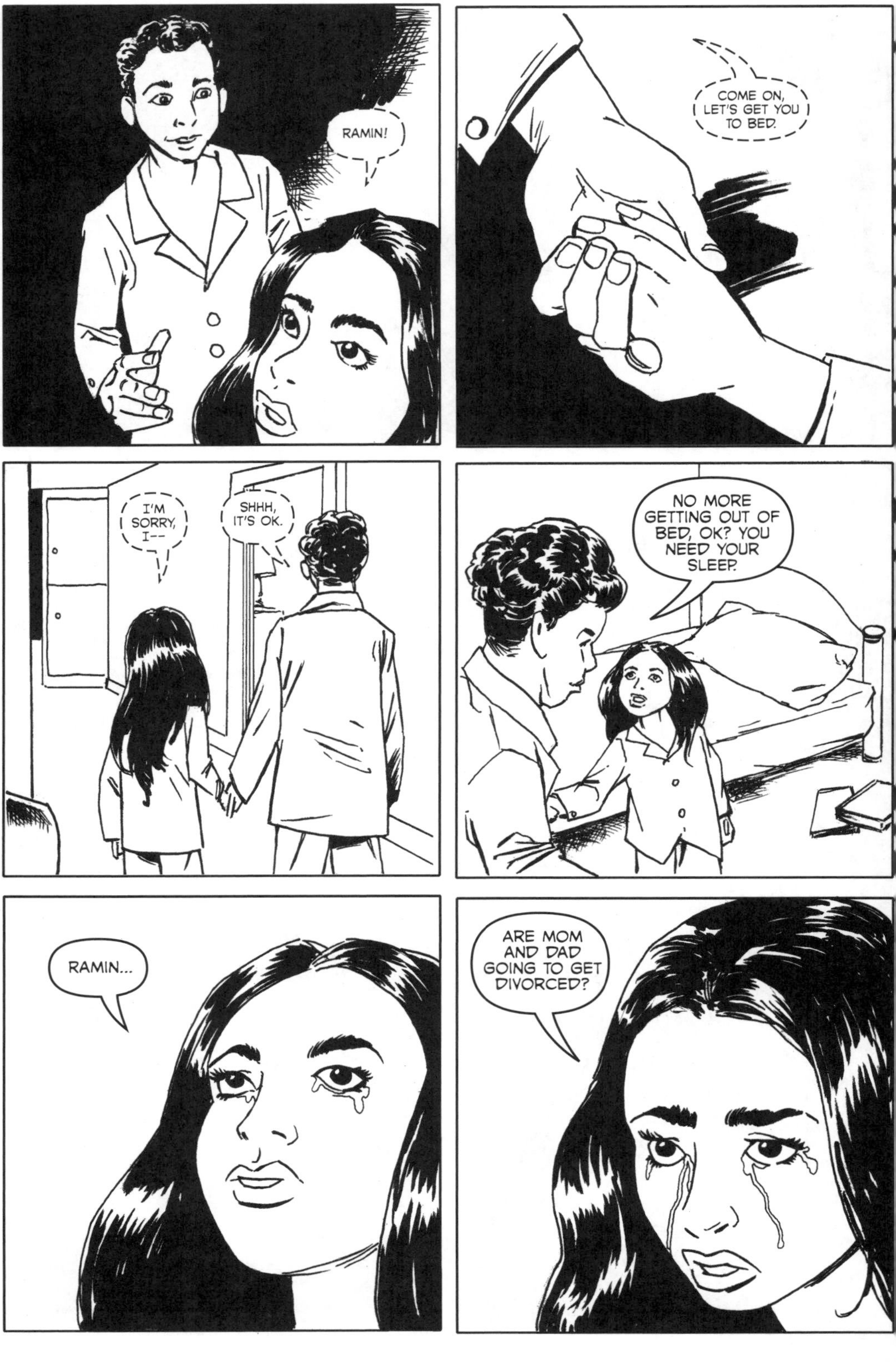
RAMIN!
COME ON, LET'S GET YOU TO BED.
I'M SORRY, I--
SHHH, IT'S OK.
NO MORE GETTING OUT OF BED, OK? YOU NEED YOUR SLEEP.
RAMIN...
ARE MOM AND DAD GOING TO GET DIVORCED?

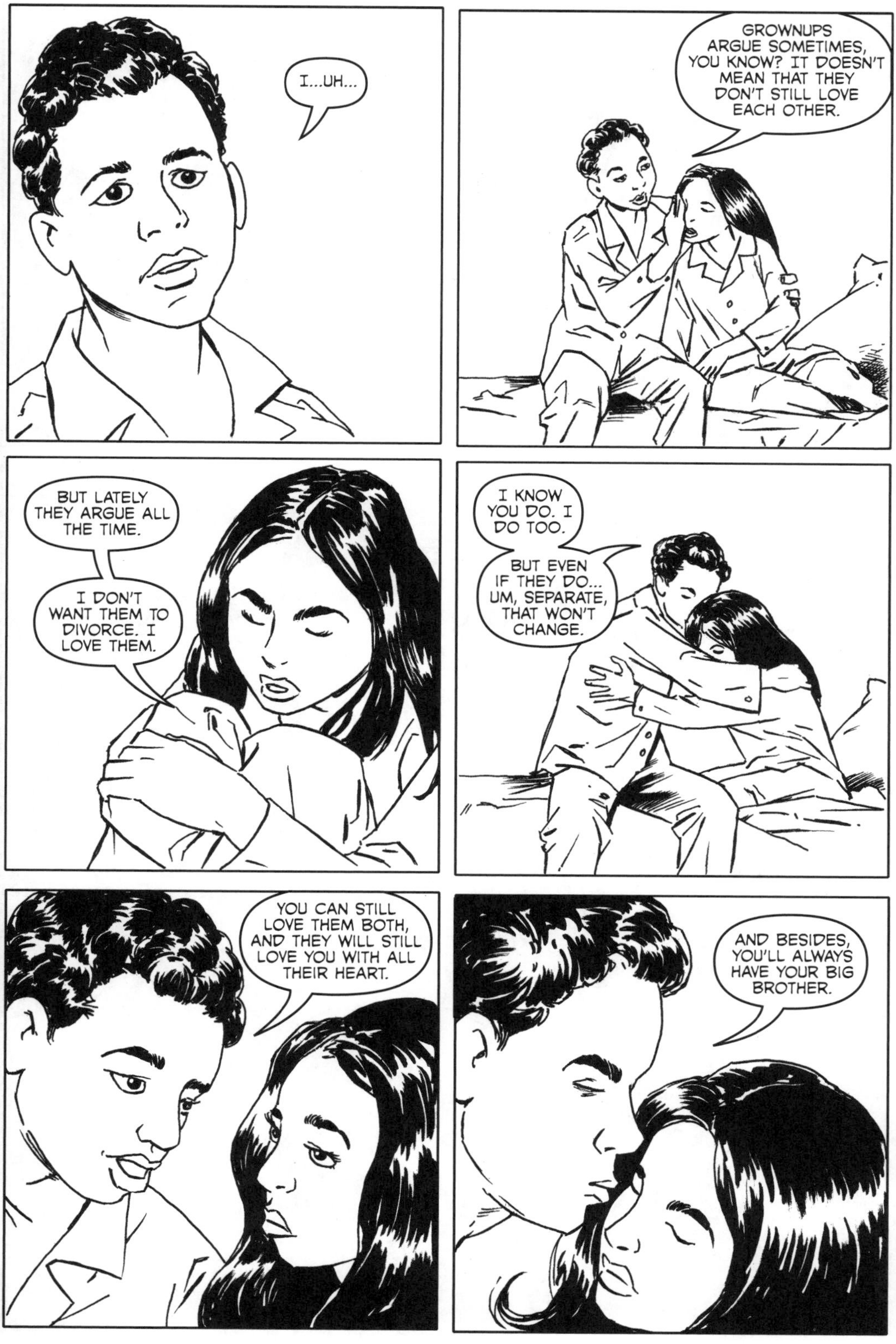
I...UH...
GROWNUPS ARGUE SOMETIMES, YOU KNOW? IT DOESN'T MEAN THAT THEY DON'T STILL LOVE EACH OTHER.
BUT LATELY THEY ARGUE ALL THE TIME.
I DON'T WANT THEM TO DIVORCE. I LOVE THEM.
I KNOW YOU DO. I DO TOO.
BUT EVEN IF THEY DO... UM, SEPARATE, THAT WON'T CHANGE.
YOU CAN STILL LOVE THEM BOTH, AND THEY WILL STILL LOVE YOU WITH ALL THEIR HEART.
AND BESIDES, YOU'LL ALWAYS HAVE YOUR BIG BROTHER.

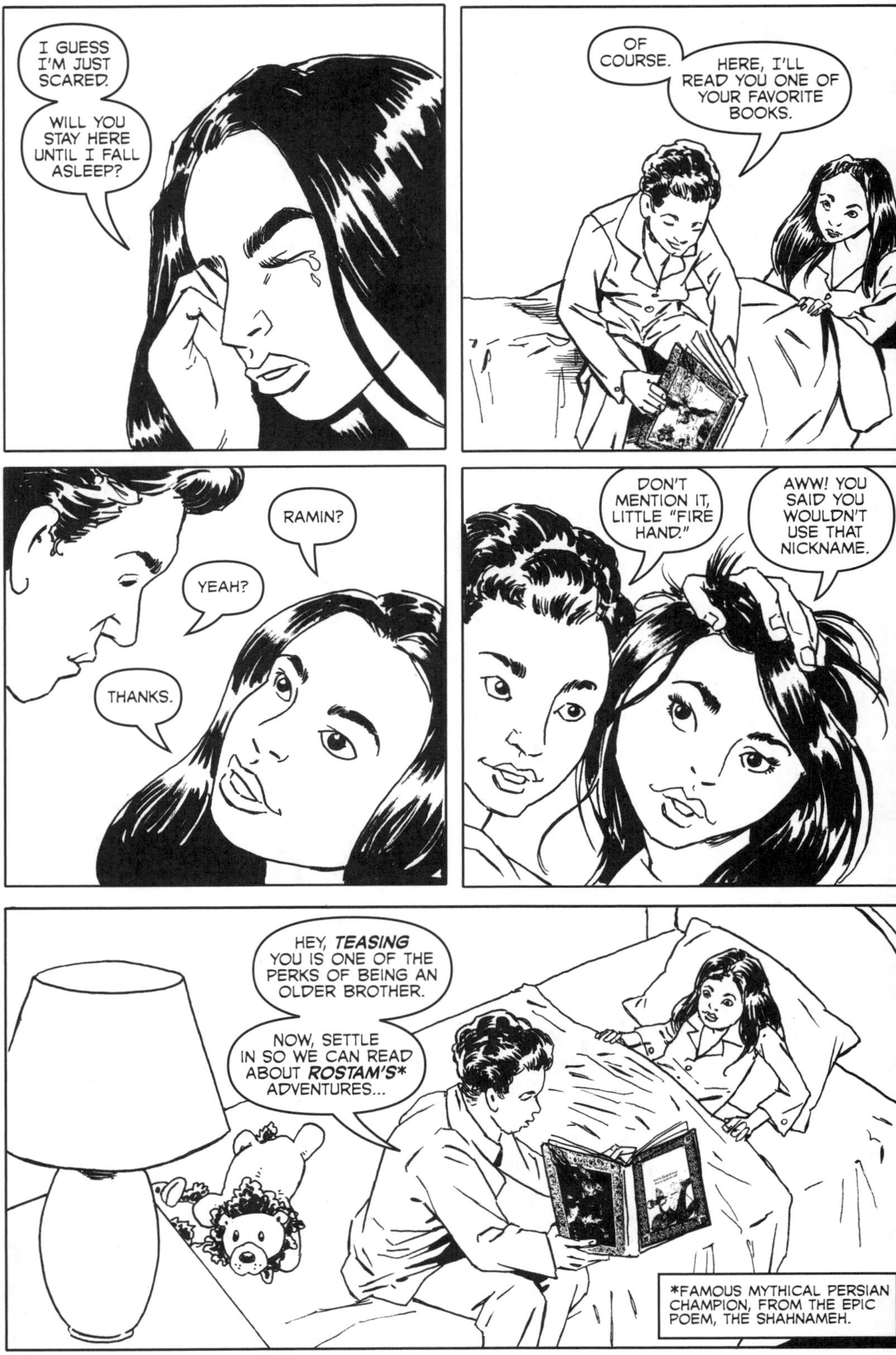
I GUESS I'M JUST SCARED.
WILL YOU STAY HERE UNTIL I FALL ASLEEP?
OF COURSE.
HERE, I'LL READ YOU ONE OF YOUR FAVORITE BOOKS.
RAMIN?
YEAH?
THANKS.
DON'T MENTION IT, LITTLE "FIRE HAND."
AWW! YOU SAID YOU WOULDN'T USE THAT NICKNAME.
HEY, TEASING YOU IS ONE OF THE PERKS OF BEING AN OLDER BROTHER.
NOW, SETTLE IN SO WE CAN READ ABOUT ROSTAM'S* ADVENTURES...
*FAMOUS MYTHICAL PERSIAN CHAMPION, FROM THE EPIC POEM, THE SHAHNAMEH.

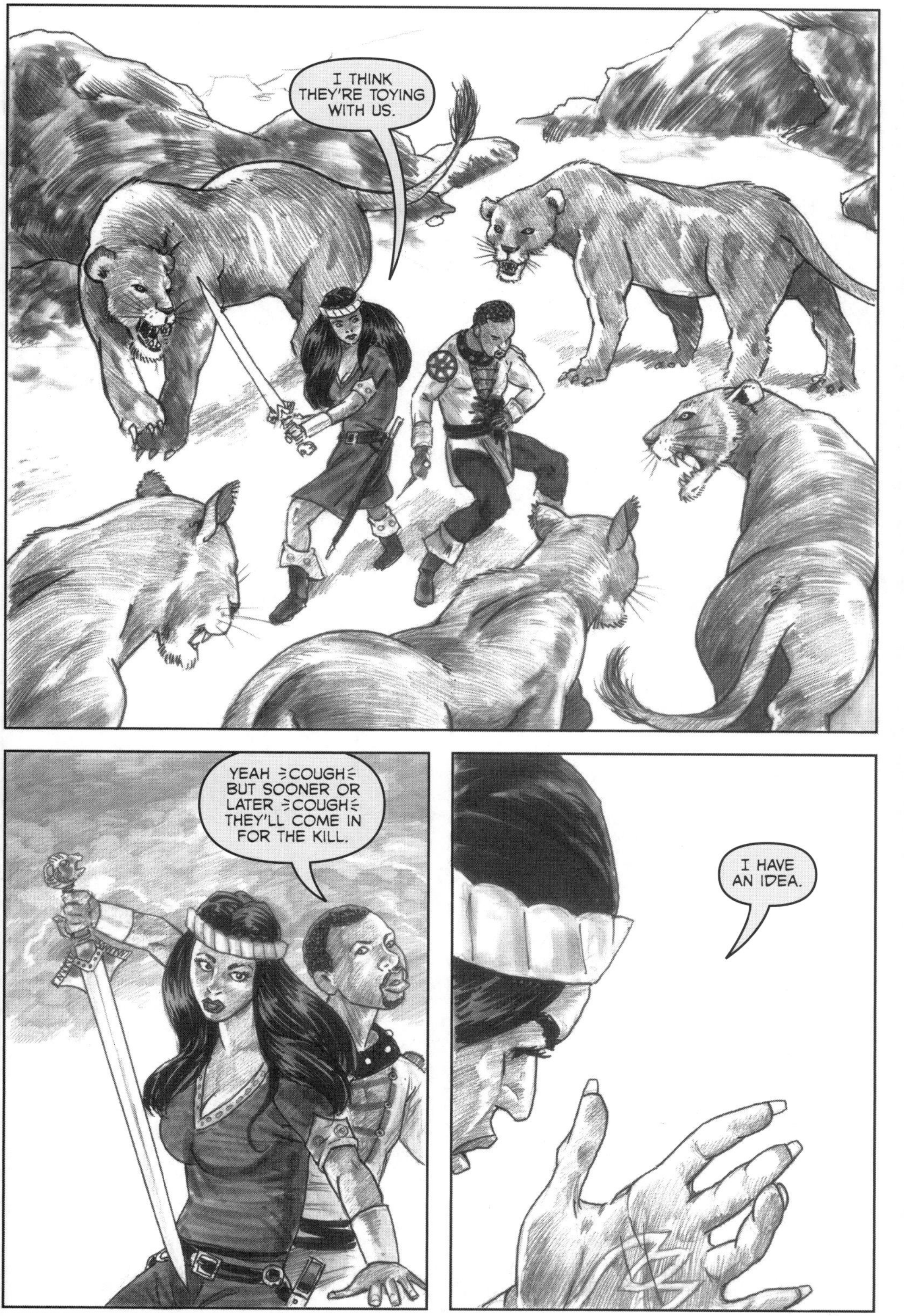
I THINK THEY'RE TOYING WITH US.
YEAH ≋COUGH≋ BUT SOONER OR LATER ≋COUGH≋ THEY'LL COME IN FOR THE KILL.
I HAVE AN IDEA.

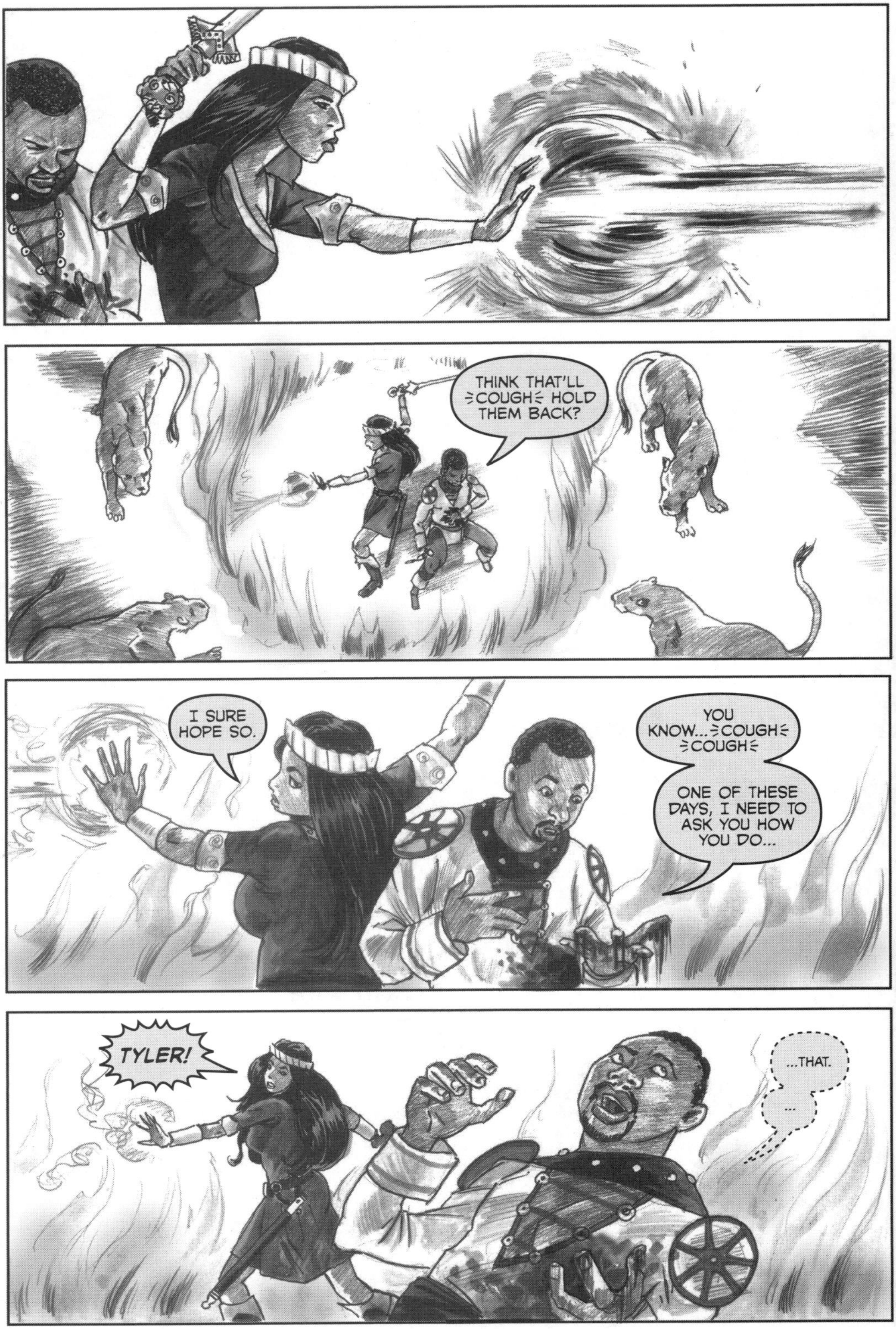
THINK THAT'LL ≈COUGH≈ HOLD THEM BACK?
I SURE HOPE SO.
YOU KNOW... ≈COUGH≈ ≈COUGH≈
ONE OF THESE DAYS, I NEED TO ASK YOU HOW YOU DO...
TYLER!
...THAT.
...

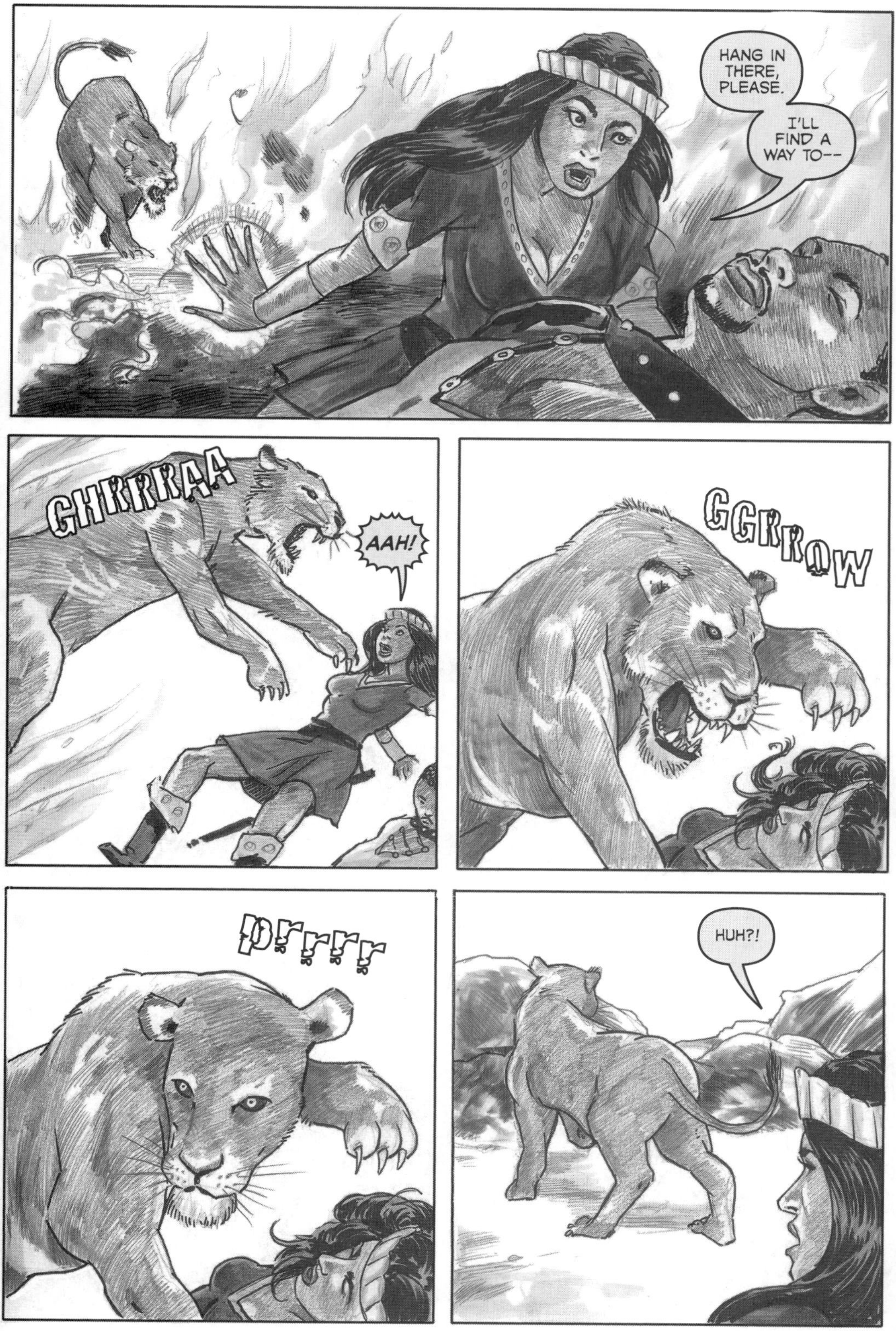
HANG IN THERE, PLEASE.
I'LL FIND A WAY TO--
GHRRRAA
AAH!
GGRROW
Prrrr
HUH?!

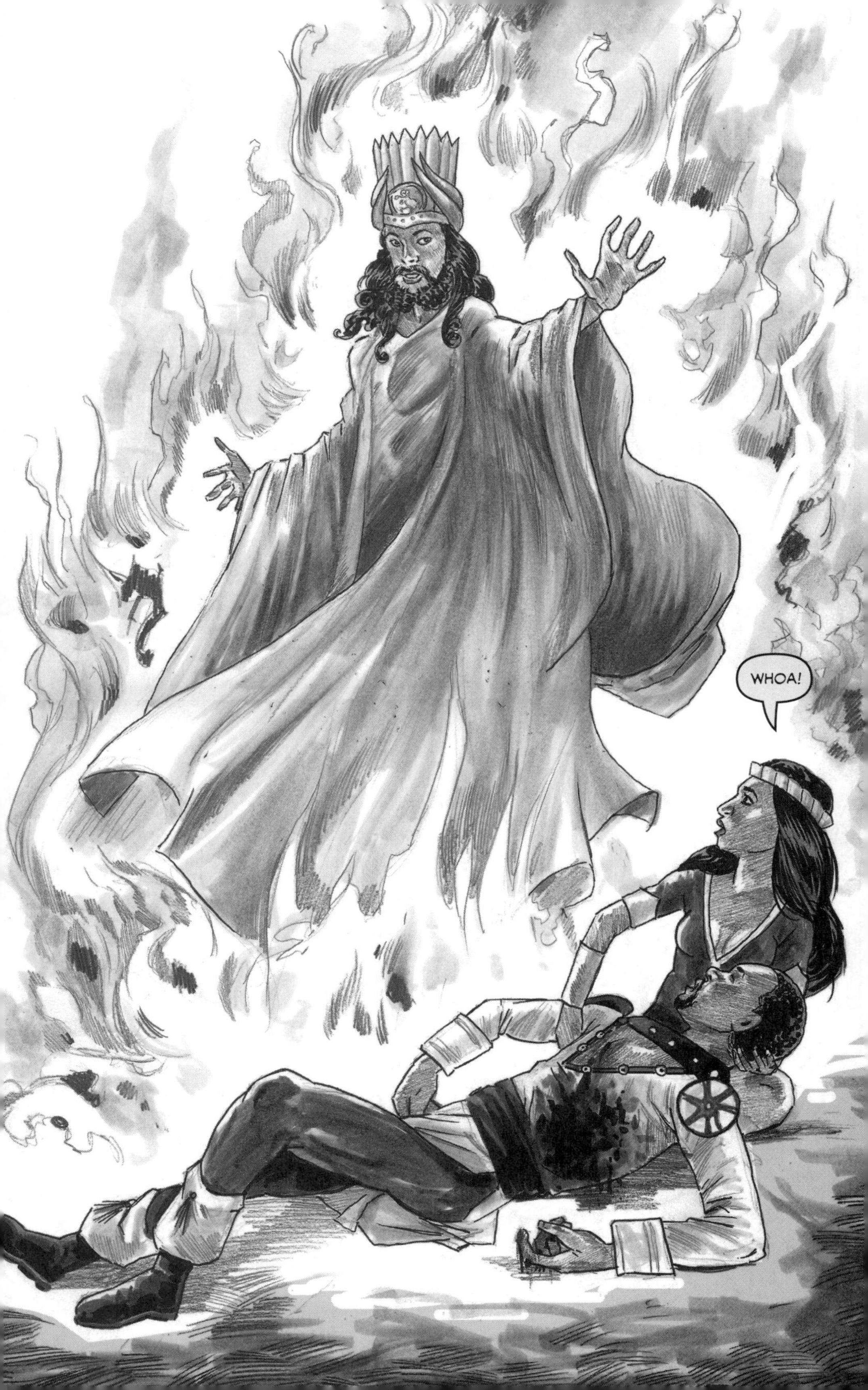
WHOA!

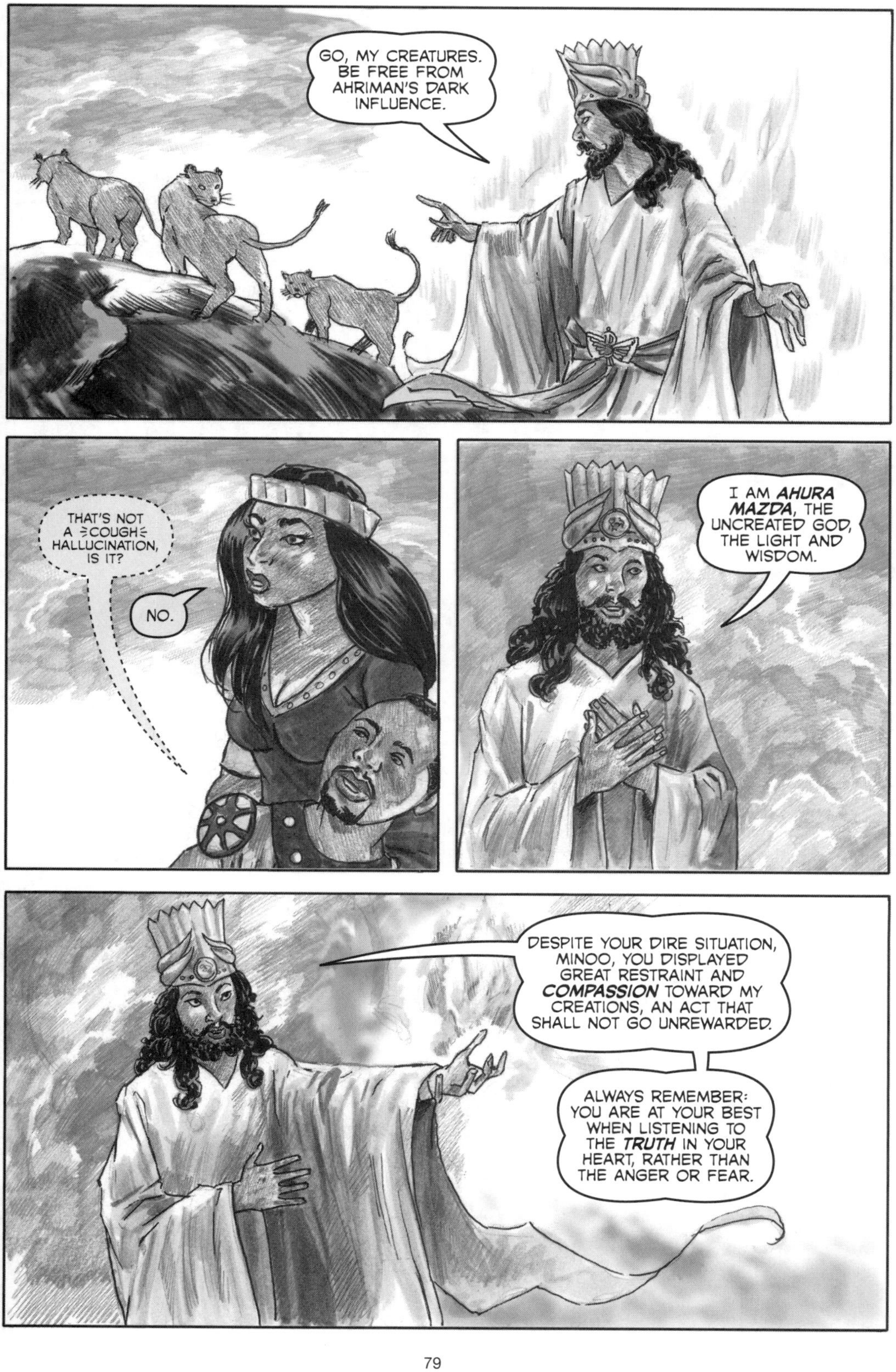
GO, MY CREATURES. BE FREE FROM AHRIMAN'S DARK INFLUENCE.
THAT'S NOT A =COUGH= HALLUCINATION, IS IT?
NO.
I AM AHURA MAZDA, THE UNCREATED GOD, THE LIGHT AND WISDOM.
DESPITE YOUR DIRE SITUATION, MINOO, YOU DISPLAYED GREAT RESTRAINT AND COMPASSION TOWARD MY CREATIONS, AN ACT THAT SHALL NOT GO UNREWARDED.
ALWAYS REMEMBER: YOU ARE AT YOUR BEST WHEN LISTENING TO THE TRUTH IN YOUR HEART, RATHER THAN THE ANGER OR FEAR.

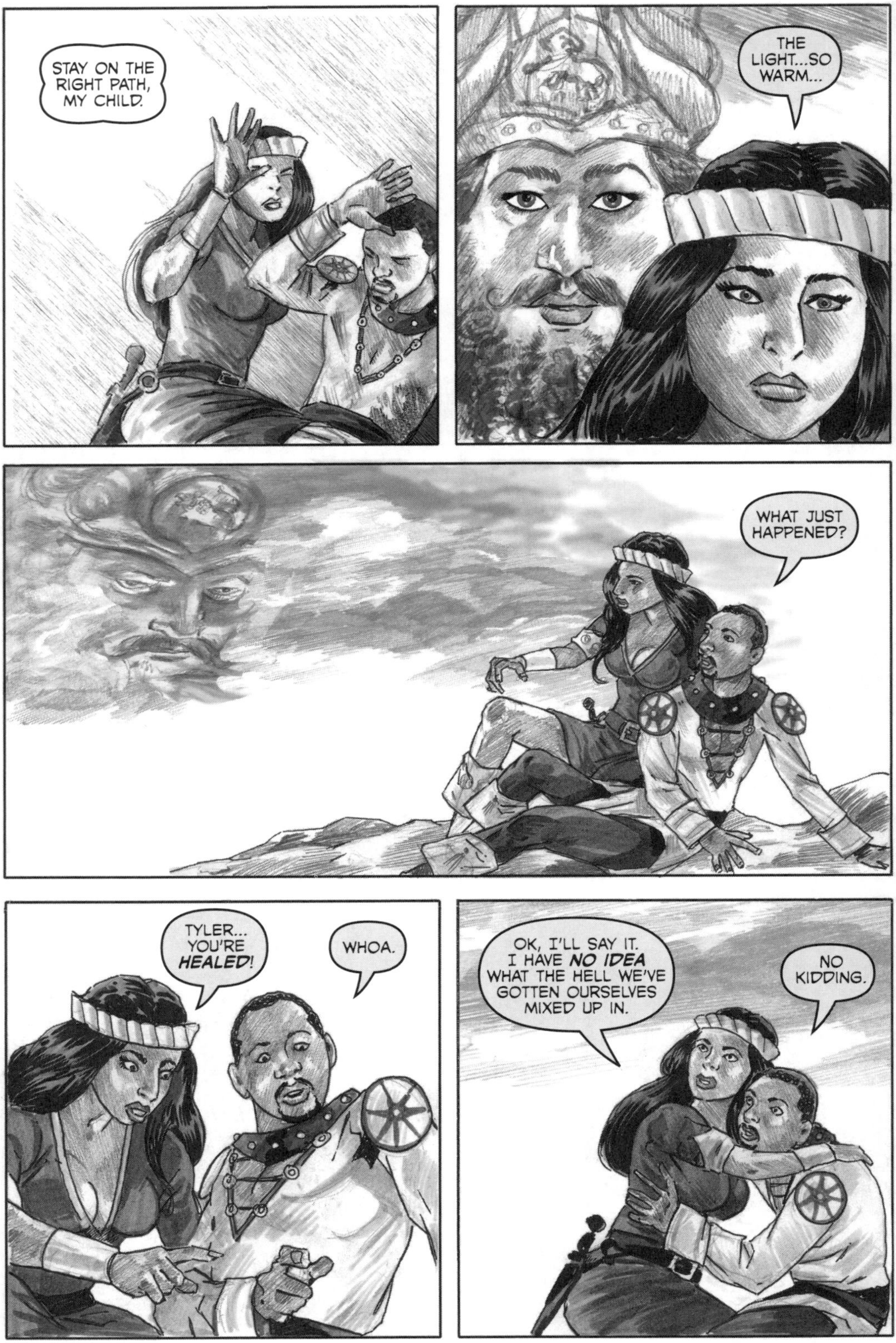
STAY ON THE RIGHT PATH, MY CHILD.
THE LIGHT...SO WARM...
WHAT JUST HAPPENED?
TYLER... YOU'RE ***HEALED***!
WHOA.
OK, I'LL SAY IT. I HAVE ***NO IDEA*** WHAT THE HELL WE'VE GOTTEN OURSELVES MIXED UP IN.
NO KIDDING.

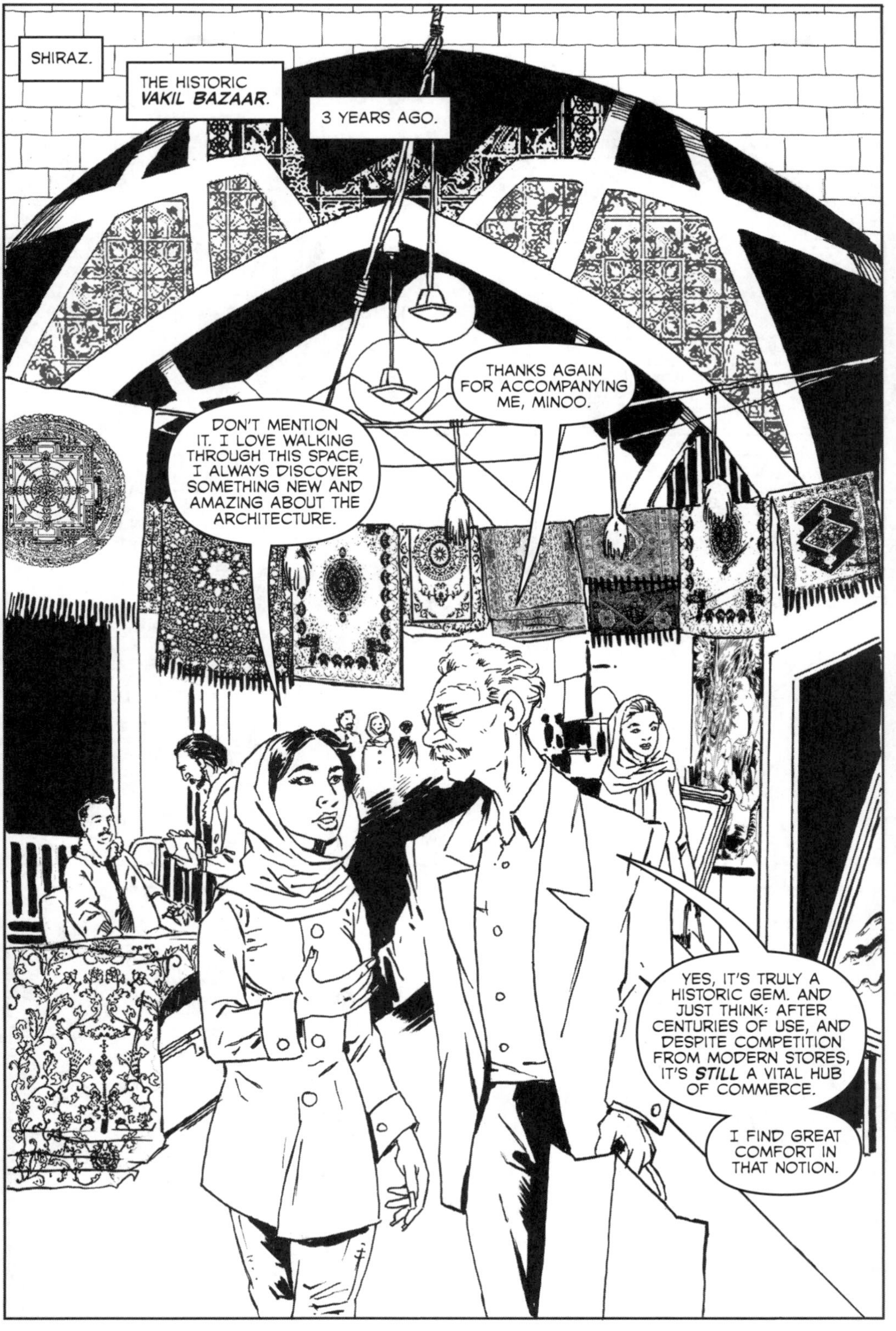

SHIRAZ.
THE HISTORIC *VAKIL BAZAAR*.
3 YEARS AGO.
THANKS AGAIN FOR ACCOMPANYING ME, MINOO.
DON'T MENTION IT. I LOVE WALKING THROUGH THIS SPACE, I ALWAYS DISCOVER SOMETHING NEW AND AMAZING ABOUT THE ARCHITECTURE.
YES, IT'S TRULY A HISTORIC GEM. AND JUST THINK: AFTER CENTURIES OF USE, AND DESPITE COMPETITION FROM MODERN STORES, IT'S *STILL* A VITAL HUB OF COMMERCE.
I FIND GREAT COMFORT IN THAT NOTION.

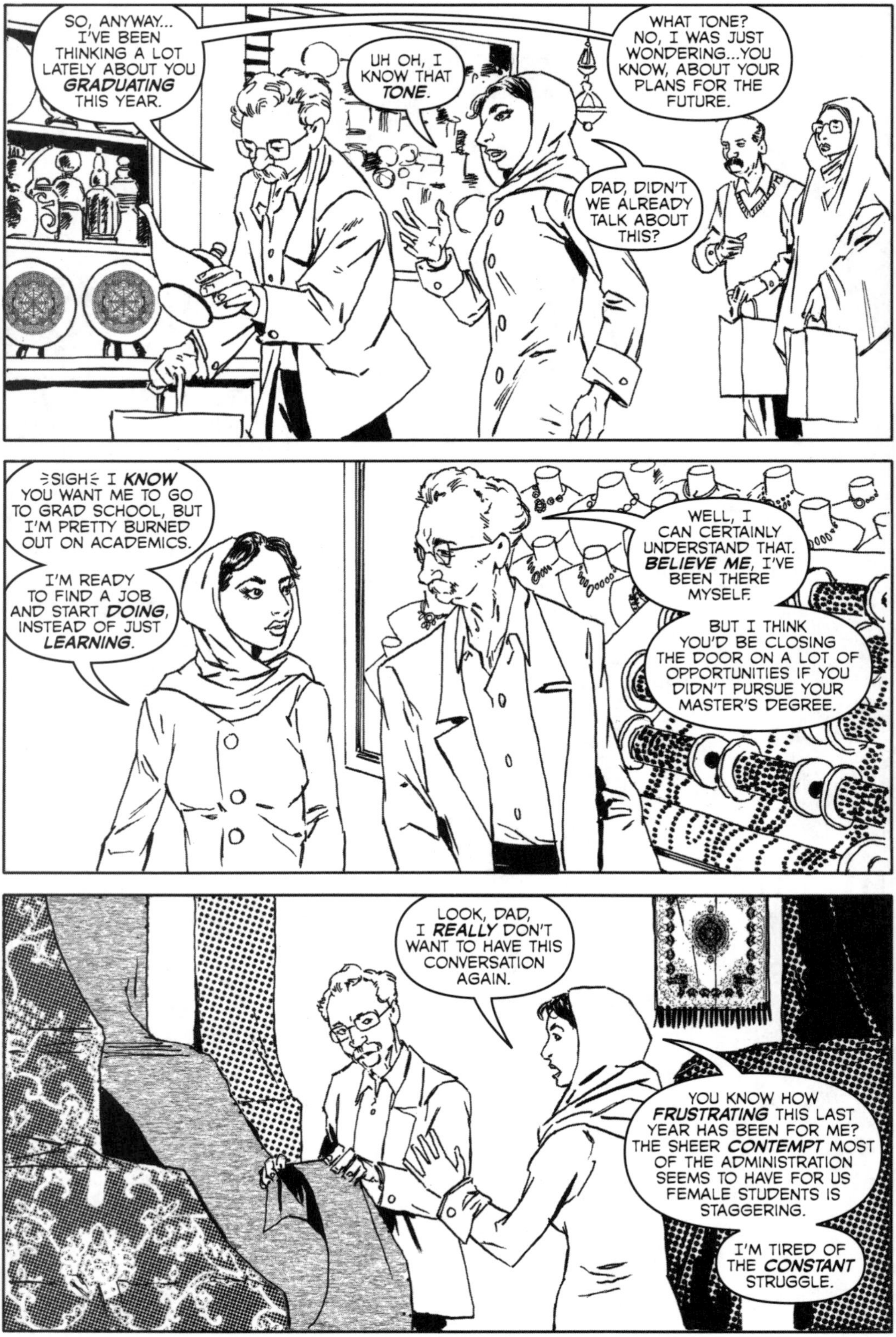
SO, ANYWAY... I'VE BEEN THINKING A LOT LATELY ABOUT YOU GRADUATING THIS YEAR.
UH OH, I KNOW THAT TONE.
WHAT TONE? NO, I WAS JUST WONDERING...YOU KNOW, ABOUT YOUR PLANS FOR THE FUTURE.
DAD, DIDN'T WE ALREADY TALK ABOUT THIS?
SIGH I KNOW YOU WANT ME TO GO TO GRAD SCHOOL, BUT I'M PRETTY BURNED OUT ON ACADEMICS.
I'M READY TO FIND A JOB AND START DOING, INSTEAD OF JUST LEARNING.
WELL, I CAN CERTAINLY UNDERSTAND THAT. BELIEVE ME, I'VE BEEN THERE MYSELF.
BUT I THINK YOU'D BE CLOSING THE DOOR ON A LOT OF OPPORTUNITIES IF YOU DIDN'T PURSUE YOUR MASTER'S DEGREE.
LOOK, DAD, I REALLY DON'T WANT TO HAVE THIS CONVERSATION AGAIN.
YOU KNOW HOW FRUSTRATING THIS LAST YEAR HAS BEEN FOR ME? THE SHEER CONTEMPT MOST OF THE ADMINISTRATION SEEMS TO HAVE FOR US FEMALE STUDENTS IS STAGGERING.
I'M TIRED OF THE CONSTANT STRUGGLE.

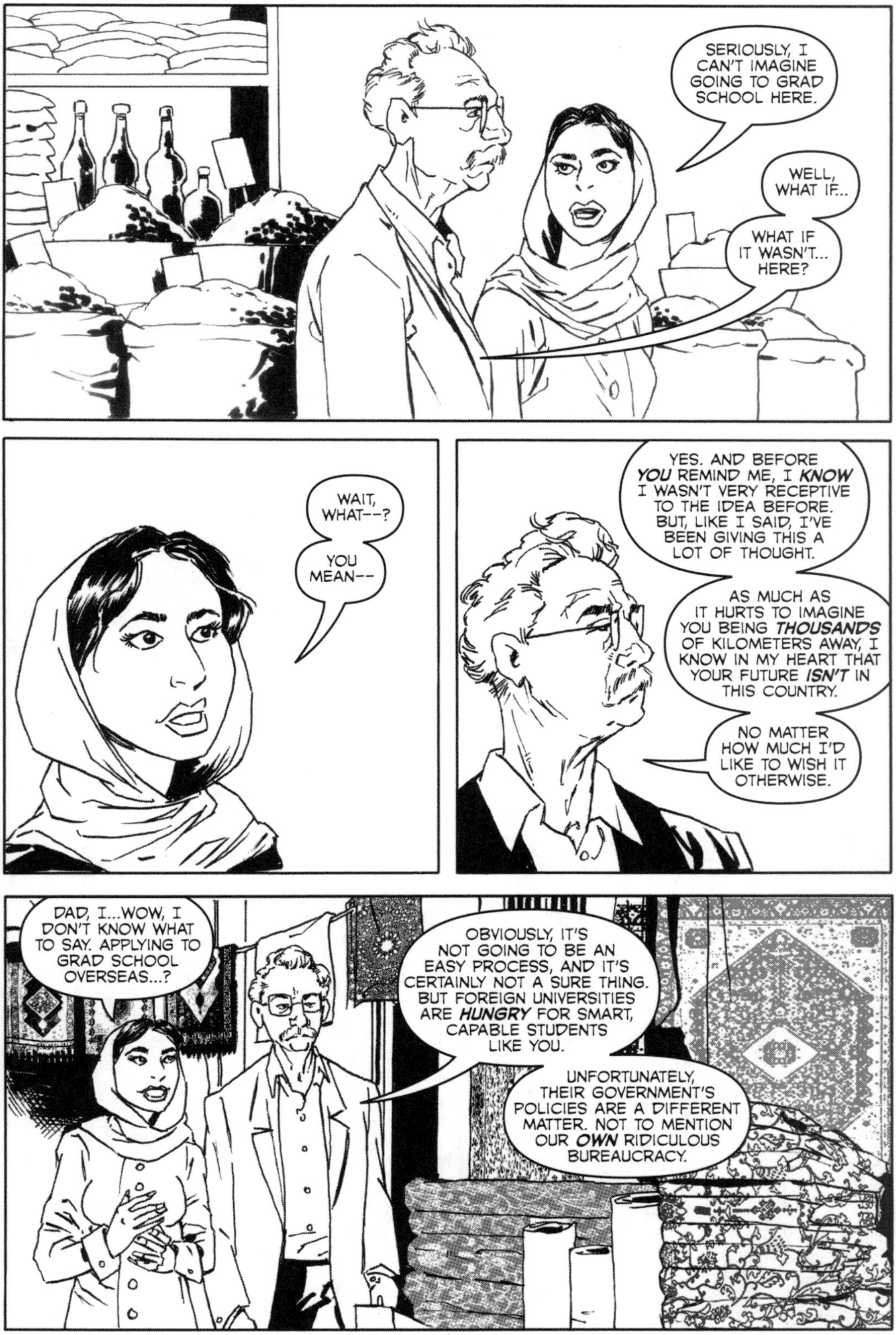
SERIOUSLY, I CAN'T IMAGINE GOING TO GRAD SCHOOL HERE.
WELL, WHAT IF...
WHAT IF IT WASN'T... HERE?
WAIT, WHAT--?
YOU MEAN--
YES. AND BEFORE *YOU* REMIND ME, I *KNOW* I WASN'T VERY RECEPTIVE TO THE IDEA BEFORE. BUT, LIKE I SAID, I'VE BEEN GIVING THIS A LOT OF THOUGHT.
AS MUCH AS IT HURTS TO IMAGINE YOU BEING *THOUSANDS* OF KILOMETERS AWAY, I KNOW IN MY HEART THAT YOUR FUTURE *ISN'T* IN THIS COUNTRY.
NO MATTER HOW MUCH I'D LIKE TO WISH IT OTHERWISE.
DAD, I...WOW, I DON'T KNOW WHAT TO SAY. APPLYING TO GRAD SCHOOL OVERSEAS...?
OBVIOUSLY, IT'S NOT GOING TO BE AN EASY PROCESS, AND IT'S CERTAINLY NOT A SURE THING. BUT FOREIGN UNIVERSITIES ARE *HUNGRY* FOR SMART, CAPABLE STUDENTS LIKE YOU.
UNFORTUNATELY, THEIR GOVERNMENT'S POLICIES ARE A DIFFERENT MATTER. NOT TO MENTION OUR *OWN* RIDICULOUS BUREAUCRACY.

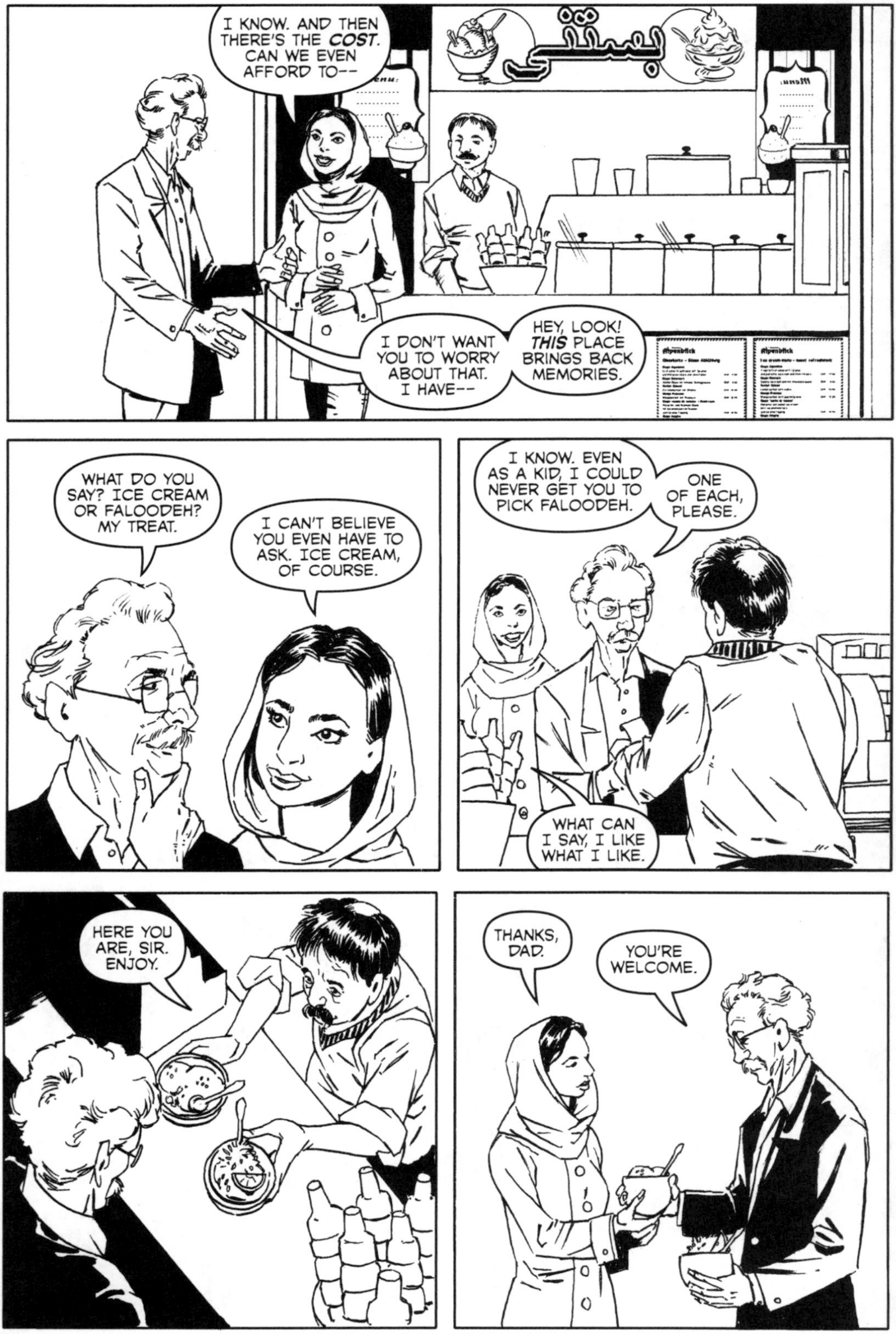
I KNOW. AND THEN THERE'S THE *COST*. CAN WE EVEN AFFORD TO--
I DON'T WANT YOU TO WORRY ABOUT THAT. I HAVE--
HEY, LOOK! *THIS* PLACE BRINGS BACK MEMORIES.
WHAT DO YOU SAY? ICE CREAM OR FALOODEH? MY TREAT.
I CAN'T BELIEVE YOU EVEN HAVE TO ASK. ICE CREAM, OF COURSE.
I KNOW. EVEN AS A KID, I COULD NEVER GET YOU TO PICK FALOODEH.
ONE OF EACH, PLEASE.
WHAT CAN I SAY, I LIKE WHAT I LIKE.
HERE YOU ARE, SIR. ENJOY.
THANKS, DAD.
YOU'RE WELCOME.

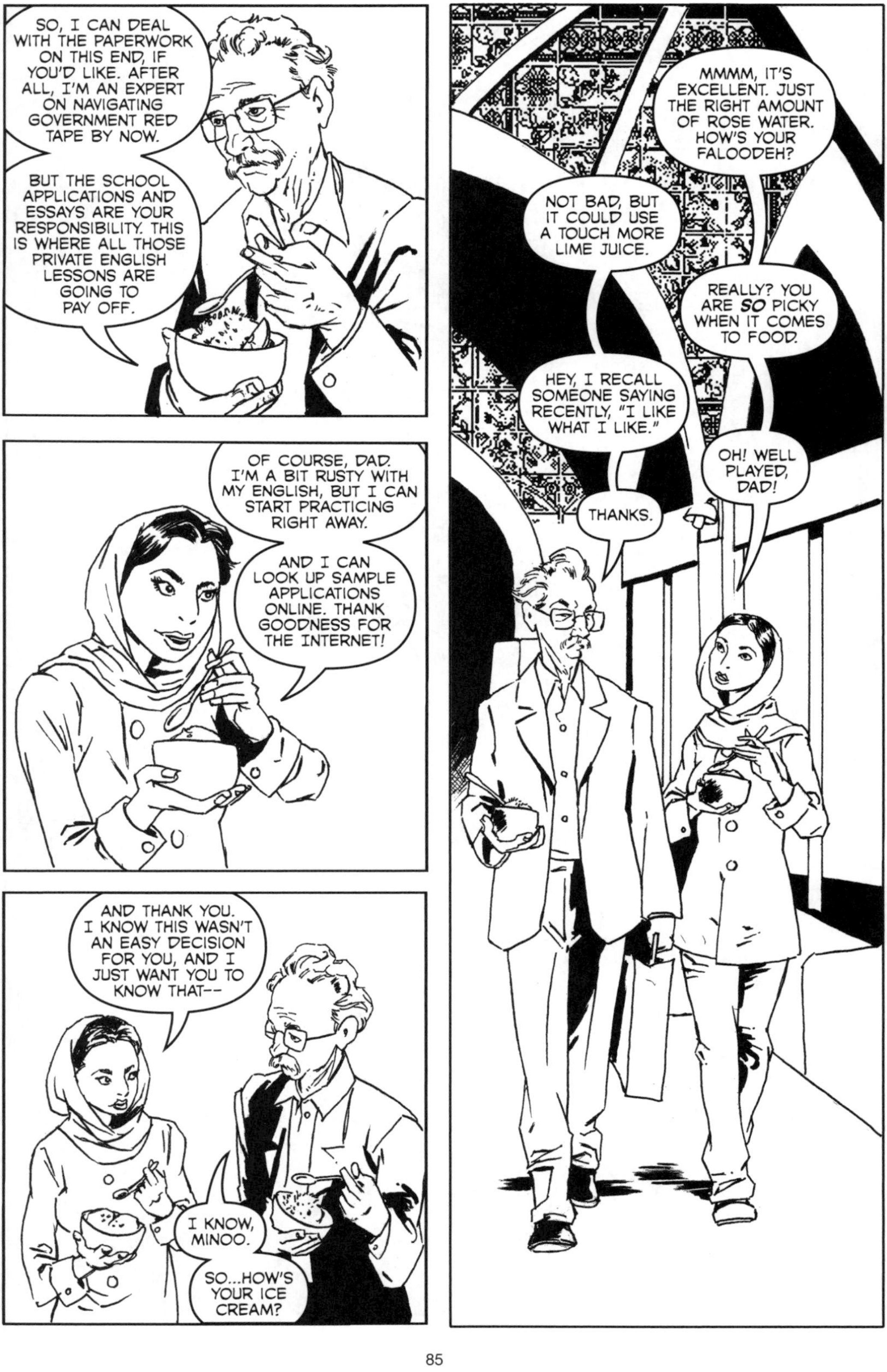
SO, I CAN DEAL WITH THE PAPERWORK ON THIS END, IF YOU'D LIKE. AFTER ALL, I'M AN EXPERT ON NAVIGATING GOVERNMENT RED TAPE BY NOW.
BUT THE SCHOOL APPLICATIONS AND ESSAYS ARE YOUR RESPONSIBILITY. THIS IS WHERE ALL THOSE PRIVATE ENGLISH LESSONS ARE GOING TO PAY OFF.
OF COURSE, DAD. I'M A BIT RUSTY WITH MY ENGLISH, BUT I CAN START PRACTICING RIGHT AWAY.
AND I CAN LOOK UP SAMPLE APPLICATIONS ONLINE. THANK GOODNESS FOR THE INTERNET!
AND THANK YOU. I KNOW THIS WASN'T AN EASY DECISION FOR YOU, AND I JUST WANT YOU TO KNOW THAT--
I KNOW, MINOO.
SO...HOW'S YOUR ICE CREAM?
MMMM, IT'S EXCELLENT. JUST THE RIGHT AMOUNT OF ROSE WATER. HOW'S YOUR FALOODEH?
NOT BAD, BUT IT COULD USE A TOUCH MORE LIME JUICE.
REALLY? YOU ARE **SO** PICKY WHEN IT COMES TO FOOD.
HEY, I RECALL SOMEONE SAYING RECENTLY, "I LIKE WHAT I LIKE."
OH! WELL PLAYED, DAD!
THANKS.

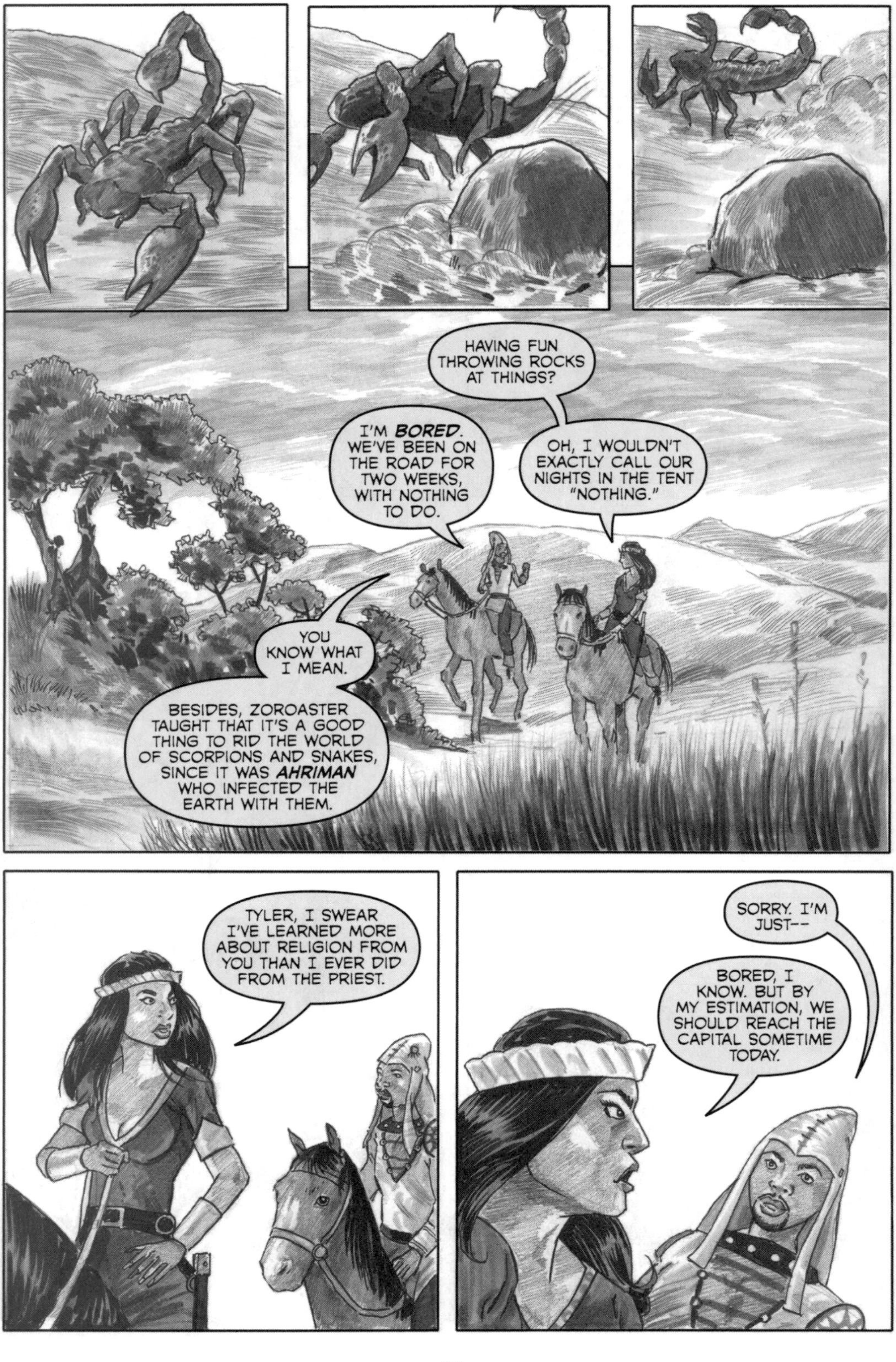
HAVING FUN THROWING ROCKS AT THINGS?
I'M **BORED**. WE'VE BEEN ON THE ROAD FOR TWO WEEKS, WITH NOTHING TO DO.
OH, I WOULDN'T EXACTLY CALL OUR NIGHTS IN THE TENT "NOTHING."
YOU KNOW WHAT I MEAN.
BESIDES, ZOROASTER TAUGHT THAT IT'S A GOOD THING TO RID THE WORLD OF SCORPIONS AND SNAKES, SINCE IT WAS **AHRIMAN** WHO INFECTED THE EARTH WITH THEM.
TYLER, I SWEAR I'VE LEARNED MORE ABOUT RELIGION FROM YOU THAN I EVER DID FROM THE PRIEST.
SORRY. I'M JUST--
BORED, I KNOW. BUT BY MY ESTIMATION, WE SHOULD REACH THE CAPITAL SOMETIME TODAY.

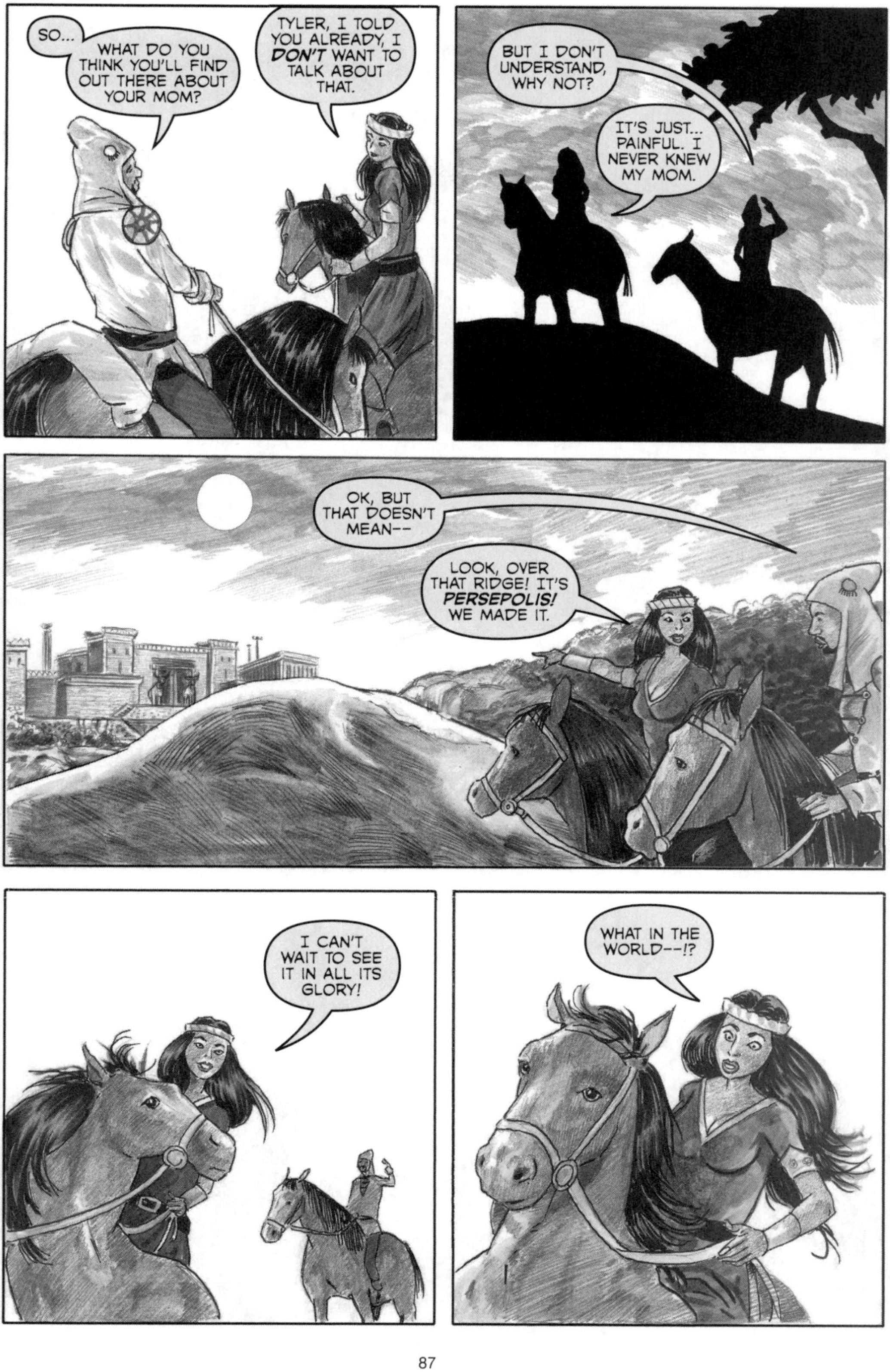
SO...
WHAT DO YOU THINK YOU'LL FIND OUT THERE ABOUT YOUR MOM?
TYLER, I TOLD YOU ALREADY, I ***DON'T*** WANT TO TALK ABOUT THAT.
BUT I DON'T UNDERSTAND, WHY NOT?
IT'S JUST... PAINFUL. I NEVER KNEW MY MOM.
OK, BUT THAT DOESN'T MEAN--
LOOK, OVER THAT RIDGE! IT'S ***PERSEPOLIS!*** WE MADE IT.
I CAN'T WAIT TO SEE IT IN ALL ITS GLORY!
WHAT IN THE WORLD--!?

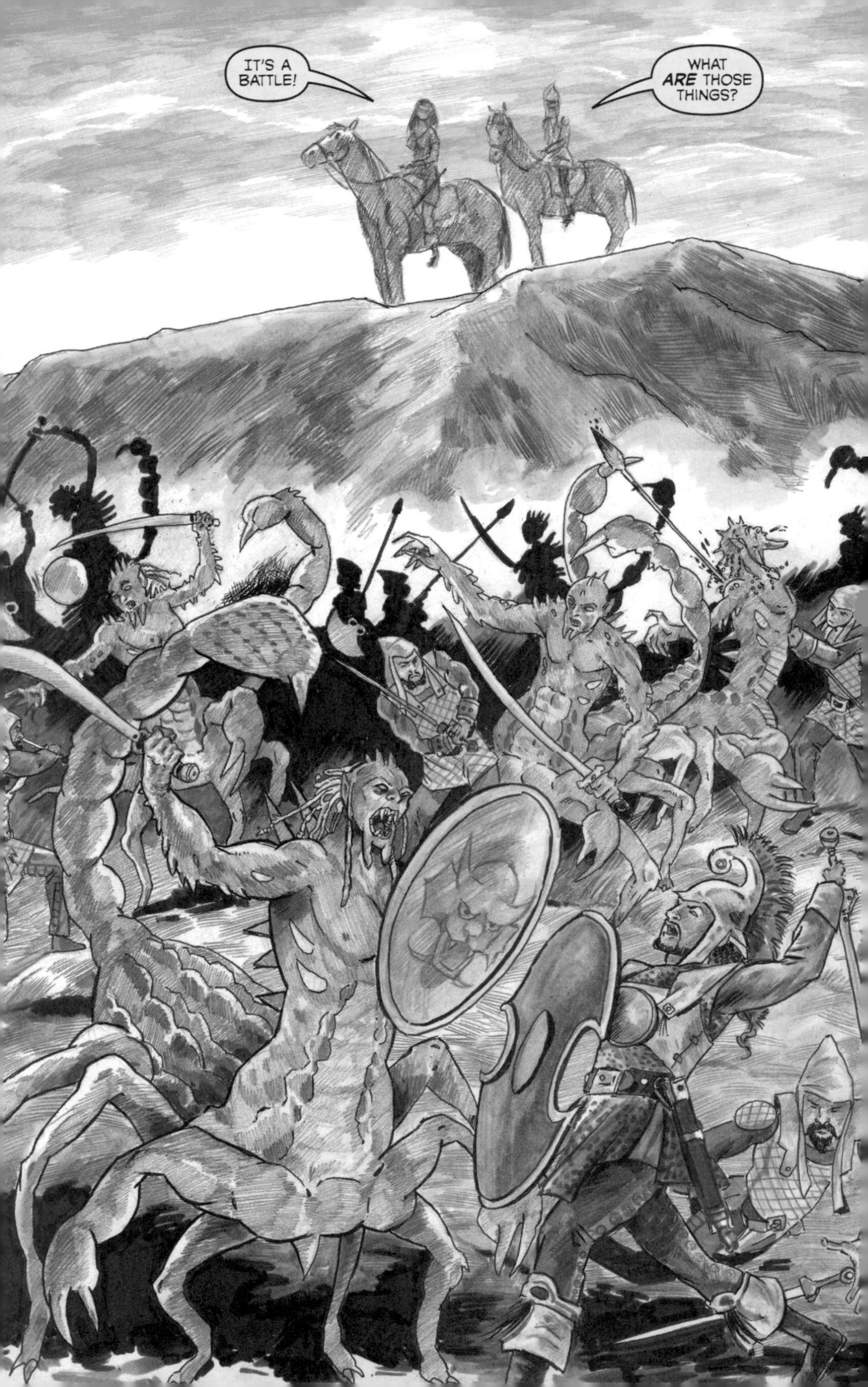
IT'S A BATTLE!
WHAT ARE THOSE THINGS?

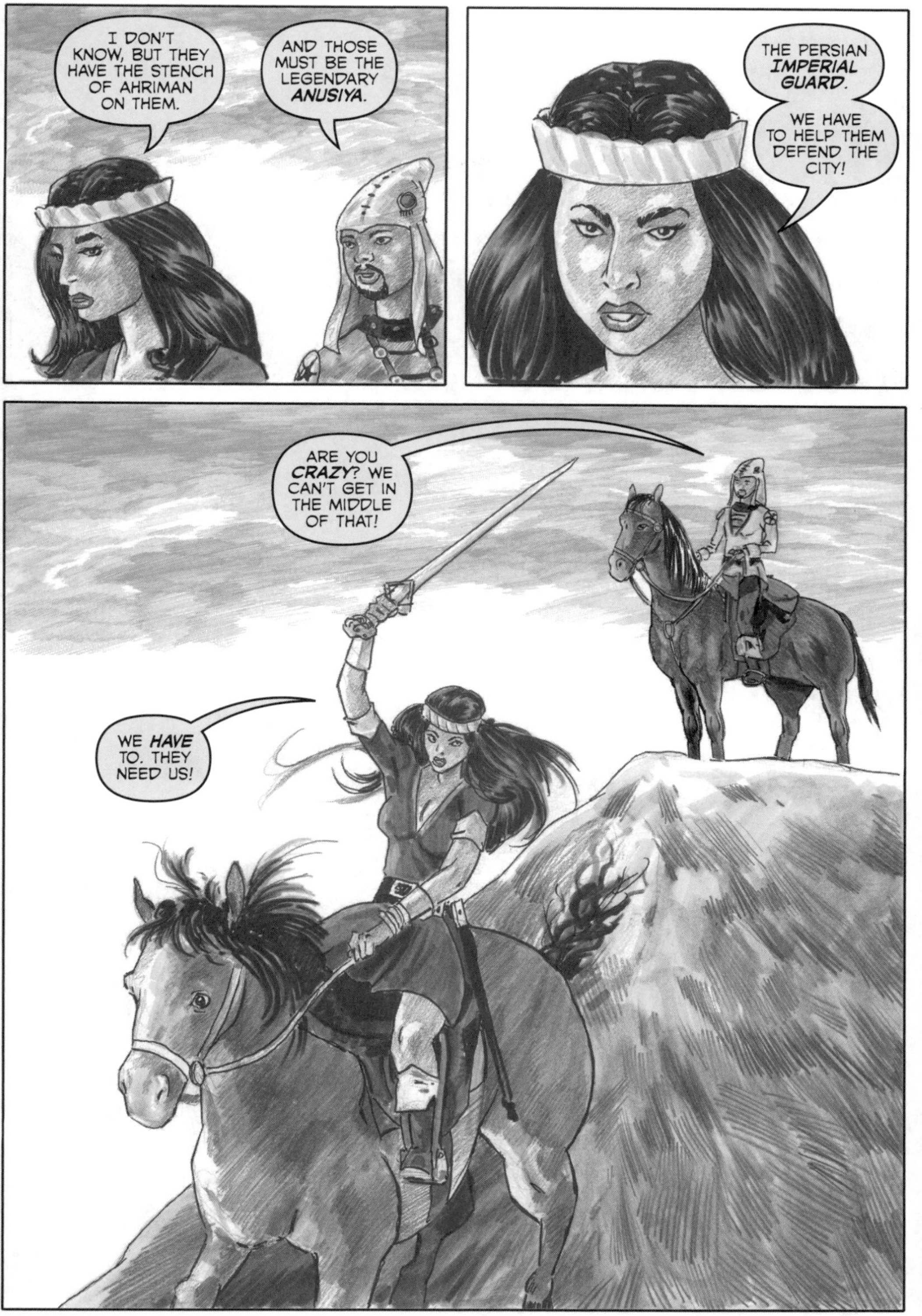
I DON'T KNOW, BUT THEY HAVE THE STENCH OF AHRIMAN ON THEM.
AND THOSE MUST BE THE LEGENDARY ANUSIYA.
THE PERSIAN IMPERIAL GUARD.
WE HAVE TO HELP THEM DEFEND THE CITY!
ARE YOU CRAZY? WE CAN'T GET IN THE MIDDLE OF THAT!
WE HAVE TO. THEY NEED US!

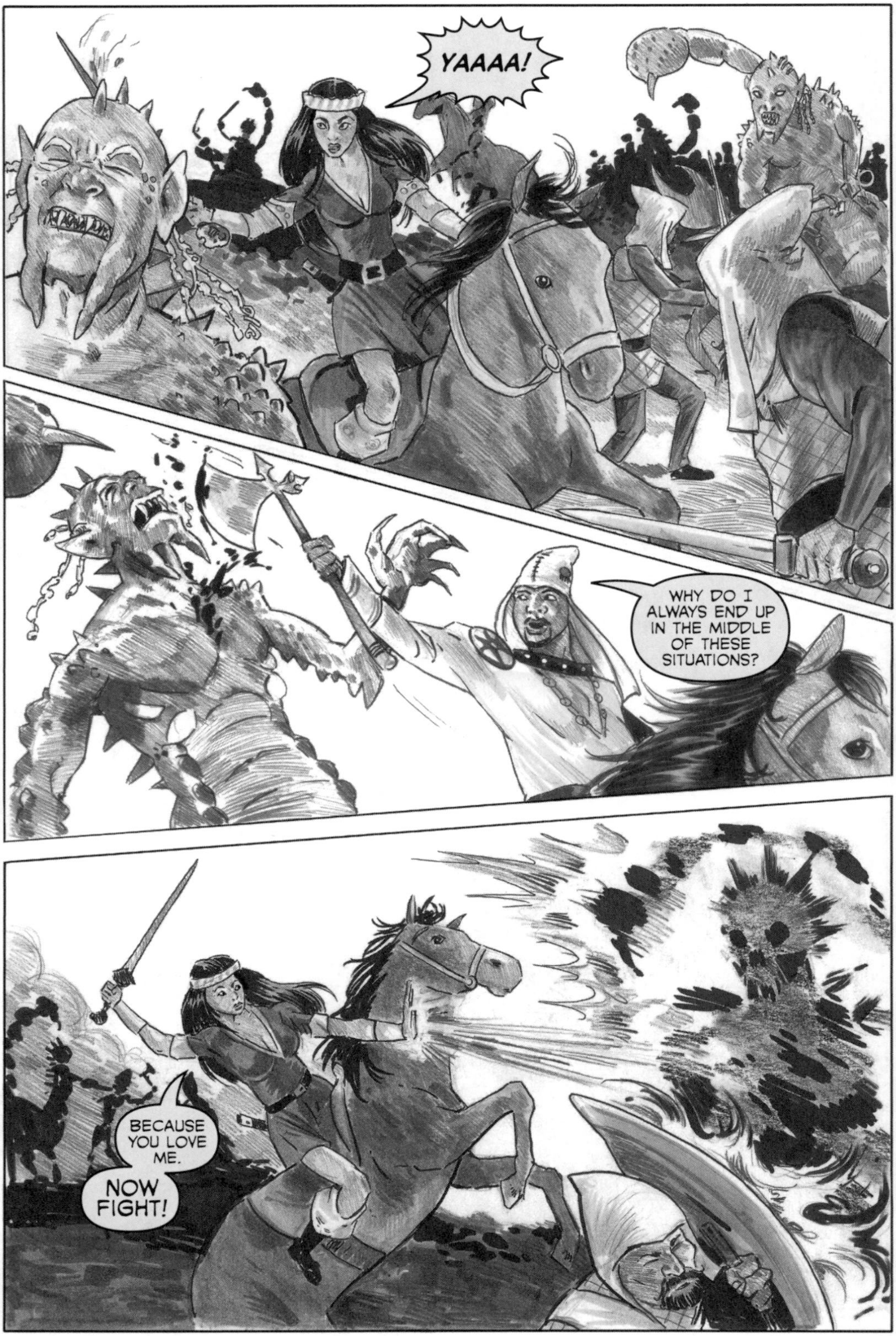
YAAAA!
WHY DO I ALWAYS END UP IN THE MIDDLE OF THESE SITUATIONS?
BECAUSE YOU LOVE ME.
NOW FIGHT!

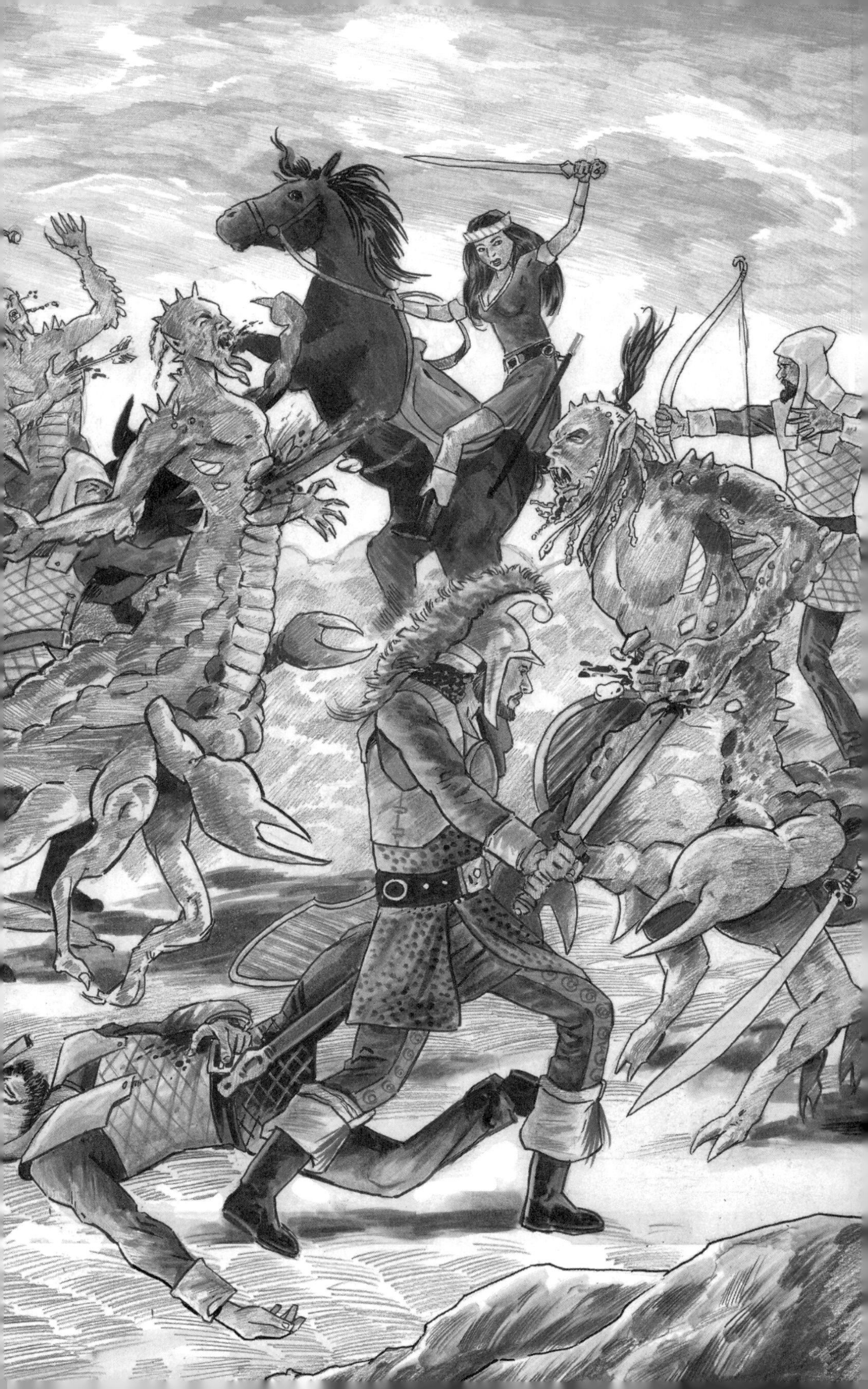

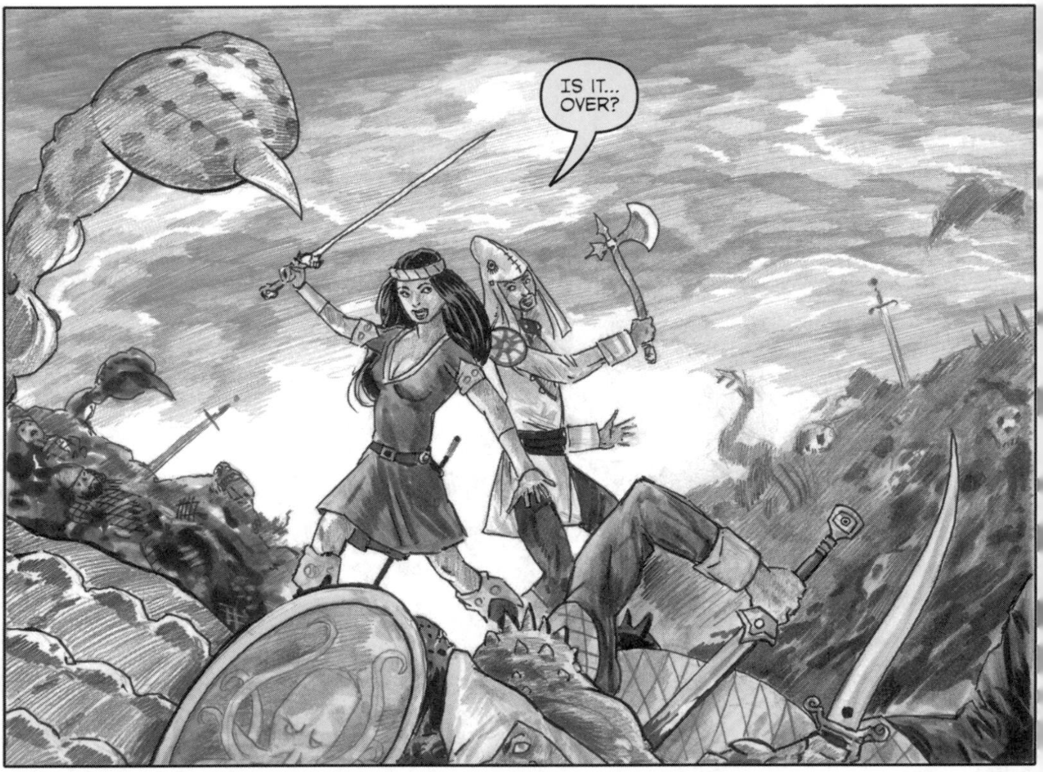
IS IT... OVER?

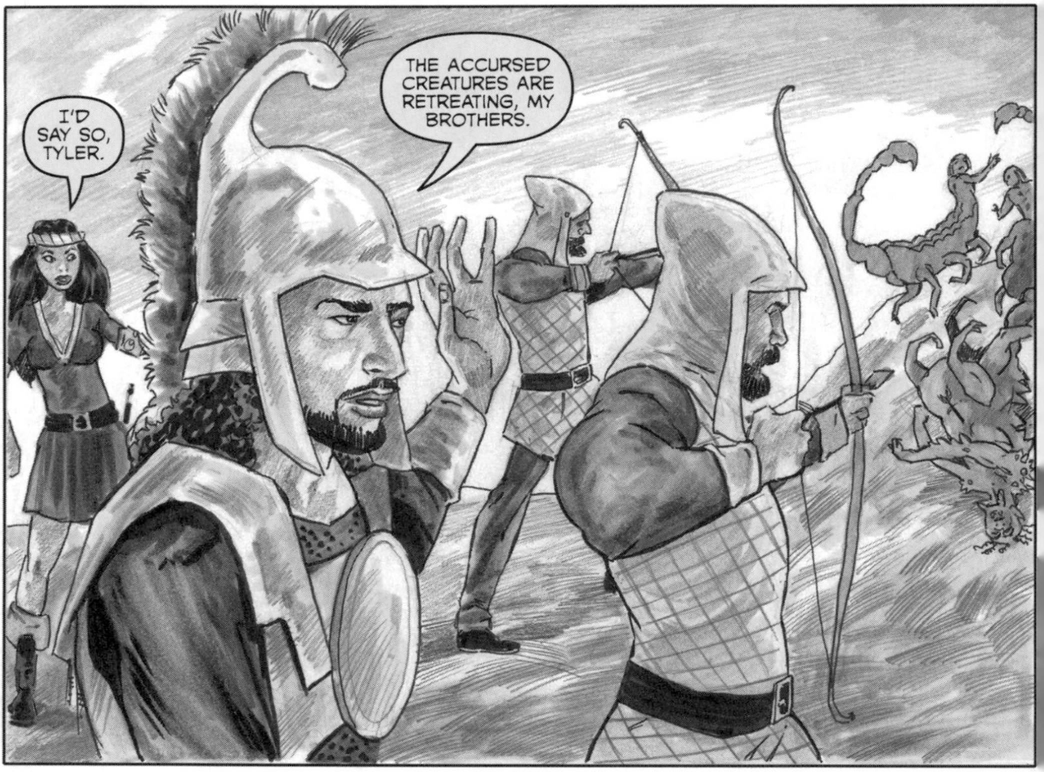
I'D SAY SO, TYLER.
THE ACCURSED CREATURES ARE RETREATING, MY BROTHERS.

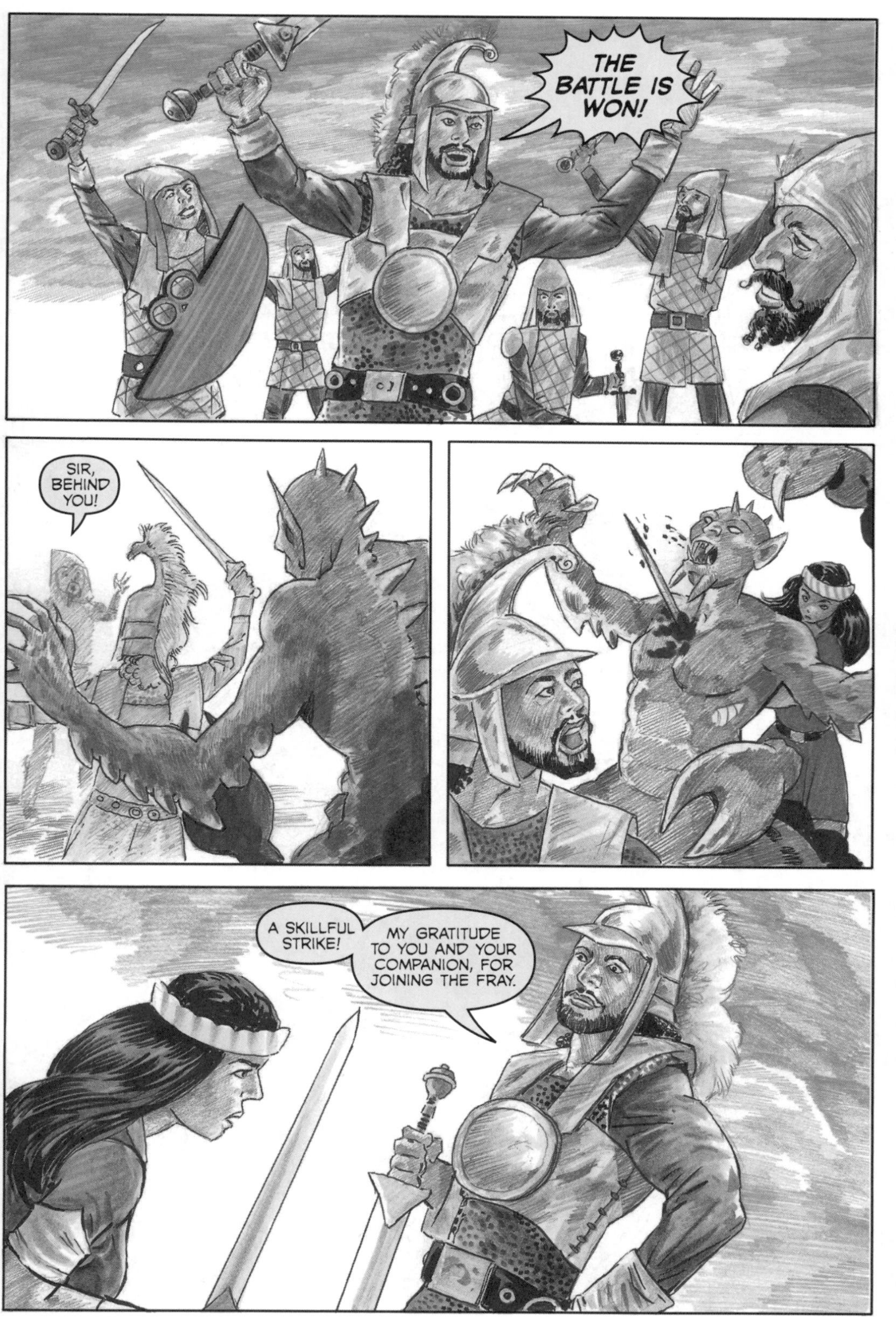
THE BATTLE IS WON!
SIR, BEHIND YOU!
A SKILLFUL STRIKE!
MY GRATITUDE TO YOU AND YOUR COMPANION, FOR JOINING THE FRAY.

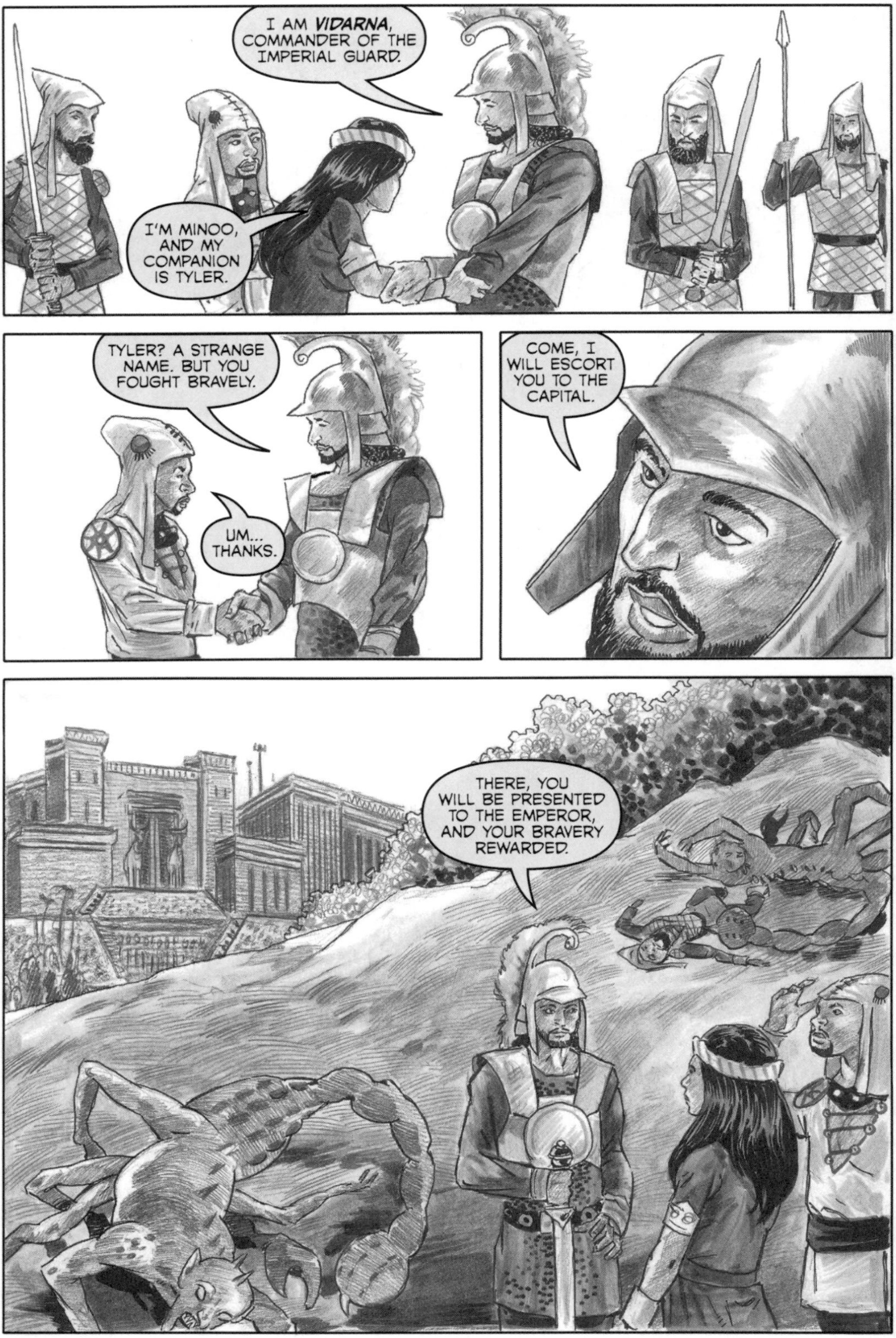
I AM VIDARNA, COMMANDER OF THE IMPERIAL GUARD.
I'M MINOO, AND MY COMPANION IS TYLER.
TYLER? A STRANGE NAME. BUT YOU FOUGHT BRAVELY.
UM... THANKS.
COME, I WILL ESCORT YOU TO THE CAPITAL.
THERE, YOU WILL BE PRESENTED TO THE EMPEROR, AND YOUR BRAVERY REWARDED.

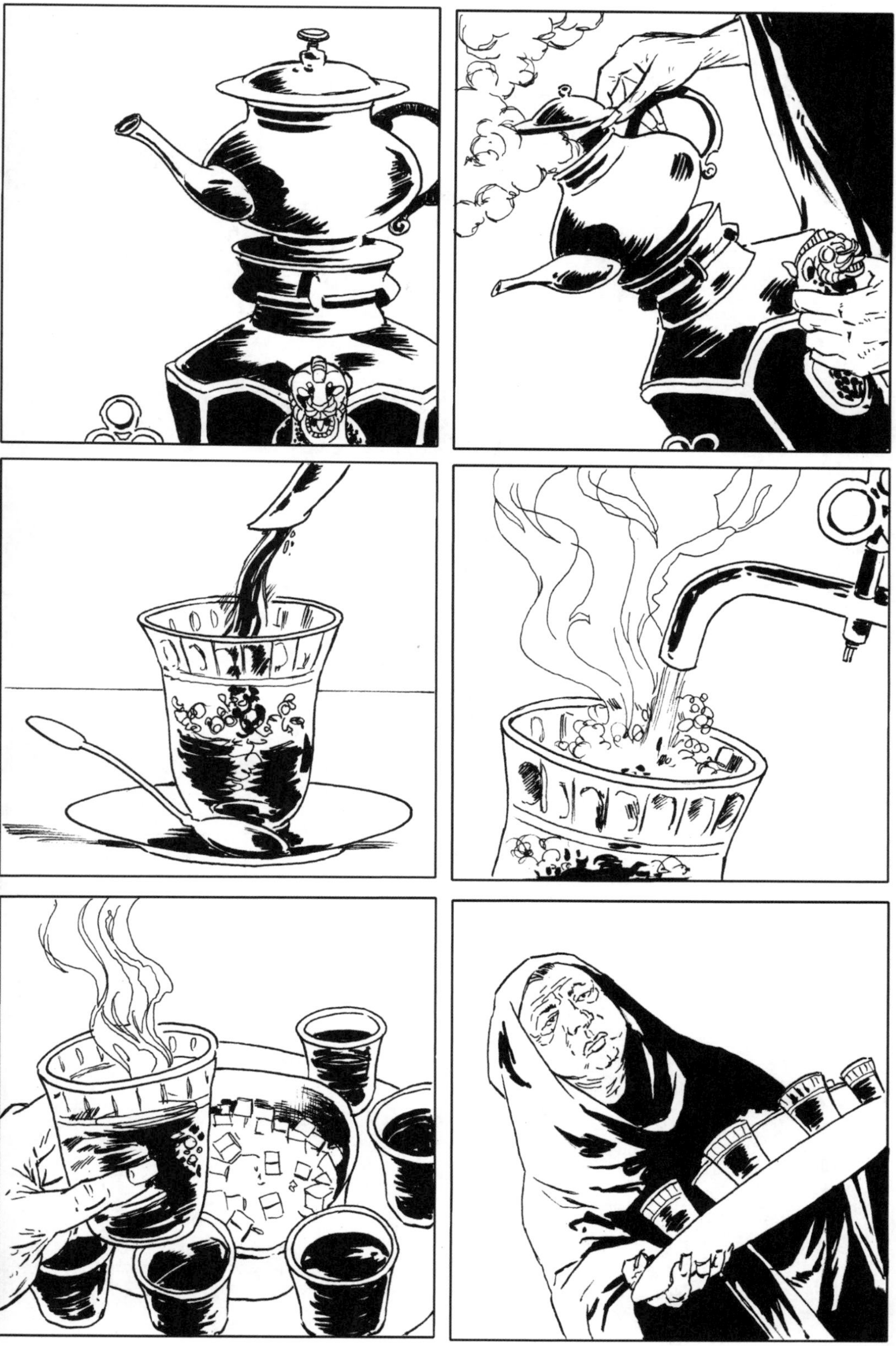

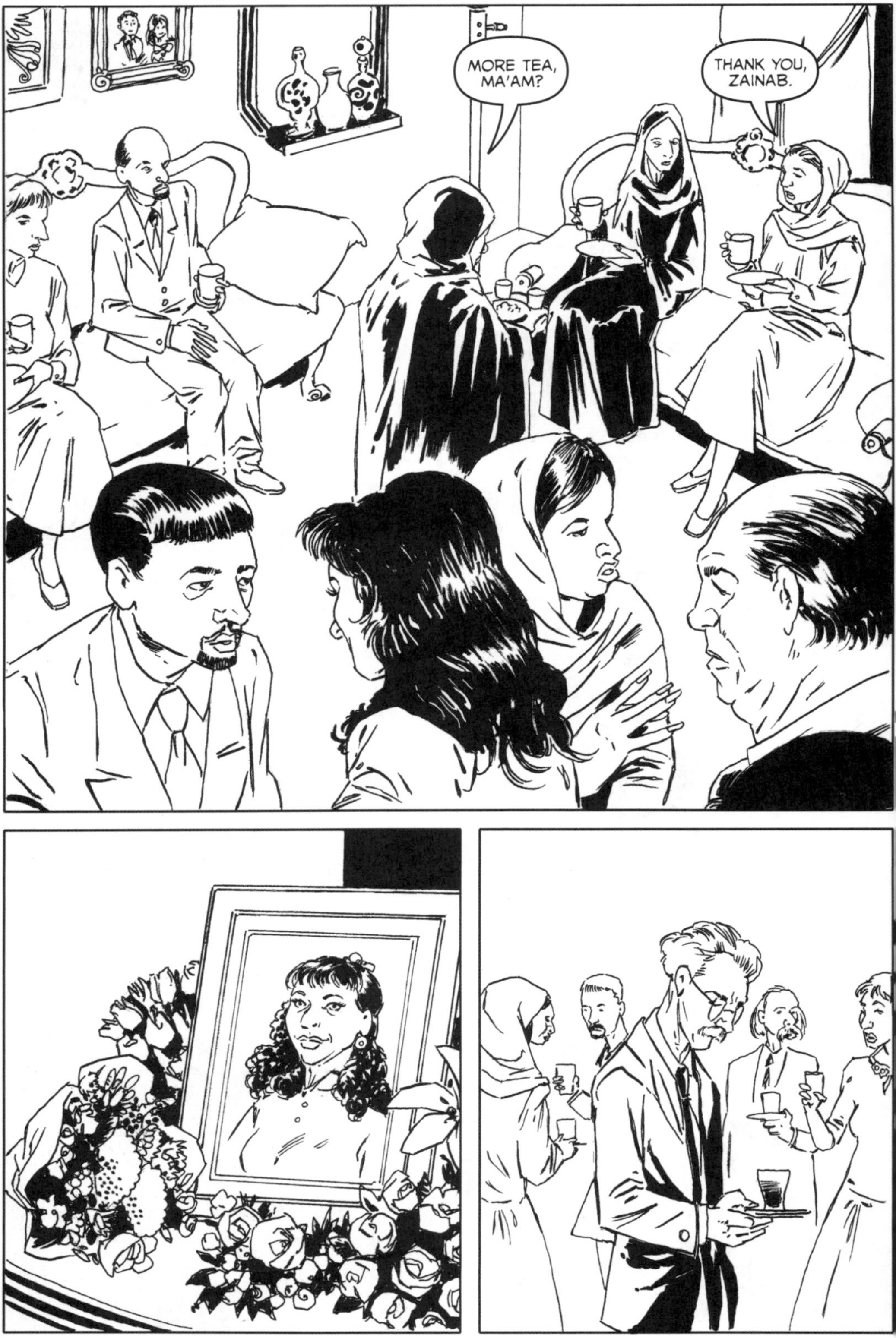
MORE TEA, MA'AM?
THANK YOU, ZAINAB.

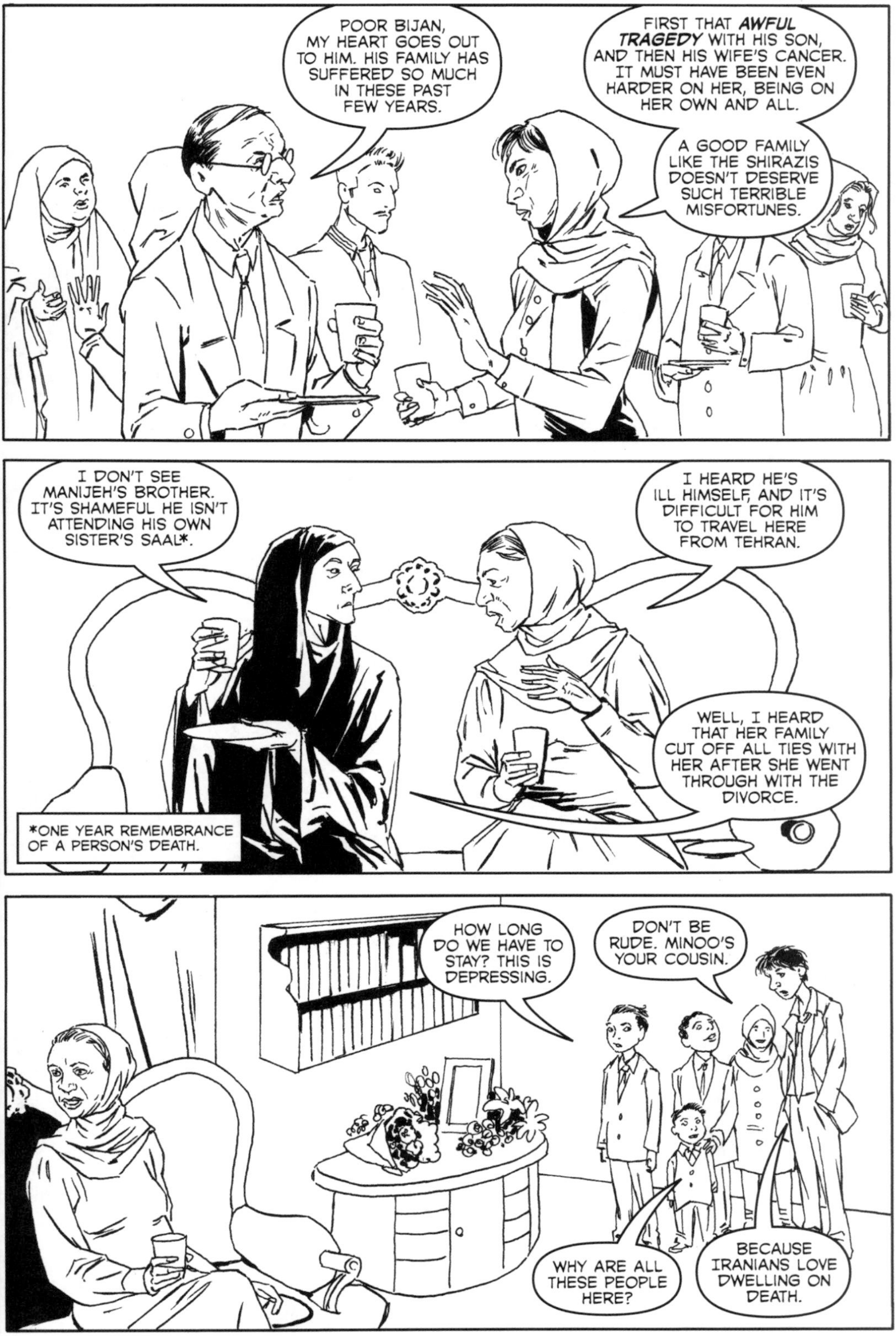
POOR BIJAN, MY HEART GOES OUT TO HIM. HIS FAMILY HAS SUFFERED SO MUCH IN THESE PAST FEW YEARS.
FIRST THAT ***AWFUL TRAGEDY*** WITH HIS SON, AND THEN HIS WIFE'S CANCER. IT MUST HAVE BEEN EVEN HARDER ON HER, BEING ON HER OWN AND ALL.
A GOOD FAMILY LIKE THE SHIRAZIS DOESN'T DESERVE SUCH TERRIBLE MISFORTUNES.
I DON'T SEE MANIJEH'S BROTHER. IT'S SHAMEFUL HE ISN'T ATTENDING HIS OWN SISTER'S SAAL*.
I HEARD HE'S ILL HIMSELF, AND IT'S DIFFICULT FOR HIM TO TRAVEL HERE FROM TEHRAN.
WELL, I HEARD THAT HER FAMILY CUT OFF ALL TIES WITH HER AFTER SHE WENT THROUGH WITH THE DIVORCE.
*ONE YEAR REMEMBRANCE OF A PERSON'S DEATH.
HOW LONG DO WE HAVE TO STAY? THIS IS DEPRESSING.
DON'T BE RUDE. MINOO'S YOUR COUSIN.
WHY ARE ALL THESE PEOPLE HERE?
BECAUSE IRANIANS LOVE DWELLING ON DEATH.

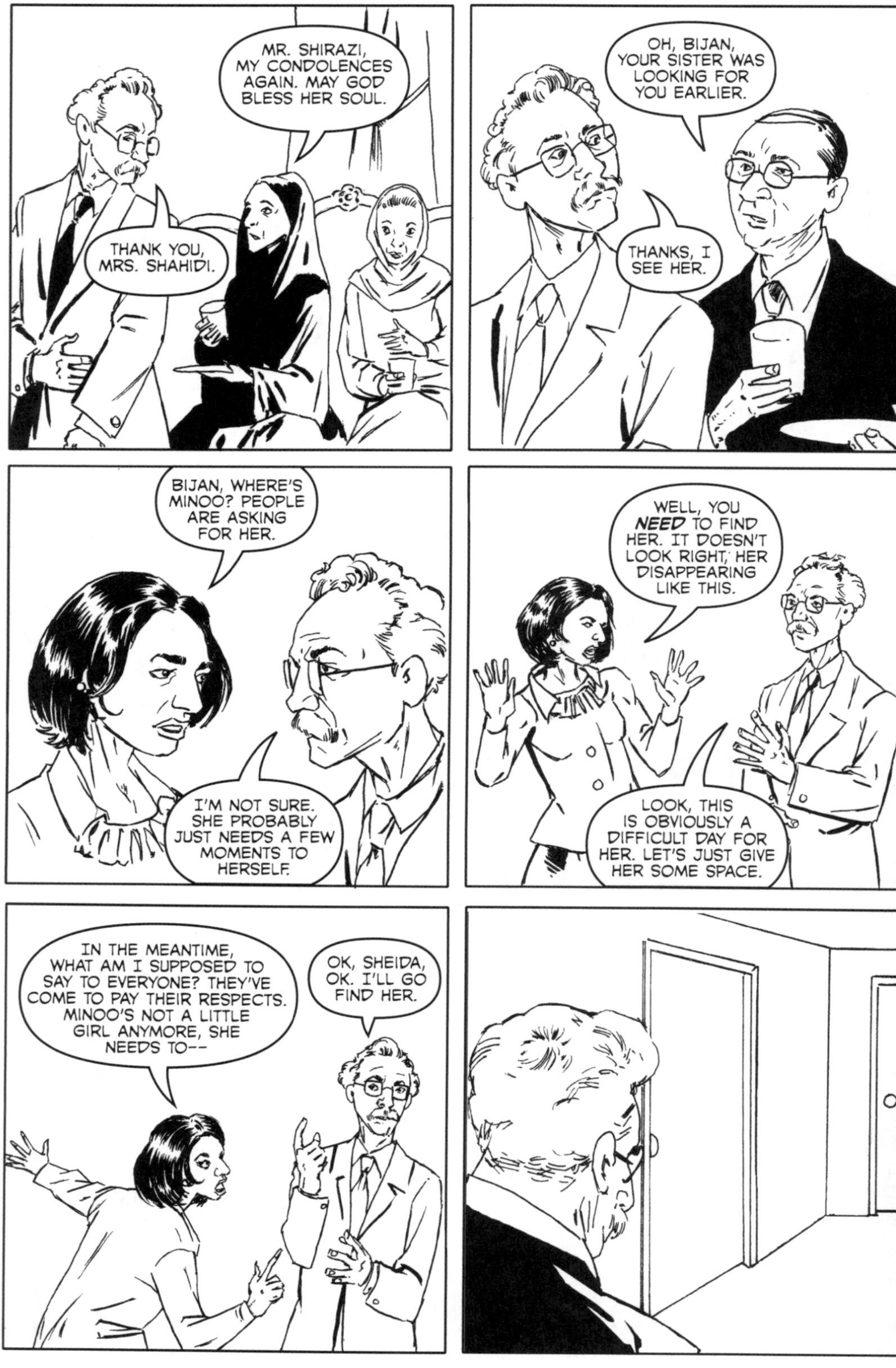
MR. SHIRAZI, MY CONDOLENCES AGAIN. MAY GOD BLESS HER SOUL.
THANK YOU, MRS. SHAHIDI.
OH, BIJAN, YOUR SISTER WAS LOOKING FOR YOU EARLIER.
THANKS, I SEE HER.
BIJAN, WHERE'S MINOO? PEOPLE ARE ASKING FOR HER.
I'M NOT SURE. SHE PROBABLY JUST NEEDS A FEW MOMENTS TO HERSELF.
WELL, YOU NEED TO FIND HER. IT DOESN'T LOOK RIGHT, HER DISAPPEARING LIKE THIS.
LOOK, THIS IS OBVIOUSLY A DIFFICULT DAY FOR HER. LET'S JUST GIVE HER SOME SPACE.
IN THE MEANTIME, WHAT AM I SUPPOSED TO SAY TO EVERYONE? THEY'VE COME TO PAY THEIR RESPECTS. MINOO'S NOT A LITTLE GIRL ANYMORE, SHE NEEDS TO--
OK, SHEIDA, OK. I'LL GO FIND HER.

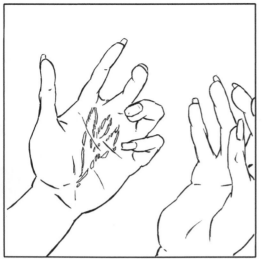

MINOO?

GREEN DAY

YOUR AUNT IS...WORRIED ABOUT YOU. WHY DON'T YOU COME OUT AND MEET SOME FOLKS?

I ALREADY DID. I DON'T WANT TO TALK TO ANYONE ELSE.

I KNOW YOU DON'T, BUT SOMETIMES YOU HAVE TO DO THINGS YOU MAY NOT NECESSARILY--

NO, I DON'T.

I SHOULDN'T HAVE TO *OWE* THOSE PEOPLE ANYTHING.

NOT ON *THIS* DAY.

MINOO, I--

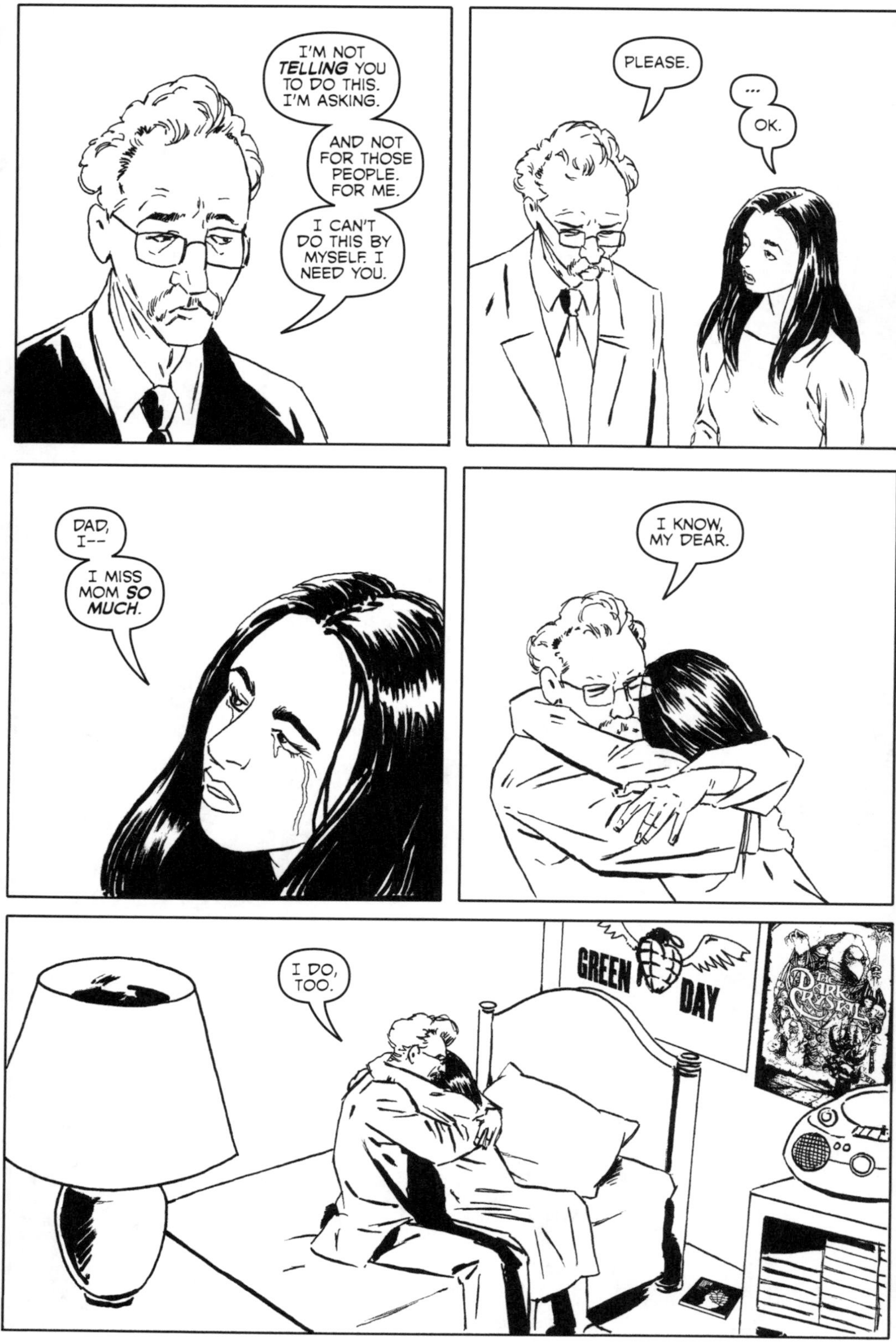
I'M NOT **TELLING** YOU TO DO THIS. I'M ASKING.
AND NOT FOR THOSE PEOPLE. FOR ME.
I CAN'T DO THIS BY MYSELF. I NEED YOU.
PLEASE.
...
OK.
DAD, I--
I MISS MOM **SO MUCH**.
I KNOW, MY DEAR.
I DO, TOO.
GREEN DAY

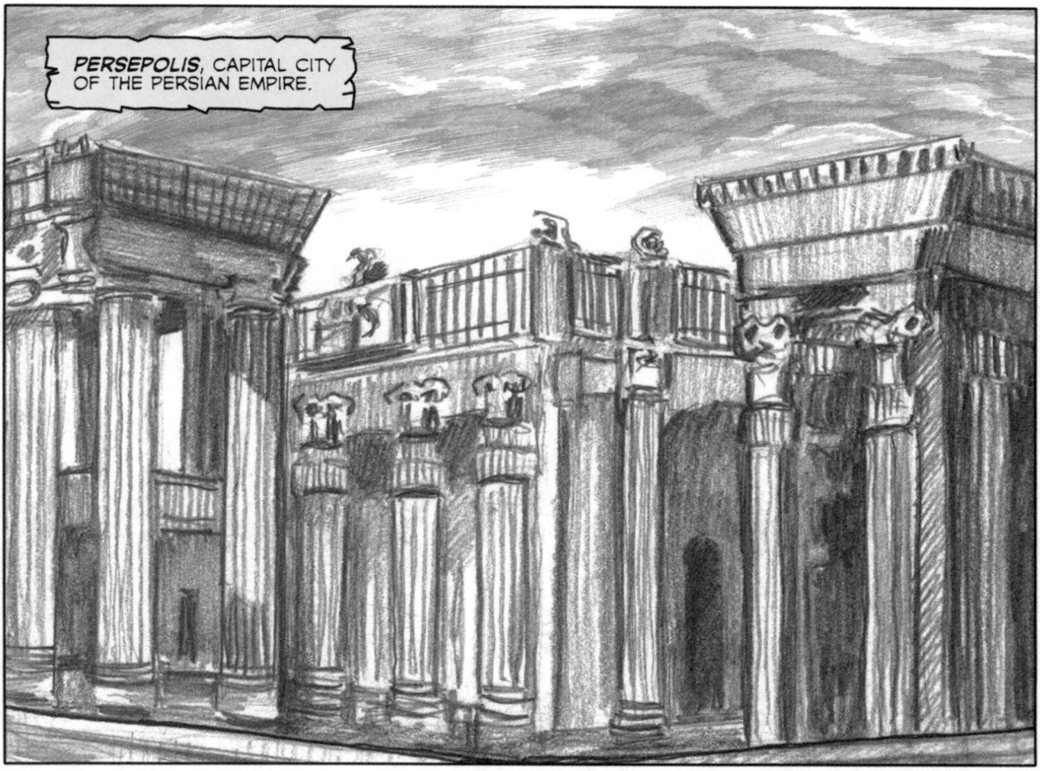
PERSEPOLIS, CAPITAL CITY OF THE PERSIAN EMPIRE.

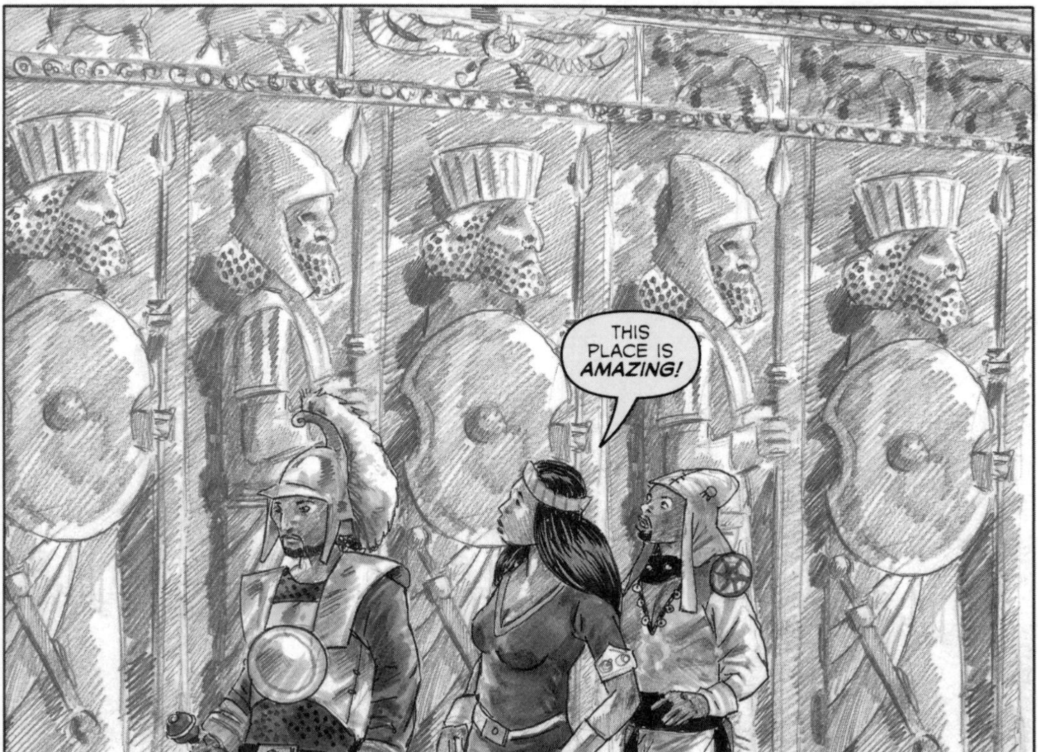
THIS PLACE IS AMAZING!

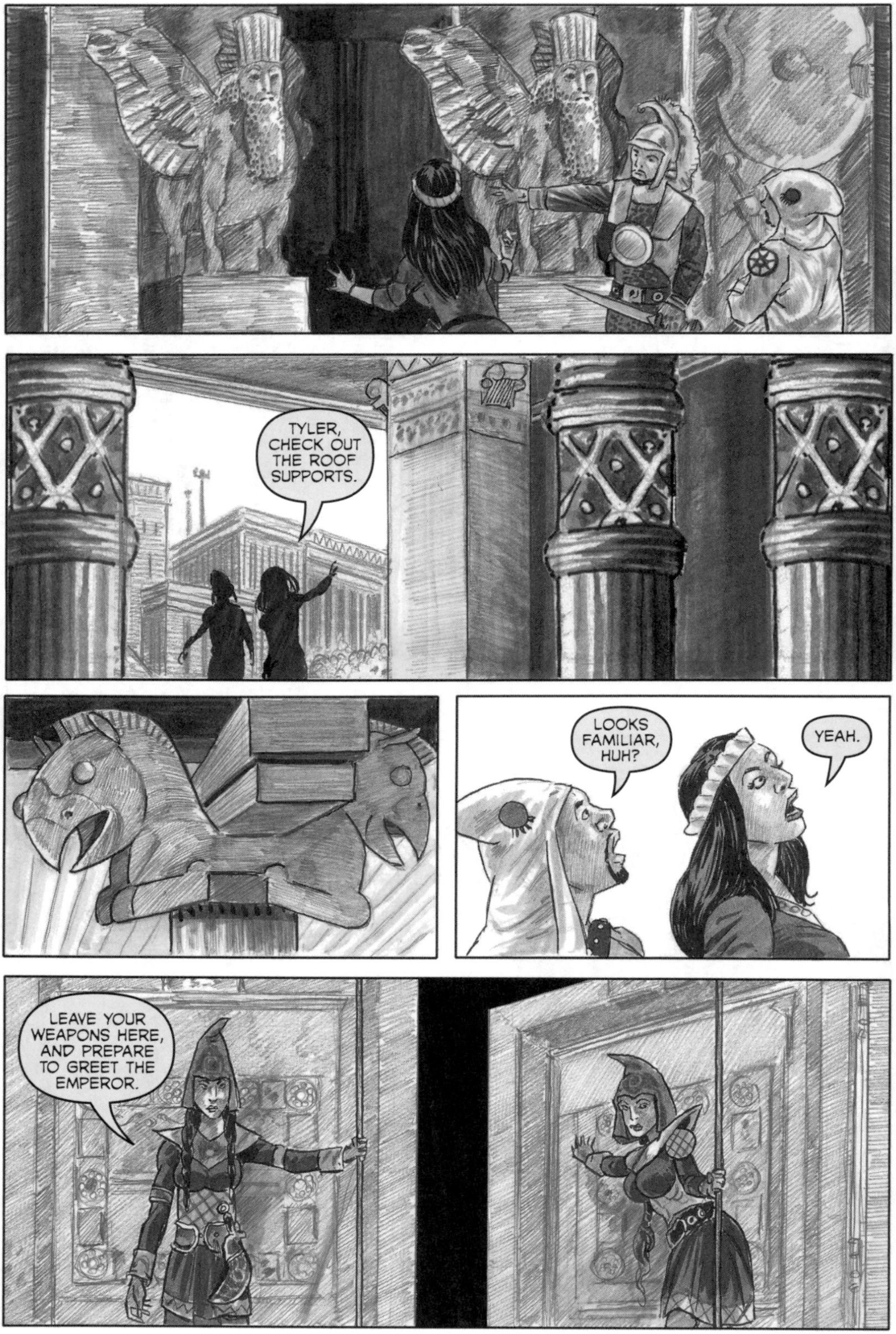
TYLER, CHECK OUT THE ROOF SUPPORTS.
LOOKS FAMILIAR, HUH?
YEAH.
LEAVE YOUR WEAPONS HERE, AND PREPARE TO GREET THE EMPEROR.

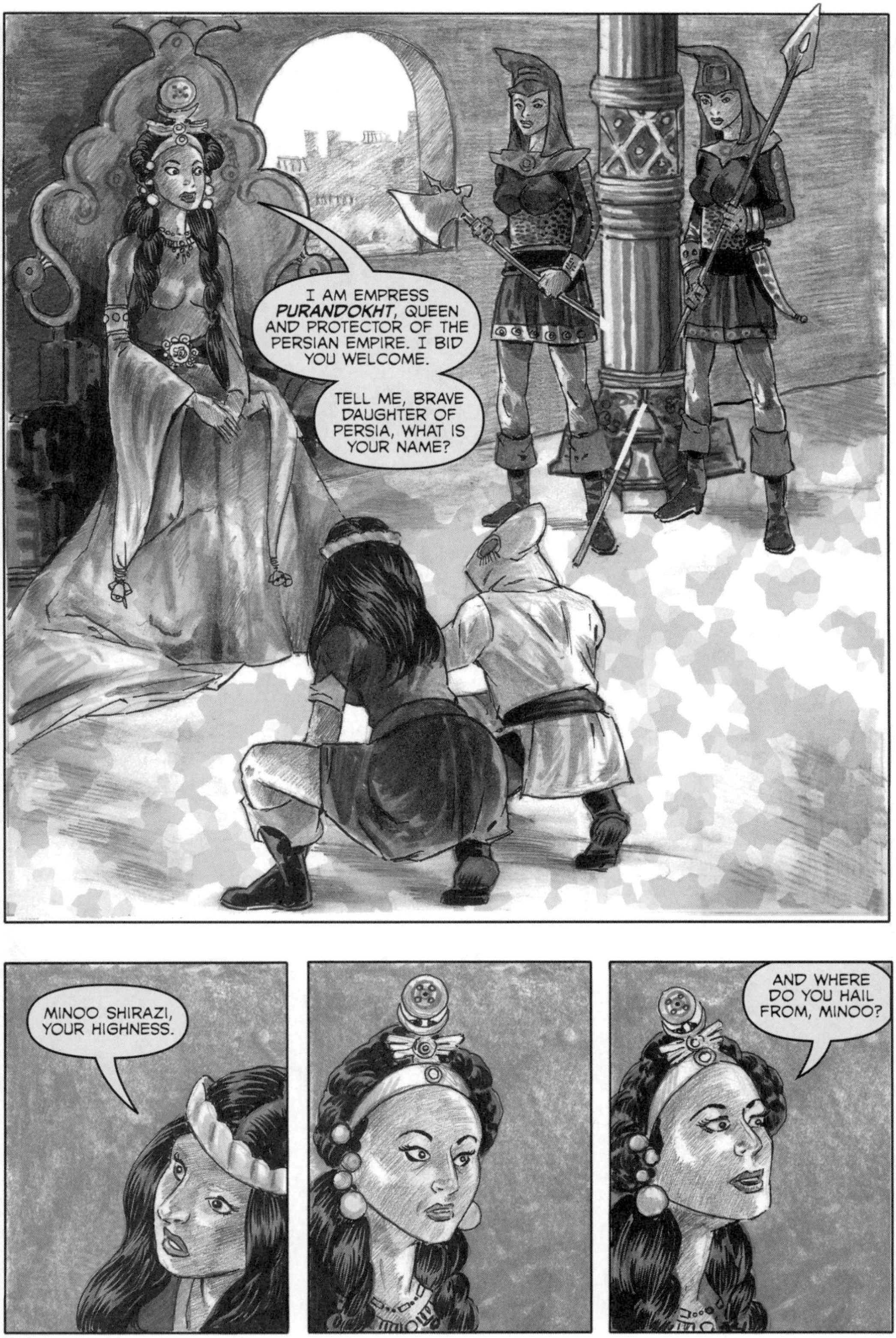
I AM EMPRESS *PURANDOKHT*, QUEEN AND PROTECTOR OF THE PERSIAN EMPIRE. I BID YOU WELCOME.
TELL ME, BRAVE DAUGHTER OF PERSIA, WHAT IS YOUR NAME?
MINOO SHIRAZI, YOUR HIGHNESS.
AND WHERE DO YOU HAIL FROM, MINOO?

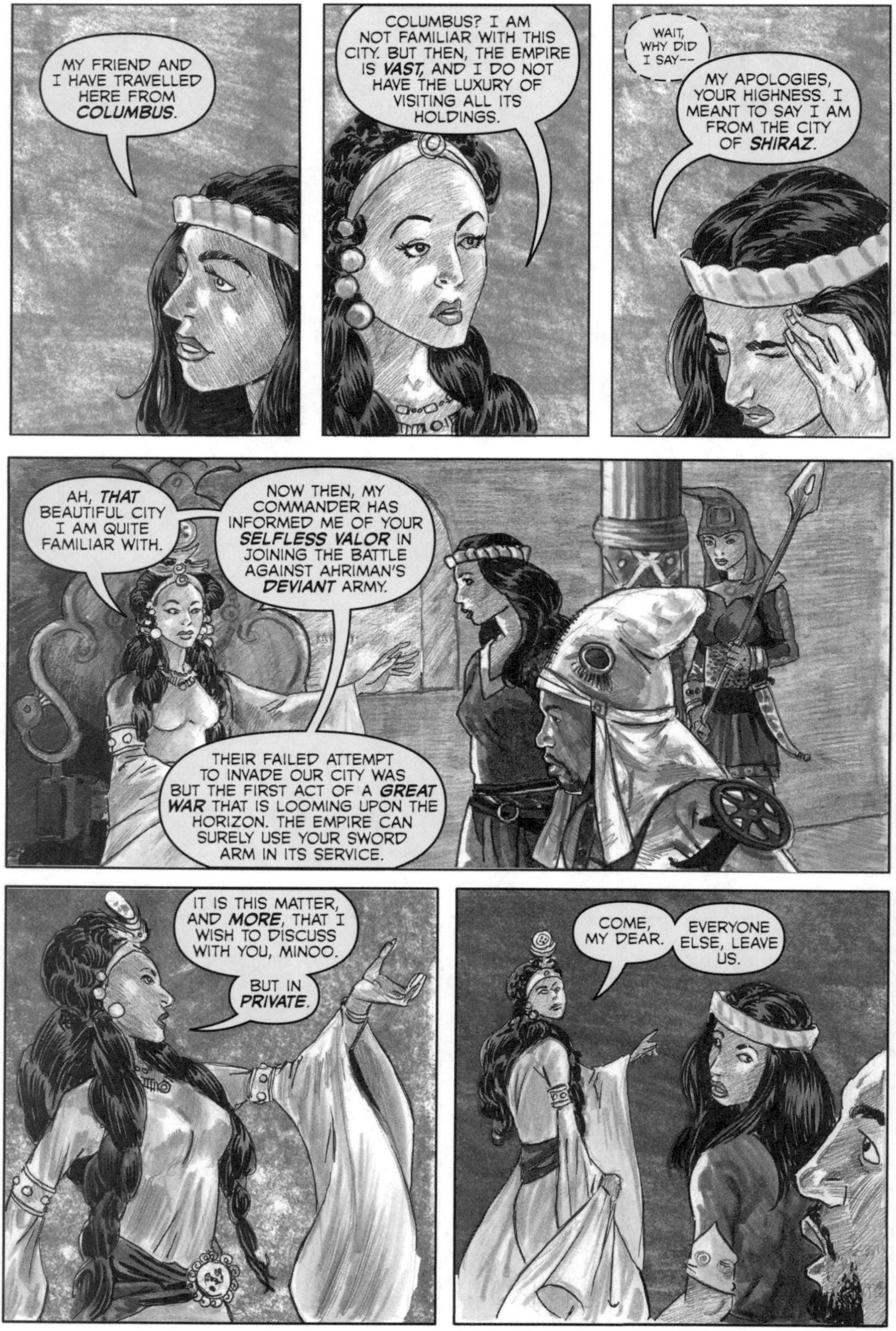
MY FRIEND AND I HAVE TRAVELLED HERE FROM COLUMBUS.
COLUMBUS? I AM NOT FAMILIAR WITH THIS CITY. BUT THEN, THE EMPIRE IS VAST, AND I DO NOT HAVE THE LUXURY OF VISITING ALL ITS HOLDINGS.
WAIT, WHY DID I SAY--
MY APOLOGIES, YOUR HIGHNESS. I MEANT TO SAY I AM FROM THE CITY OF SHIRAZ.
AH, THAT BEAUTIFUL CITY I AM QUITE FAMILIAR WITH.
NOW THEN, MY COMMANDER HAS INFORMED ME OF YOUR SELFLESS VALOR IN JOINING THE BATTLE AGAINST AHRIMAN'S DEVIANT ARMY.
THEIR FAILED ATTEMPT TO INVADE OUR CITY WAS BUT THE FIRST ACT OF A GREAT WAR THAT IS LOOMING UPON THE HORIZON. THE EMPIRE CAN SURELY USE YOUR SWORD ARM IN ITS SERVICE.
IT IS THIS MATTER, AND MORE, THAT I WISH TO DISCUSS WITH YOU, MINOO.
BUT IN PRIVATE.
COME, MY DEAR.
EVERYONE ELSE, LEAVE US.

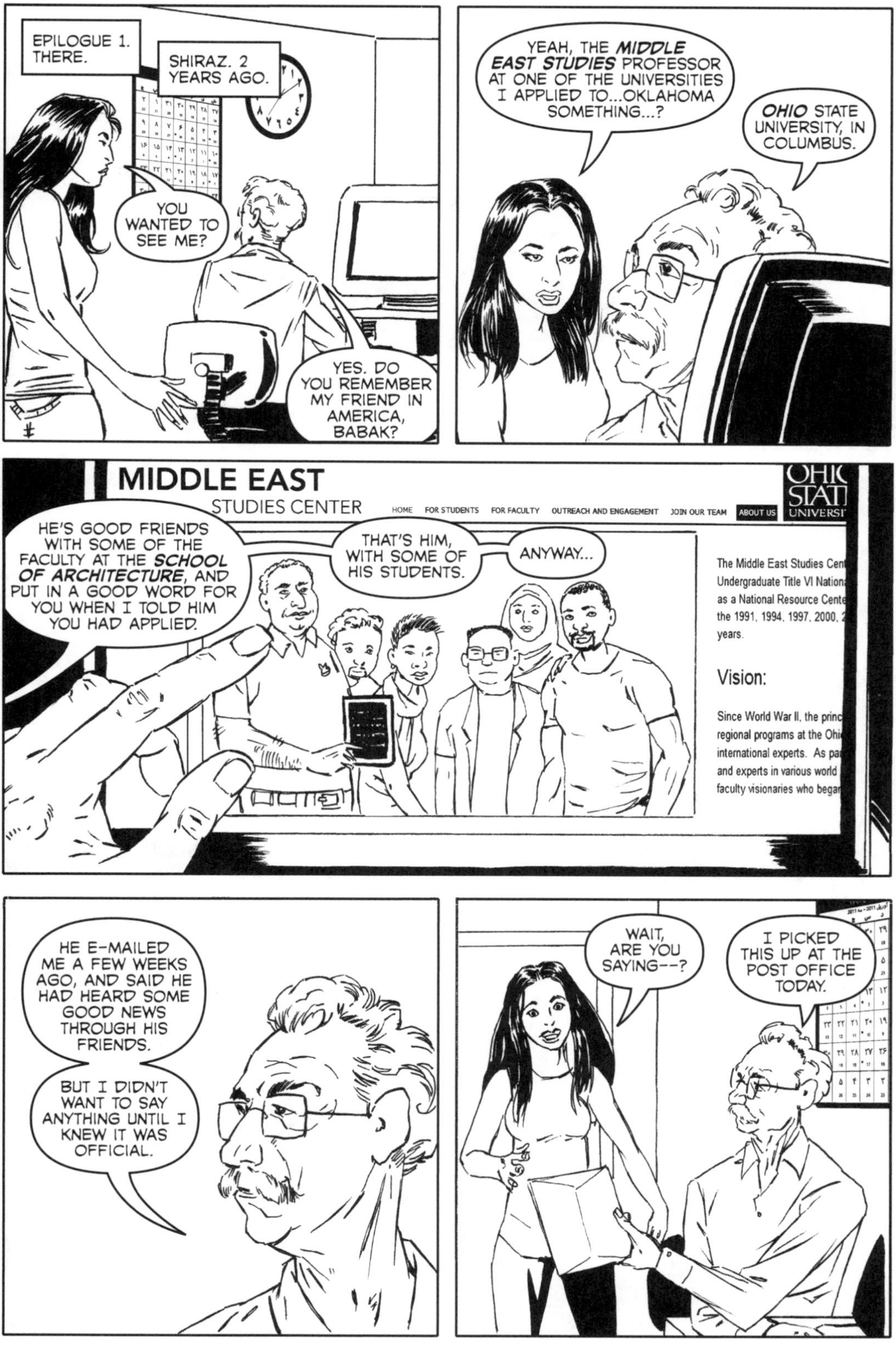
EPILOGUE 1. THERE.
SHIRAZ. 2 YEARS AGO.
YOU WANTED TO SEE ME?
YES. DO YOU REMEMBER MY FRIEND IN AMERICA, BABAK?
YEAH, THE MIDDLE EAST STUDIES PROFESSOR AT ONE OF THE UNIVERSITIES I APPLIED TO...OKLAHOMA SOMETHING...?
OHIO STATE UNIVERSITY, IN COLUMBUS.
MIDDLE EAST
STUDIES CENTER
HOME FOR STUDENTS FOR FACULTY OUTREACH AND ENGAGEMENT JOIN OUR TEAM ABOUT US
HE'S GOOD FRIENDS WITH SOME OF THE FACULTY AT THE SCHOOL OF ARCHITECTURE, AND PUT IN A GOOD WORD FOR YOU WHEN I TOLD HIM YOU HAD APPLIED.
THAT'S HIM, WITH SOME OF HIS STUDENTS.
ANYWAY...
Vision:
HE E-MAILED ME A FEW WEEKS AGO, AND SAID HE HAD HEARD SOME GOOD NEWS THROUGH HIS FRIENDS.
BUT I DIDN'T WANT TO SAY ANYTHING UNTIL I KNEW IT WAS OFFICIAL.
WAIT, ARE YOU SAYING--?
I PICKED THIS UP AT THE POST OFFICE TODAY.

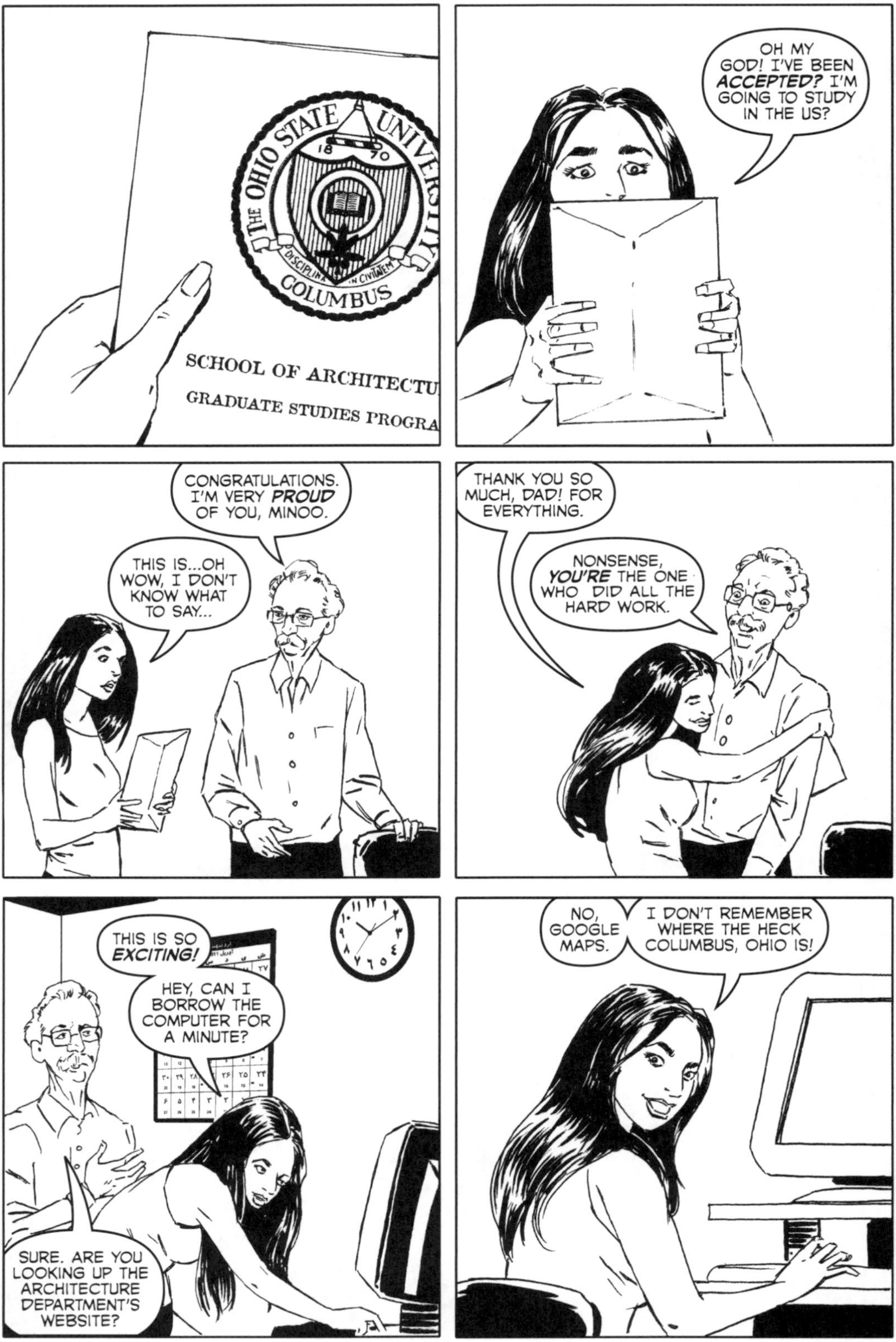
THE OHIO STATE UNIVERSITY
1870
DISCIPLINA IN CIVITATEM
COLUMBUS
SCHOOL OF ARCHITECTU
GRADUATE STUDIES PROGRA
OH MY GOD! I'VE BEEN *ACCEPTED?* I'M GOING TO STUDY IN THE US?
CONGRATULATIONS. I'M VERY *PROUD* OF YOU, MINOO.
THIS IS...OH WOW, I DON'T KNOW WHAT TO SAY...
THANK YOU SO MUCH, DAD! FOR EVERYTHING.
NONSENSE, *YOU'RE* THE ONE WHO DID ALL THE HARD WORK.
THIS IS SO *EXCITING!*
HEY, CAN I BORROW THE COMPUTER FOR A MINUTE?
SURE. ARE YOU LOOKING UP THE ARCHITECTURE DEPARTMENT'S WEBSITE?
NO, GOOGLE MAPS.
I DON'T REMEMBER WHERE THE HECK COLUMBUS, OHIO IS!

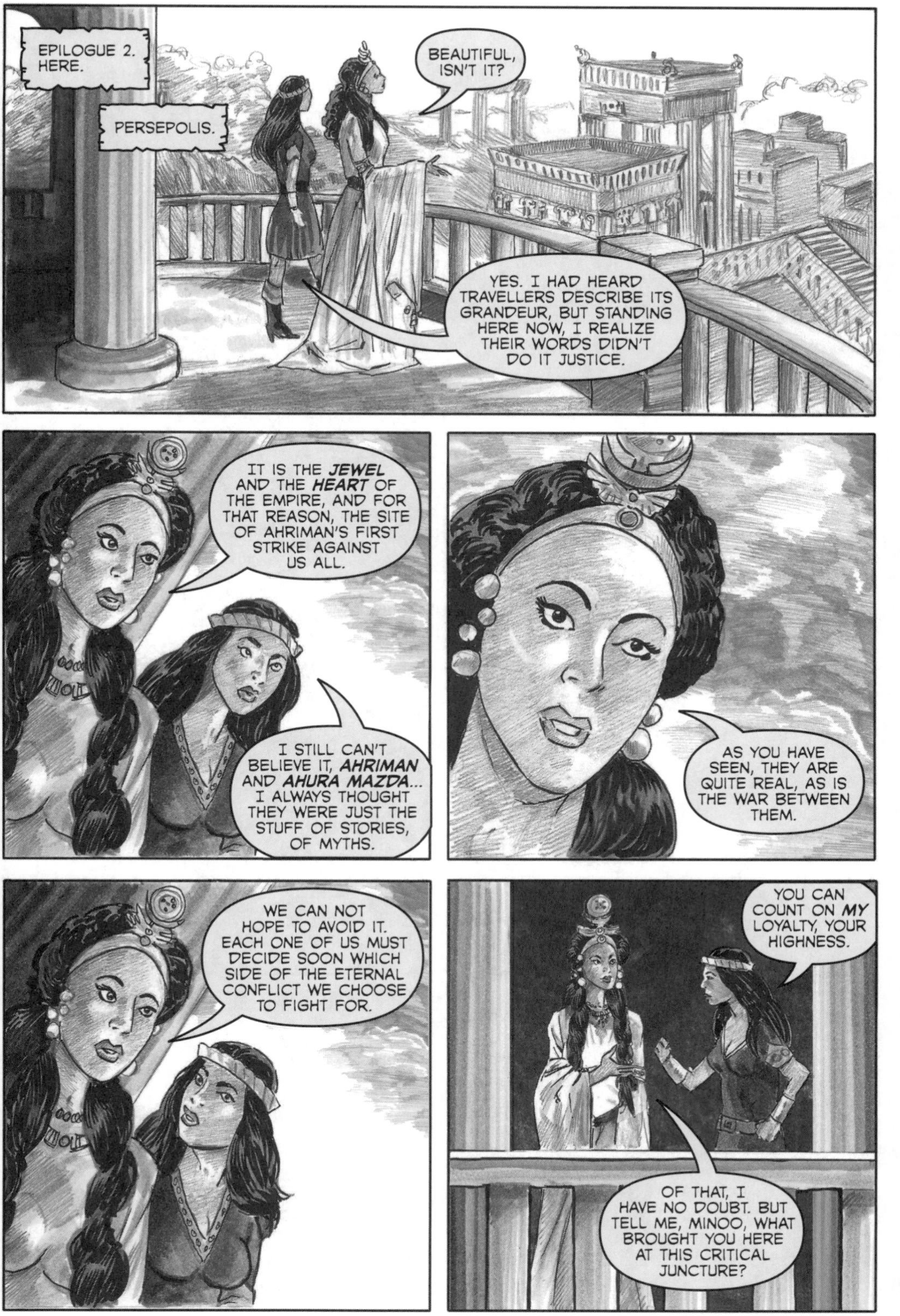
EPILOGUE 2. HERE.
PERSEPOLIS.
BEAUTIFUL, ISN'T IT?
YES. I HAD HEARD TRAVELLERS DESCRIBE ITS GRANDEUR, BUT STANDING HERE NOW, I REALIZE THEIR WORDS DIDN'T DO IT JUSTICE.
IT IS THE *JEWEL* AND THE *HEART* OF THE EMPIRE, AND FOR THAT REASON, THE SITE OF AHRIMAN'S FIRST STRIKE AGAINST US ALL.
I STILL CAN'T BELIEVE IT, *AHRIMAN* AND *AHURA MAZDA*... I ALWAYS THOUGHT THEY WERE JUST THE STUFF OF STORIES, OF MYTHS.
AS YOU HAVE SEEN, THEY ARE QUITE REAL, AS IS THE WAR BETWEEN THEM.
WE CAN NOT HOPE TO AVOID IT. EACH ONE OF US MUST DECIDE SOON WHICH SIDE OF THE ETERNAL CONFLICT WE CHOOSE TO FIGHT FOR.
YOU CAN COUNT ON *MY* LOYALTY, YOUR HIGHNESS.
OF THAT, I HAVE NO DOUBT. BUT TELL ME, MINOO, WHAT BROUGHT YOU HERE AT THIS CRITICAL JUNCTURE?

IT'S A LONG STORY, BUT A DYING PRIEST IN MY TOWN TOLD ME TO DO SO. HE SAID THAT I WOULD FIND MY MOTHER HERE.

I'M GLAD I CAME, BUT I MUST ADMIT, I STILL FEEL SILLY ABOUT THE WHOLE THING.

WHY IS THAT?

BECAUSE IT SEEMS LIKE A FOOL'S ERRAND. I MEAN, HOW DO I GO ABOUT FINDING SOMEONE I DON'T EVEN KNOW, IN A CITY THIS LARGE?

SHOW ME YOUR LEFT HAND, MINOO.

TRUST ME.

W-WHAT? I DON'T UNDERSTAND...

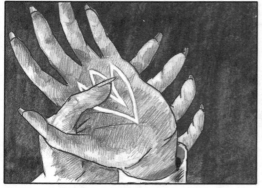

MY SCAR? DO YOU THINK IT CAN HELP ME FIND MY MOTHER?

IT ALREADY HAS...

...MY *DAUGHTER*.

END OF BOOK 1.

We would like to acknowledge and thank the following people, who generously supported the creation of this book via the crowd funding site, Kickstarter. Whether family, friends, or total strangers, your belief in this book means the world to us.
Sincerely,
Dara & Brent

Susan Adami
Hassan Alamdari
Ashley Aminian
Andy Bennett
Gib Bickel
Nathan Blumenfeld
Stergios Botzakis
Susan Bradt
Ted Brown
Leilani Cantu
Leighton Connor
Bob Corby
Megan Crawford
Robert Davis
Margreet de Heer
Matt Dembicki
Dr. Dineh
Nand Dussault
Ken Eppstein
Reza Farivar
Timothy Fischer
Marnie Galloway
The Gibbons Family
Mike Gilson
Tony Goins
Daryn Guarino
Steven Hager
Jessi Hersey
Jason Hissong
Casey Hoch
Christian Hoffer
Travis Horseman
Tony Isabella
Dr. Kambiz
Katharine Kan
Sean Kelly
Tim Kenyon
Matthew Kish
K Kisner
Sean Kleefeld

Harry Knight
Richard Krauss
Mark Latture
Thad Linson
Adam Luchjenbroers
Ali Akbar Mahdi
Shaun Manning
Mark Martel
Sean T McBeth
Tim McClurg
Rachel McDonald
Judy McGuire
Sean McGurr
Randy Meredith
Josh Miller
Shahrokh Minoui
Bahram Mirfendereski
James Moore
Michael Shaudon Paktinat
Eric Palicki
Ebrahim Paydar
W.R. Printz
Mitra Rahnamai
Rafer Roberts
Thomas Rood
Rafael Rosado
Arsia Rozegar
Diana Sofariu
Sabrina Spruitenburg
KT Swartz
Cody Thompson
Christo van Wyk
Annalisa Ventola
Rob Vollmar
Markus Zwinger
Robert & Kelly Zwink
Elika & Cody
Mandana & Bahram
Marlene and Manouher

Special thanks to Terry Nantier at NBM Publishing for additional support of our Kickstarter campaign.

Dara Naraghi was born in Iran and educated in the United States. An Ohio State University alum, he works in the information technology field, but his passion is for the comics medium. His debut graphic novel, Lifelike, has garnered many positive reviews. His other notable graphic novels include the Terminator Salvation official movie prequel, and Witch & Wizard: Battle for Shadowland (both New York Times Bestsellers), as well as works for Image Comics, IDW Publishing, Dark Horse, and DC Comics. Dara is also a founding member of the comic book writers/artists collective known as PANEL, with whom he has produced 20 volumes of their comics anthology. Dara lives in Columbus, Ohio with his wife, daughter, and the world's sweetest hound dog. www.DaraNaraghi.com

Brent Bowman is a graduate of the Columbus College of Art And Design with a degree in Illustration. A lifelong comics fan, Brent has been drawing since he was old enough to pick up a pencil. His work has appeared in publications by Image Comics and Caliber Press, as well as the collectible card game Age of Empires. He's a contributing member of PANEL, a local comics collective that publishes two anthologies a year. Brent has been nominated for the small press SPACE prize in 2008, 2010 and 2011 for both his PANEL work and his own original self-published comics. He lives in Columbus Ohio with his wife and two boys. www.PersiaBlues.com

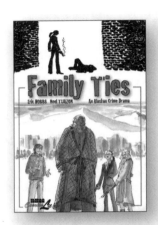 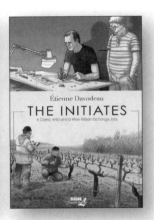

Also available from Comics Lit:
Family Ties, *An Alaskan Crime Drama*, by Eric Hobbs and Noel Tuazon, $14.99
The Initiates, *A Comic Artist And a Wine Artisan Exchange Jobs*,
by Etienne Davodeau, $29.99 cloth

See previews and more at nbmpub.com
We have over 200 graphic novels available, order online or from:
NBM
160 Broadway, Suite 700, East Wing,
New York, NY 10038
P&H: $4 1st item, $1 each addt'l.
Catalog available upon request.